THE UNRELIEVED PARADOX

The Unrelieved Paradox

Studies in the Theology of Franz Bibfeldt

Edited by

Martin E. Marty and Jerald C. Brauer

WILLIAM B. EERDMANS PUBLISHING COMPANY
GRAND RAPIDS, MICHIGAN

Copyright © 1994 by Wm. B. Eerdmans Publishing Co.
255 Jefferson Ave. S.E., Grand Rapids, Michigan 49503

Printed in the United States of America

00 99 98 97 96 95 94   5 4 3 2 1

Library of Congress Cataloging-in-Publication Data

The unrelieved paradox: studies in the theology of Franz Bibfeldt /
edited by Martin E. Marty and Jerald C. Brauer.
p.   cm.
Includes bibliographical references.
ISBN 0-8028-0745-3 (pbk.)
1. Theology, Doctrinal — History — 20th century — Humor.
2. Theology, Doctrinal — History — 20th century — Miscellanea.
I. Marty, Martin E., 1928–   . II. Brauer, Jerald C.
BT28.U57   1994
230'.0207 — dc20   94-21934
CIP   .

To Robert Howard Clausen, inventor

Contents

III. The Pastoral Theology of Franz Bibfeldt

IV. Culture and Art in Bibfeldt

V. Landmarks and Landmines in Bibfeldt Scholarship

Appendices

Preface

At mid-century, the golden age of modern theology, the names of most prominent theologians began with the letter *B*: Baillie, Balthasar, Barth, Bea, Berdyaev, Bibfeldt, Bonhoeffer, Brunner, Buber, Bultmann. Only a few names like Niebuhr and Tillich were exceptions to the *B* rule.

Near the century's end, only one of the mid-century *B*'s survives and even thrives: Franz Bibfeldt. Some prefatory words about him and the occasion for this book may well be necessary and will certainly be helpful.

The idea for this book came from the publisher, whose *B* is in his middle name, and from a bookseller, also a *B*. They have prodded the Bibfeldt Foundation, of which the two of us are custodians, to set his papers in order and to allow them to produce this volume. (The papers, as will be seen, are now in the Special Collections of Regenstein Library at the University of Chicago, and can be consulted by scholars who have the proper credentials.)

That the initiative came from others is very much in keeping with the ethos of Franz Bibfeldt and the Foundation. The world comes to Bibfeldt; he does not go to the world. With the exception of an occasional invitation to a Chicago religion newswriter or two, beckoned as friends but sometimes moved to write, the Foundation engages in no public relations efforts. An annual Bibfeldt festival, held on the Wednesday nearest April 1st, occurs some years and is neglected through long stretches of others. Some years an enterprising lecturer appears with something to say; in other years, when no one appears with something to say, someone still says it; and then no one appears for a length of time. A special 1988 session of the American Academy of Religion devoted to his thought resulted from planning by his devotees, not by the Foundation. The Foundation, needless to say, is nonprofit.

What follows is largely explanatory or self-explanatory, so there is not much need for explanation — only apology — in this preface. The collection of materials here gives evidence of a random character; this results from the hit-or-miss way in which Bibfeldtiana makes its appearances. Books on chaos theory are necessarily full of chaos: think of this as a theological book on chaos theory, as personified in one person and his work. The concept of an ordered Bibfeldt is oxymoronic.

What is Bibfeldt all about? Why, for the better half of this century, have international gatherings awaited his presence and devoted themselves to his words and ways? What ecological niche does he fill? We like to urge upon writers of essays or books a paraphrase of Eugen Rosenstock-Huessy's line: "One book is about one thing; at least the good ones are." Carry that further into analogy: "One life is about one thing; at least the good ones are." Thus Buber is about "I and Thou" and Schweitzer about "Reverence for Life" and Tillich about "The Courage to Be," and so on.

Bibfeldt is "about" Proteanism, as his coat of arms demonstrates (see later in this book). It is about being able to affirm and negate, to change. Scholars of Bibfeldt, by studying him carefully, have been able to track one of the main elements in twentieth-century theology. One might ask: how could one be a Barthian ("God as Wholly Other") one year, a death-of-God theologian the next, and a Barthian again a year later? Why is it that so many of the theologians who were on the far left in the late 1960s turned to the right in the 1980s? Bibfeldtians know: it is the *Zeitgeist*, the spirit of the times, to whose whistlings many theologians dance. Bibfeldt is a virtuoso in the theological art of making things come out right, or changing his sails to meet the winds, of saving face after it has been slapped by shifts in fashion.

Bibfeldt, admittedly, is not everyone's cup of tea. Better for him had he been born a suave French savant. Then he could have bent with the winds, as some French theologians have done, from devotion to *Raillement* through integralism and neo-scholasticism to Sartreism to modernism to structuralism to deconstruction to postmodernism to poststructuralism to postdeconstruction, never missing a beat, raising an eyebrow, or evoking the slap of a thigh. Better for him had he been born a British thinker, so his winds of change would have taken him through the cool waters of logical positivism through language analysis to who knows what new metaphysics. Alas for him, he was born German, so when he is being dead serious, as his scholars also tend to be, the expression sometimes sounds like an effort at Teutonic humor. Now *there's* an oxymoron if there ever was one.

An apology: since there have been more sightings of Bibfeldt at the University of Chicago than elsewhere, inevitably there are traces of local color, unfunny analogues to "family jokes," references of the "you have to have been there" sort. We as editors purged as many of these as possible, but we still ask the indulgence of readers who are not familiar with some of the names, places, and nuances referred to in these materials. We are confident that they will find plenty of congenial items that are nonspecific in respect to place or time, as is Bibfeldt himself.

One more apologetic note: it goes without saying, but still needs saying, that Bibfeldt is *not* an alter ego for either of the undersigned. It happens that two artists, frustrated in their attempts to get Franz Bibfeldt to sit still for his portrait, have made some composites that bear some resemblance to one or another of us, but this kind of portrayal is born of rage and coincidence, not out of efforts at creating verisimilitudes. Look up the word "invention" in the dictionary: you will find that it means to come across, to discover, as much as it means to make up. We, along with others, are comers across of Bibfeldt, discoverers of Bibfeldtiana, not of ourselves. If he is a mirror to be held up to anyone, we will hold him up to ourselves as much as to anyone else, but will see little but cracks, waves, and distortions, as one sees in amusement parks.

That Bibfeldt is not to everyone's taste does not disturb him or his Foundation executives. On the other hand, everyone is to *his* taste, it has to be said. He is capable of affirming everything that he denies or should deny; but that catholicity is not always shared. We persist in believing that by his example of mutability and his embrace of the coincidence of opposites he has much to say to our times. Some of that gets said in this book.

We thank Reinder Van Til and Wayne Bornholdt for assembling and encouraging the work, and Judy Lawrence for typing scraps of Bibfeldt materials that came to the University of Chicago on bread wrappers, bottoms of six-pack cartons, Sunday church bulletins, and the like. And, of course, we thank the contributors, none of whom has received royalties, except for those who received $29.95, the annual yield from the Donnelley Stool of Bibfeldt Studies. Since that is prize money, it has not been reported to the IRS, which is busy enough without having to track Bibfeldt and his Foundation and Stool.

JERALD C. BRAUER
MARTIN E. MARTY

I. The Quest for the Historical Bibfeldt

The history of the world is a record of Divine judgment; the history of Christianity displays the wonder of Divine mercy; the history of the Church reveals the depth of Divine patience.

FRANZ BIBFELDT,
The Crooked Way

Portrait of Franz Bibfeldt by Siegfried Reinhardt

Franz Bibfeldt: Theologian for Our Time

MARTIN E. MARTY

This essay is a slightly revised and updated version of what the Foundation has come to call the *Ur*-paper on Bibfeldt. It was delivered early in the 1970s at the first of the occasional annual observances, and goes a long way toward explaining the theologian. Let it be noted that many items in subsequent essays do not and will not square with details of some of the materials in this one. In the case of inconsistencies and contradictions among the authors, the reader should know that they are both, and all, as correct as each other. — ED.

Franz Bibfeldt was born in the early morning hours of November 1, 1897, at Sage-Hast bei Groszenkneten, Oldenburg, Niedersachsen, Germany, and was baptized later the same day. His birth was one day premature, since he was conceived on February 2 after a Candlemas party. His father, Friedrich Bibfeldt, happened to be home that day and evening at a time when he was traveling to represent Friedrich Naumann during the latter's efforts to establish the *Nationalsoziale Verein*. This meant that his father was a Protestant Christian, a liberal, a Democrat, and a non-Marxian socialist — certainly the proper background for the future theologian.

The baptism was performed on the birthdate, November 1, because that was All Saints' Day, dedicated to "all the apostles, martyrs, confessors and all the just and perfect who are at rest." Franz's parents did not want to offend any of the saints, hence their effort to please all of them by choosing this date for their son's christening. This willing-

3

ness to please everybody was a personality trait the parents passed on to their son, and it served him well in his chosen calling.

Not much is known of a biographical character, but before that little bit is detailed, it is important to establish Bibfeldt's central position, since he is not widely recognized in America. To the heart of it: his is known as the theology of "Both/And," based on the suggestion that it is possible for the contemporary theologian to be relevant to everything and to adapt to anything. Something of this thinker's position is evident from the title of his best-known pamphlet: within a decade after Karl Barth had written one called *Nein!* (No!), Bibfeldt responded with *Vielleicht?* (Perhaps?).

Bibfeldt, having studied the history of the subject intensely, defines theology as "the art of making things come out right." His motto is *Respondeo ergo sum*, "I respond, therefore I am." This phrase styles him perfectly for the role we have designated for him, "theologian for our time, or our times." The Bibfeldt family coat of arms shows the god Proteus rampant on a weathervane, an excellent symbol for these decades. One should recall that Proteus was the herdsman of the many seals that belonged to Poseidon, the sea god. He hated to prophesy and in order to avoid it he would change his shape, appearing as a lion, a dragon or even fire. Ordinarily he looked like an old, old man. The motto on the coat of arms corresponds to the one Bibfeldt chose personally. An old Spanish proverb, it reads, "I dance to the tune that is played."

Bibfeldt's thesis is that the theologian should and can reconcile everything to everything. "If God can do it, why can't we?" he asked. This thought occurred to him as a student while he pondered the ejaculation of Eunomius, the fourth-century bishop of Cyzicus and patron of so many subsequent theologians, "I know God as well as He knows Himself!" The man whom we now honor consolidated his viewpoint in the best-known of his translated works, *The Relieved Paradox* (Howard Press, 1951). The words that best characterize the thought of this *Sic et Non* man are "be relevant," "adapt," "accommodate," "adjust," "compromise," "come to terms with," and the like.

The admirable consistency of Bibfeldt's application of these less-than-original principles has occasioned some of the attention given him. He likes to quote Archilochur: "The fox knows many things, but the hedgehog knows one big thing." While he is first of all the hedgehog since he knows "one big thing" about the nature of much of the theological enterprise, he is also the fox, knowing "many things." He has, therefore, commented on many subjects and as these comments become better known there is no doubt that he will become a household word. After only forty years of exposure to America, he has already attracted several followers.

Details of his life are meager, though more may be known after the interview of him by Howard Hughes appears in a popular American magazine. We do know that in his hometown he joined the *Turnverein* "Gut Heil" (good health). This may have seemed a strange choice, since the Turners were and are a semi-anticlerical, semi-secret, semi-athletic society. But Bibfeldt has always been attracted to entities which we characterize with the prefix *semi* and, in any case, it was his nature to "play both sides of the street." He became an expert equilibrist and tightrope walker and was an excellent gymnast on the balance beams. But ultimately he was to be disgraced and to turn from athletics.

The German Turners all tried to get dueling scars to match those of their militaristic contemporaries in the university fraternities. When Bibfeldt's turn came, it happened that he jumped just as his opponent swung for his cheek, and the young athlete was cut in a place which he was never able to show to the public. It is thought that this event led him to write the famous essay "Empathy with the Circumcised," the article that later induced James Robinson to classify him in the "empathist" school of later Heideggerians and may have stood behind his long record of good relations with Jews, from his sanctuary in Switzerland through the Nazi period.

Having failed at the *Turnverein*, Bibfeldt was seventeen years old. It was 1914, and war was brewing; soon he would be in the military. W. H. Auden's poem about the "unknown citizen" perfectly characterized him: "Our researchers into Public Opinion are content that he held the proper opinions for the time of year/When there was peace, he was for peace, when there was war, he went." Bibfeldt went to Switzerland; for that reason he came to be known as a pacifist theologian. Having failed at athletics and having avoided the military, there was not much for him to do, so he went to the University of Bern to study church history. In order to balance the reputation he was gaining for arrogance during the time when Eunomius was his model, he chose to think of himself as humble and called himself "Exiguus."

Reading Cassiodorus one day — reading Cassiodorus is the kind of thing church history students did in those times — he came across another "Exiguus," in this case Dionysius Exiguus, the sixth-century Scythian monk who did much work on the Christian calendar. This serendipitous discovery led Bibfeldt to write his doctoral thesis, "The Problem of the Year Zero." He came to be disturbed over the fact that,

as the *Encyclopaedia Britannica* says, "chronologers admit no year between 1 B.C. and A.D. 1." The man who wanted to reconcile all subjects
and to make things come out right did not believe it fair to move the
calendar two years when really only one had passed. In the course of
this work he became so adapted to thinking in terms of "one year
earlier," that he has been one year off for many events. For all we know,
he may have been here a year ago today or will be here a year from
today for this festive observance!

The thesis was not well received and was never published. The
years were passing and this great man had not found himself. Then he
learned of the fact that theologians could entertain the *coincidentia oppositorum*, the "coincidence of opposites." A new discipline and voca-
tion lay ahead of him. Athletics, the military, church history — none of
these fields permitted him to excel. So he became a theologian, devoting
himself to epistemology. It was his contention that it "makes no difference whether something is known or not known, because knowing and
not knowing are both dimensions of the same faculty, the knowing-not-
knowing faculty."

His ability to speak this way made him popular with the followers
of Martin Heidegger, and for some time he attended conferences of the
Heideggerian theologians. However, when he contended that the
geschicklich (fateful) and *geschichtlich* (historic) were identical, he was
excluded and entered his silent years. We know that he wrote and was
for some time a parish pastor; but it is through his writings that he
gained what measure of fame has come to him, culminating in the
publication of *The Relieved Paradox*.

It might be well to comment on Bibfeldt's relationship with this
city and this university. While he was first cited in a course paper by
Robert Howard Clausen in the autumn of 1947 at Concordia Seminary
in St. Louis, most of the Bibfeldtian lore has lived on at Chicago. Were
it not for the attention paid him by Jerald C. Brauer, the first American
professional to cite Bibfeldt in a formal lecture, it is possible that a
number of eminent religionists would have overlooked him. Among
those introduced by Professor Brauer to Bibfeldt's approach have been
Paul Tillich, Helmut Thielicke, Joseph Sittler, Karl Barth, Cardinal Leo-
Josef Suenens and Mircea Eliade; regrettably, his influence has never
really surfaced in their work.

His first trip to America came in the early years of the United
Nations. It is believed that he gave the United States' U.N. ambassador,
Warren Austin, the suggestion that an Arab-Israeli dispute at the U.N.
could be resolved if only the Arab delegates and Israeli delegates would

come out with him into the hall to settle the affair "like Christian gentlemen." The Chicago visit is believed to have occurred on July 1, 1970, the day after Professor Brauer completed his tenure as dean of the Divinity School. (Recall that Bibfeldt is often one year off in his commitments.) The only evidence we have of that visit was a graffito in the Swift Hall men's room, the epigraph of Bibfeldt's popular book, *The Crooked Way*. It reads: "God grades on the curve."[1]

The only time Bibfeldt is known to have referred to a member of the Chicago faculty in print came when he reviewed Professor Robert M. Grant's *U-Boats Destroyed*. In that review Bibfeldt argued that "destroyed" was too radical a concept. Since he had lived in Switzerland, he was sure that his criticism was not based in chauvinism; but Bibfeldt would have preferred *U-Boats Damaged*. Not finding his supporters at Swift Hall on that July day — indeed, finding no one in the Divinity School in midsummer — he went to a place called the Urban Training Center, since he had long sought Emerging Structures of Viable Ministry, and "took the plunge." This was a UTC program that called for its students to be on their own without funds or identity papers for a week in Chicago.

It is known that Bibfeldt, in his "sixties" mode, went to Esalen, where he read Norman O. Brown's writings on "polymorphous perversity." Desiring to be relevant to this, and now having found his goal, the place "where the action was," he went on to develop a variation of the Brown theme. (Theologians rarely plagiarize; they usually "adapt themes.") Bibfeldt favored "polyperverse morphology." A reviewer of his paper on this subject was later to say: "Baron von Hügel once said, 'I kiss my daughter not only because I love her but in order to love her.' Bibfeldt would kiss his daughter because he is a dirty old man." Bibfeldt, by the way, never had a daughter, so far as we know.

While in California, he also devoted himself to a study of Charles Schulz's work, to which Robert Short had drawn him. Bibfeldt always favored the Schulzian concept of "the wishy-washy," a phrase that loses something in translation (*saft- und kraft-los, läppisch, geringfügig*). No other record of Bibfeldt's second American visit is available to us.

While it is not possible to briefly give the content of Bibfeldt's

---

1. This is the place to acknowledge my indebtedness. Most scholarly papers — and the reader can tell this is a scholarly paper because now it has a footnote — apprise others of the authors' debts to the Guggenheim Foundation or to the Fulbright Program. I would like to thank the University of Chicago Building and Grounds department for leaving the graffito there for many months until it was brought to my attention.

protean thought, something should be said about its manner, style, and relation to other modern theology. Eunomius and Dionysus he left behind. "Historical theology takes too long to write," said Bibfeldt after he finished both his dissertation and his *Habilitationsschrift*. They took so long, in fact, that he finally chose to dedicate them after the long scholarly sit to St. Fiacre, patron of hemorrhoid sufferers.

Bibfeldt turned to the moderns when he read Neander to the effect that Friedrich Daniel Schleiermacher was the true shaper of modern theology, and that his was both a *Gefühlstheologie* and a "pectoral theology." *(Pectus est quod facit theologum.)* Favoring the pectoral approach, he read further when he heard that Schleiermacher "is neither for absoluteness nor against it." The Schleiermacherian concept of religion as the feeling of absolute dependence was too much for Bibfeldt's *läppisch* approach, and he revised this to "relative dependence."

Søren Kierkegaard disturbed him most. One would have expected that Bibfeldt's reply to Kierkegaard's *Either/Or* would have been *Both/And*; but that represented too drastic a choice for the man who elevated the *saftlos* to high status. His second treatise was called *Either/Or and/or Both/And*. Having heard that Kierkegaard was always haunted by the fact that his father had always been haunted by the fact that he, the father, had once stood on a heath in Jutland and cursed God, Bibfeldt decided to even things out; he went to Jutland and cursed the heath.

He agreed with Adolf Harnack concerning the Hegelians at Tübingen: "The work of the Tübingen School was an episode in which we have learned much, but after which we must unlearn more." Bibfeldt virtually made unlearning a life passion. He found little in Albrecht Ritschl, another nineteenth-century giant. Asked what he thought of Ritschl's response, "Where I find mystery, I say nothing about it," Bibfeldt as a theologian of mystery — some would say of bewilderment — replied, "Where I find Ritschl, I say nothing about him."

Having heard of Ludwig Feuerbach's materialist antitheology and its condensation in the phrase, "Man ist was er iszt" (man is what he eats), he recalled the New Testament saying about that which issues forth from a man as characterizing the man, and developed an anthropology parallel to Feuerbach's in his famous essay translated into English under the title "Scatology and Eschatology."

Bibfeldt was not content with Karl Barth's adoption of the Kierkegaardian concept of the "infinite qualitative difference" between time and eternity, between God and man, and spoke of the "relative quantitative similarity" between them. He knew that Barth's famous commentary on Romans had made theological history, and was told of his fellow Swiss's recall of that event: "As I look back upon my course, I seem to myself as one who, ascending the dark staircase of a church tower and trying to steady himself, reached for the bannister, but got hold of the bell rope instead." Bibfeldt's response: "Hold to the bannister." Given his attack on Barth in *The Relieved Paradox*, it is a sign of Barth's graciousness that he so enjoyed the work of Bibfeldt, who seemed to represent no threat to him.

Americans may wonder about Bibfeldt's attitude toward American theology. For example, what was his opinion of the Chicago School, of process thought, of theology that depicted an evolving God? This suited Bibfeldt fine, but he also wanted to give equal time to the opposition, as was his wont, and quoted Dean W. R. Inge, "You forget, said the Devil with a twinkle, that I have been evolving too." He was attracted to Unitarianism because he had read of Ralph Waldo Emerson's dismissal of it for its "pale negations." Bibfeldt thought there was nothing wrong with "pale," but wanted negations to be balanced with affirmations.

Attracted to American political theology in his "fifties" mode, he favored the late Senator Everett M. Dirksen of Illinois, since he could find no record of that Senator's ever having taken a firm and consistent position on anything. But that was mere politics, and he was interested in civil religion. Thus he came across Dwight D. Eisenhower: hearing that Nelson Algren called Eisenhower "that man who melted like cotton candy in the mouth of history," Bibfeldt asked that this pleasant saying be his own epitaph one day. Who better than Eisenhower had summarized so well the "adaptation theology" when he had said that government must be "founded in a deeply felt religious faith — *and I don't care what it is.*"

So far as formal modern theology is concerned, he liked some of the radicals of the 1960s, notably Thomas J. J. Altizer for his position on the *coincidentia oppositorum*, since it enabled Bibfeldt to speak on both sides of all issues and still seem to be taking a stand. His first reading of J. A. T. Robinson's *Honest to God* impressed him, since Robinson wanted to replace a God "up there" or "out there" with a God in the dimension of depth, which must mean "down here" or "in here." Bibfeldt worked out the idea of "God on the average," more or less transcendent. On Robinson he was to paraphrase a line of Peter DeVries that later became a cliché: "On the surface, he's profound. Deep down, he's shallow."

Having read the two best-known books of Harvey Cox and having been told that the theses of the two were contradictory, he was asked, "Is *Secular City* or *The Feast of Fools* correct?" Bibfeldt's answer was "Yes!" This oracular style stood him in good stead during the old death-of-God controversy. When asked "Is God dead?" it was he who answered, "God ——— Is." Incidentally, not having come across the October 1965 issues of the *New York Times* and *Time* magazine until April 7, 1966, he almost missed out on the death-of-God movement, so he had only one day in which to become relevant to it, since the April 8, 1966 *Time* cover story on God marked the end of the movement in the sense of a phenomenon to which Bibfeldt felt the need to adapt.

On Roman Catholic thought he has had much to say, but space permits little opportunity to develop it here. I am told that Father Andrew Greeley is researching the Catholic counterparts to these Bibfeldtian themes. Bibfeldt has shown interest in the workings of the hierarchy, and has generally liked the American ecclesiastical style. He felt, on the basis of having read a chess rule book, that most bishops are living up to their obligations: "A bishop can move diagonally only." He has commented on the burning issue of celibacy, and made a constructive proposal: "I think Roman Catholicism should keep celibacy — but should make it a little easier for everybody."

The "new morality" and situation ethics pleased him most, and he was grateful to Joseph Fletcher for resurrecting St. Augustine's maxim for ethics, "Love with care and then what you will, do," especially when he heard it in Latin: *Dilige et quod vis, fac.* "I like that!" he exclaimed.

H. R. Mackintosh has said that "a great man condemns the world to the task of explaining him." We Bibfeldtians gladly take on the explanatory task to which we have been condemned by this great man. What makes this task possible is Bibfeldt's consistency. When the theological world was neoorthodox, he adapted himself to it. When theologians half a generation later all wanted to accommodate themselves to the secular, his weathervane turned him there. When they moved toward the new religious enthusiasms and transcendence, Proteus as a symbol came again to his rescue. Now in an age of anomie and acedia and apathy, his time seems certainly to have come, and he will be relevant to still another age.

F. Scott Fitzgerald once said that "the test of a first-rate intelligence is the ability to hold two opposed ideas in the mind at the same time, and still retain the ability to function." On those terms, Franz Bibfeldt is the genius of our time, the proper theologian for tomorrow.

Franz Bibfeldt's Bicentennial Legacy

ROBERT M. GRANT

Robert M. Grant, the Carl Darling Buck Professor Emeritus, an expert on New Testament and early Christian literature, used the occasion of the nation's bicentennial to recall a story of Bibfeldt ancestry and then moved on to discuss some of Bibfeldt's implications for hermeneutics. — ED.

Franz Bibfeldt has sent me the outline of remarks he was to give today and asked me to bring this message to his friends old and new. He claims he has no enemies; this illusion must be due to advancing years or even to hardening of the arteries. What he wanted to talk about on this bicentennial occasion was what he considered the real heroes of the Revolution, one of whom was his ancestor Martin Bibfeldt. These heroes were not the Yankees or the British, nor even the Hessians whom the British brought with them. They were the quiet Pennsylvania Dutchmen whom the Hessians hired. History has little to tell us about them, and this is why we always need revisionist history or even historical revisionism.

Martin Bibfeldt was born in Paradise, Pennsylvania, on February 22, 1732. After getting run out of Paradise at a fairly early age, he moved to the nearby town of Intercourse and proceeded to raise a family. In the typical early American manner, failure succeeded failure, and by 1776 he was ready for a declaration of independence. The revolutionary army refused his services. The recruiter told him they "weren't worth a Continental." Martin thereupon turned loyalist and since he knew German much better than English, though that's not saying much, he

11

attached himself to a Hessian regiment that tried to prevent Washington from crossing the Delaware. As we all know from the picture of the man or divine being in the boat, crossing the ice as the British or Hessian dogs pursued, with the red glare of Martin Bibfeldt's rockets in the background, Washington did cross the Delaware. Bibfeldt surrendered. This was just about two hundred years ago, and it marked the beginning of Bibfeldt's Revolution that has meant so much in the local histories of eastern Pennsylvania.

Naturally he was soon freed by the colonials, for they noticed that his appetite for knackwurst, sauerkraut, and even Wiener schnitzel was a terrible burden on the treasury. Once on his own, he took colonial aptitude tests, and it was discovered that he had an aptitude for absolutely nothing. Once more we find him to be a truly typical early American sage. Moreover, his memory was poor. He tried to achieve fame by memorizing things from Dr. Franklin's thoughts, but he could not even get "Early to bed, early to rise" into his head. He claimed to have invented electricity, but people thought he had simply been struck by lightning. He lived on, finally, in the poorhouse at Lancaster, Pennsylvania, until 1812, when he got out and was shot as he tried to join the British again.

What is the message of Martin Bibfeldt for our trying times? First of all, keep trying. Or, if you are trying enough, you may succeed and you may not. As a matter of fact, his little-known "Notebook of 1798" contains exactly these thoughts.

In 1799, however, Martin was lucky enough to come upon a book of poems and in that year's notes he inscribed words that his descendent Franz Bibfeldt and, indeed, all worthwhile theologians or administrators were to find meaningful: "Whatever is, is right." Here is the essence of Martin Bibfeldt's theological message, the words not so much Protestant as popish, that were to overarch hermeneutically and to mesmerize the thought of his successors. "Whatever is, is right" is a thought that has always meant much to Franz Bibfeldt and is surely the essence of whatever we learn here in his name. With it goes the sublime philosophical axiom inculcated by all our professors and most of our students: "Change is decay." Had Martin Bibfeldt lived to see our university with its absolute devotion to Christianity — the primitive and pure Christianity of St. Clement and the immortal phoenix — he would have gone on to draw the last and most logical conclusion: if "Change is decay," then "Decay is change." And this we learn from the story of the phoenix itself, the central myth of the Christian religion.

I recall the last time I saw Franz Bibfeldt, his quavering lips barely enunciating the basic principles of his ancestors. "Whatever is, is right," he said and then he added, with an unexpected declension into modern vulgarism: "Tell them to tell it like it is. This is what I have tried to do."

Since I am the emissary of this Bibfeldt lecture, let me now simply pass it on to you as I received it.

Distinguished colleagues:

The thought of Franz Bibfeldt needs no introduction, or even apology, for this audience and readership. The *Ur*-Bibfeldt essay [see previous chapter] shows that the command of Jesus to his disciples was obviously applicable, "Let not your right hand know what your left hand is doing." No adequate picture of Bibfeldt was available to scholars at that time. Only the combination of certain letters written by him and certain reports leaked from government files makes it possible to say what his real contribution to the official renewal has been since about 1933. At that time, you will recall, Bibfeldt was about thirty-six.

It is not generally known that in the late thirties Bibfeldt taught New Testament theology at the University of Graustark. Though he advanced only briefly to the rank of *ordinarius*, his students, and even some of his colleagues, were well aware of his merits; and although like other New Testament fantasies his new method of *Numerologiegeschichte* collapsed, it was highly regarded for a time, at least by Party members. In the methodological spectrum it lay between *Schallanalyse* and *Formgeschichte*; indeed, it looked ahead toward other *Geschichtes* of our time. It involved counting the letters in various New Testament passages, using the presupposition or *Ding an sich* that to express a theological thought requires no fewer than forty letters and no more than fifty. On this basis Bibfeldt was able to revise much of the rubbish his predecessors had produced. Many of his calculations have survived, chiefly because the OSS thought they might contain a new German cipher.

After the War

After the war there were many Germans who thought that perhaps they had been misled by the Party and the Movement. Bibfeldt was among them. He could express himself freely as favoring the French, the British, the Americans, and the Russians. One of his deepest expressions, however, favored none of these powers. It was produced in a time of angst — apparently during the Berlin airlift — and is a sermon preached in a small church in Graustark. The text was taken from the Psalms (75:6): "Neither from the east, nor from the west, nor yet from the South, cometh lifting up." Bibfeldt, with other neoorthodox theologians of his time, was rather fond of allegorization. This is to say that he used the Bible as he had used *Mein Kampf*, as a book of spells. And in this verse from the Psalms he found a reference to the 1948 political situation. His people should promote close relations with Scandinavia; lifting up would obviously come from the North if not from East, West or South.

When his applications to teach at Uppsala, Lund, or Aarhus were rejected, he turned with renewed vigor to biblical criticism. The most important article in the new period was of course the hermeneutical study of Psalm 75, based no longer on *Numerologiegeschichte* but on the theological point that God tells the hermeneut what to think. Having read just a little Pope (not the Roman one), Bibfeldt felt that whatever had been, was right; therefore, since he had not received a Scandinavian call, he would have to emend the text, however reluctantly. Relying on three magical cylinders from Ur and a gold plate in the British Museum, he decided that the psalmist must have intended to say this: "Neither from the East nor from the West (Bibfeldt was disenchanted with all the northern powers), nor yet from the North, cometh lifting up." Though only his students accepted the new reading, it was impressive enough to Bibfeldt himself. He decided, like other theologians of his era (E. Peterson, H. Schleier), to wend his way southward and see what possibilities of theological renewal lay in Italy, where one could find Rome *aeterna*, the *ecclesia* and *theologia perennis*, perhaps even a *Papa amabilis*.

Romeward

Bibfeldt arrived in Rome too soon. A few Jesuits, however, recognized his potential value as a Protestant Trojan horse or, as they liked to put it in order to confuse him, the column of Trojan. His renown as the "chameleon of the Western world" (as Barth called him) or the "forerunner of borderline theology" (Tillich) or "sexy Biebgeldt" (Thielicke) meant that for almost a decade he lived free of charge in a branch of the Banco di Santo Spirito. He was more welcome in Rome than in Athens, where the Patriarch referred to him as *ho loimos ton dusmon* (ὁ λοιμὸς τῶν δυσῶν), or The Pest of the West.

During this time he assiduously studied Italian. The result was that during several papal audiences he was heard expressing himself fluently, with the use of such expressions as "Molto bene," "presto," "pronto," and "prego." Whether or not papal policy was influenced by Bibfeldt's counsel is hard to say. At the time of the Vatican Council he firmly opposed innovation but advocated reform, thus winning from both sides almost unmitigated contempt. Such is the lot of the Bibfeldts of this world, always misunderstood or, it may be, understood.

The peak of his career seems to have been achieved around 1969, when he was flown to Chicago by misguided students who supposed that his theology as expressed at that time would help them in their attempt to take over the Divinity School. When he announced his intention of lecturing in German, much of his prospective audience vanished. His lectures in English lost the rest of it. It was not so much how he said it as what he said. Responding to the basic theological crisis produced by Thomas Altizer (on the one occasion when Altizer visited Harper Library, God appeared to him and said, "I am he who is not"), Bibfeldt boldly proclaimed the past existence or "wasness" of God. Since he had spent so much time in Rome he was able to suggest a Latin term, not the *esse* or *essence* of the divine nature but its *fuisse* or *fuissence*. This dismayed his hearers, few of whom were acquainted with the language involved. Bibfeldt also insisted that the *Blik* described by another God-is-deader was a misunderstood *Blitz*; but his further ramblings about *Krieg* in relation to this were incomprehensible.

On returning to Rome from Chicago, Bibfeldt felt that it was time for him to begin work on his magnum opus. Certainly it could not be called *Entweder/Oder*, and *Die Beide/Und* seemed a rather strange German concept. He therefore concluded that it should simply be called *Magnum Opus*; in addition, a Latin title, he wrongly supposed, might attract Roman Catholic readers. At one point he thought of keeping it anonymous and simply ascribing it to "the apostle of theological renewal," but a publisher with whom he was briefly in contact discouraged him.

The great advance in hermeneutical methodological exactitude that Bibfeldt achieved, or thought he achieved, was based on neosyllogistic existentialism. Thus if I say "God is," I have gone too far; if I say "God is not," I have not gone far enough (or vice versa); therefore I must simply say "God" and start there. Thus "if God, then" leads to the heart of the matter. (This can be rephrased as "if God, so.") From the heart of the matter we go up to the head or down to the feet by asking the precisely phrased question, "If God, so what?" After 330 pages of closely packed metaphysics, physics, metamorphosis, pseudo-morphosis, and the like, Bibfeldt's book comes to an end. A reviewer pointed to this fact as perhaps Bibfeldt's supreme achievement.

At the time it *was* his supreme achievement. A little later, however, the University of Chicago recalled its initial response to his work — none — and the faculty concluded that once again it had failed to recognize real greatness. A committee lost itself in the dank obscurity of *Magnum Opus* and recommended the unique degree of B.V.M., apparently under the impression that Bibfeldt was a Jesuit. At the convocation, in an impromptu address, Bibfeldt rose to the occasion. "During the Hitler years," he said, "I was not exactly a martyr, but on the other hand I was not firmly loyal to the Nazi party. The method of 'Both/And' set forth in my book of neosyllogistic existentialism fully justifies my position, at least insofar as it is close to that of Heidegger and the other revolutionary saints of our time." At this point even the collegiate gothic chapel had experienced more than it could tolerate. That is why it has lain in ruins from that day to this.

A Letter from Franz Bibfeldt

JERALD C. BRAUER

Also during the bicentennial seasons, Jerald C. Brauer, co-head of the Foundation, passed on to audiences and now, without updating, he passes on to readers, a letter from Bibfeldt, who was caught in the act of trying to be relevant to American politics — in this case, during the Ford administration. Here is the letter, as received and read. — ED.

July 4, 1976

Dear Professor Brauer:

Greetings on this holiest of all days. Oh day of light and splendor. Oh moment of revolution and revelation. To think that two hundred years ago a new nation immaculately conceived was brought forth dedicated to the proposition that all people are created equal. Why had I never heard this before? An invitation to a bicentennial celebration changed my whole life, my theology will never be the same. I had to write you of my experience. Surely it is a new *Turm erlebnis*.

Early in the spring of 1976 I received a special invitation from the president of the United States to attend a bicentennial celebration and deliver the keynote lecture in Washington. My first impulse was to put a nix on the whole idea. But as I sat on my balcony smoking my pipe and rereading the invitation, it dawned on me that perhaps there was a Ford in my future.

Still in reverie, I got up from my chair and as I knocked my pipe on the balcony railing, the ashes streamed downward in streaks of red,

17

white, and blue. Surely this was a special leading, but I was not convinced. Secure in my Schwartzwald hideaway, that bastion of true theology, I went in to view the evening *Fernsehen* (TV) news.

Miracle of miracles, it happened. I flicked the switch, a light flashed on the screen, and there was the message, "Ford has a better idea." Suddenly everything came together for me: first the invitation from Ford, then the red, white, and blue ashes, then a flick of the television switch and the message — Ford has a better idea. How I had underrated him. I too wanted to beg his pardon. What was Ford's better idea?

It was to invite Bibfeldt to deliver the main bicentennial lecture in Washington. I was determined to study the bicentennial, to note its relation to my theology, and to prepare the greatest theological lecture of my career. America needed Bibfeldt. What else could we poor Germans offer than our humble theological insight?

Systematically I studied the significance of the American Revolution, the bicentennial celebration. True to my time-tested method, I started by analyzing the word *bicentennial*. First, I broke it into its components. *Bi* — that connotes two, or it is a short form of farewell, or it can mean next to. Quickly I became convinced that it means all three in this context. It could not signify only two, or one, because that would contradict our trinitarian heritage; therefore, the three are meaningful in our celebration.

How then were all three meaningful? Again my Bibfeldtian method provided the answer — Washington. The bicentennial lecture was to be in Washington, Washington was father of the nation, so all three meanings of the word are related to the patriarch. *Bi* as two — Washington was president for two terms. *Bi* as a short form of farewell — Washington delivered a short farewell address. *Bi* as next to — Washington is next to the Potomac River.

My heart pounded with excitement as all things began to cohere. Furiously I knocked my pipe in the ashtray, but the burned tobacco would not come loose. I paced up and down as the significance of my insights overwhelmed me. The bicentennial was to center in Washington; Washington was the father of the nation; and the doctrine of the Trinity, the root of all our Christian theology, begins with the Father. The parallel was clear; I did not have to proceed further into an analysis of the word *bicentennial*. The first syllable was key to our entire understanding.

It was necessary to analyze the key symbol of the bicentennial — father. Raised and educated in the Lutheran tradition, I immediately turned to the bedrock of truth — Scripture and common sense. The former is clear in every age, so one can easily assume the self-evident truths of Scripture. No Christians have ever disagreed on that. Common sense presents a different matter, for each age has a different view of common sense. I am deeply committed to the concept of relevance, so I turned to our contemporary view of common sense, namely, Freudianism.

Freud had much to teach us concerning the central symbol of the bicentennial — the father. Strange that everybody has overlooked that in Freud. At least two points stand out: the Oedipus complex, the urge of every man to kill his father in order to establish his own freedom, his autonomy; and the father complex, an unusual attachment of young ladies to their father. Here was a concept grounded in common sense, which, in its essentials, gave equal rights to men and women. Now I was cooking.

What was the bicentennial all about? It concerned the father — the king who lusted after the money of the sons and the beauty of his daughters in his overseas family. This king and his minions in parliament demanded obedience from his colonial family, but they were rooted and grounded in Scripture and in common sense. In Scripture they learned they were to bow on the knee to none but God in heaven, and they were to call no man king. From common sense — implicit Freudianism — they learned about problems with father.

So the daughters of the Revolution struck off the shackles of their father complex and left daddy once and for all: they rebelled against the king and found God. The sons of that revolution had to kill their father to find their autonomy, their freedom. And so they became free for a proper relationship with their mother, Pat, better known as Patria. As I reviewed that tremendous struggle, I was struck with the fact that on Washington's left hand was that great French patriot, General Lafayette. But on his right hand was that freedom fighter from Greece, General Oedipus. These two combined — Lafayette and Oedipus — to conquer the king at a great battle symbolic of their two nations: Brandywine.

You note, Professor Brauer, that everything coheres in the Bibfeldtian hermeneutic. So we are brought to the center of my discovery based on the bicentennial theology of Revolution. I am convinced that some day theologians will learn to appreciate not only Scripture but also Freud, not only authority but also revolution. Who knows, at some distant point in the future there may develop a theology of revolution that is now receiving my full attention and is the basis for my great bicentennial lecture.

Permit me to recapitulate in one paragraph the essence of the lecture. My first great book was an answer to Karl Barth on the paradox resolved. My next book is really an answer to Karl Marx (I seem to be hung up on Karl) on the paradox returned. All this I owe to the American Revolution. Hannah Arendt reminded us that the word *revolution* really means to revolve, to turn back to, to return to, actually to come full circle. Americans were the first to learn this in their revolution: they have been going in circles ever since. I learned it from them, and so I have moved from paradox to paradox resolved (anti-Karl B.) to paradox returned (anti-K. Marx) and I too have come full circle. As another great man once said, I have returned.

Instead of being on a linear straight and narrow, my head is now spinning with new ideas. Barth is wrong: history is not *senkrecht von oben*, moving but into a final judgment. And Marx is wrong: history is not moving in a straight line toward the paradise of the proletariat. You might mention this to your colleague Eliade, who could get a new book out of that idea. The American Revolution is right: history itself is a great revolution, a constant revolving in a mad whirl of freedom and creativity, on into the wild blue yonder. Ezekiel called it a wheel within a wheel, and that is proved by the fact that only in America can one find countless wheelers and dealers.

Am I a wheeler or am I a dealer? You know me well enough to know that the answer is yes. So I join in all that your revolution represents, as well as its opposite.

Dein,
Franz Bibfeldt

The Quest for the Historical Bibfeldt

DAVID OUSLEY

Still in the bicentennial seasons there were efforts to pursue "The Quest for the Historical Bibfeldt." David Ousley, now rector at the Church of St. James the Less, Philadelphia, revisited the efforts of Robert M. Grant and presented the following revisionist experiment. — ED.

Throughout the recent quest for the historical Bibfeldt, the discussion has been marred by a universal misunderstanding: taking "Bibfeldt" to be a name rather than a title. Although the point is so obvious that it should not require argument, Bibfeldt scholars here once again demonstrate their remarkable ability to miss the obvious. Therefore, it is the purpose of this essay to demonstrate that "Bibfeldt" cannot be considered Franz's surname, but is rather a religious title given him in the course of his life.

A brief remark on methodology is necessary (or at least inevitable) at this point. In order to demonstrate this thesis, we need a hermeneutical method of some sophistication, a type of demythologizing whereby we may understand and re-express in intelligible and meaningful contemporary language the true meaning of the source texts. The warrants for this are too obvious to be cited: in particular this method is required by the nature of the texts themselves as shown by Franz's own use of *Numerologiegeschichte*.[1]

To proceed, then, with the demythologizing. First, let us consider

1. See Robert Grant's essay, pp. 11-16.

the refusal of the United States Department of State to grant Bibfeldt a visa to attend the last Bibfeldt lecture.[2] It officially cited Bibfeldt's activities in the theological reform movement which he undertook during World War II. There were also rumors current at the time of an unfortunate incident involving Bibfeldt's wife and an official of the State Department. The mythological element in both of these "reasons" is patent: the fact behind these excuses is that the State Department could find no evidence of a person named Franz Bibfeldt (there being, of course, no such person, any more than there is a person named Elizabeth Queen). At the same time, they were understandably reluctant to admit this because of the high esteem in which Bibfeldt's works were apparently held in American universities. (It has also been suggested that Bibfeldt's popularity here contributed to the State Department's negative decision.) In any case, one cannot grant a visa to a nonexistent person; to grant one to a person with only a first name is equally unthinkable.

A second instance that supports my thesis is to be found in the manuscript tradition of Franz's last work, *Magnum Opus*. Although the title page of the printed edition cites the author as "Franz Bibfeldt," the original manuscript (the autograph, as recently demonstrated by Adolf Polanski, S.J.) bears only the name "Franz." This shows that Franz himself did not use "Bibfeldt" as a name, and further that "Bibfeldt" was in common use as a title by the time of the publication of *Magnum Opus*.

The third and definitive instance involves the final pericopae of the *G* source: that during Franz's first (and, as far as I have found, only) visit to Chicago, he spoke in the campus chapel. His words on the occasion were so intolerable as to cause the destruction of the chapel, which, the *G* source relates, "lies in ruins to this day." This enigmatic story is certainly original, since it satisfies the criteria of dissimilarity, incoherence, and single attestation. Archaeological excavations on the site of the chapel indicate that while other structures have occupied the site, the chapel itself has never suffered anything approaching ruin.

Several things may be meant by the mythic language of this story: the intent may be to show the power of the historical Franz's words, extending even to the physical universe. Or the story may show how Franz fulfills the office of Bibfeldt, through the Bibfeldtian conquest of

---

2. This is a reinterpretation of Bibfeldt's stated reason for not attending the bicentennial lecture (see Jerald Brauer document, pp. 17-20), but there Bibfeldt may have been speaking allegorically.

all forms of extreme moderation, the latter symbolized by the regular preaching that goes on in the chapel, or (more likely) by the collegiate gothic of the building.

These instances could be multiplied *ad nauseam* (and probably will be) by applying the hermeneutical method to the various stories and sayings found in our two main sources, the *M* source and the *G* source. But it should be clear, even from this brief exposition, that Bibfeldt is not a name but a title. This leads ineluctably to the questions of the meaning of the title and its source.

For the answer to these questions, we must turn to an article by Ludwig Amadeus Strauss, published at Tübingen in the *Zeitschrift für Geisteswissenschaftliche Studium* (CCCXIII:2; pp. 4-67) in 1821.[3] In this seminal article Strauss discusses the evolution and history of a syncretic religious sect known as the Anophilists. The sect still survived in Tübingen at the time of his article. It was named after its founder, Anophiles, an early medieval figure about whom little is known. Since the sect was certainly heretical from the start, the absence of sources from this period is hardly surprising. A resurgence in its vitality was felt with the influence of the alchemists, both Islamic and Christian. The foremost figure during the period was the alchemist Peristalsis. As an expression of the Anophilist identification with the downtrodden (and anyone else who agreed with them), they took Pope Joan as their patroness, and Peristalsis began the movement to have her canonized.[4]

The Anophilists were remotely Christian and broadly tolerant. Apparently, their numbers included such diverse luminaries as Pope Julius II, Luther, Tetzel, Francis Bacon, Oliver Cromwell, Schleiermacher (in his earliest days at the university), and Benjamin Franklin. Theologically, they accepted anything that did not appear to commit them to something — and held it passionately. (Already the affinities with Franz become evident.) Their credo was "Anything and everything — sometimes." But their central original contribution to the history of theology is of special note for our present concern: it is the understanding of the *Bibium feltum*. This term refers to a figure (whether human or not is unknown) who will mark the end of the Age — or,

3. This obscure but significant theological journal was available in libraries until sometime last fall (1975), when it seems to have disappeared. I have been able to uncover no other trace of it, but this is a problem not unfamiliar to Bibfeldt scholars.

4. In the late middle ages Joan was thought to have become pope, having spent her life masquerading as a man. She was discovered only when she gave birth to a son during a procession to the Lateran. She died shortly thereafter.

according to some sources, the beginning — presumably by succeeding in the attempt to have Pope Joan canonized.

The derivation of the title remains obscure, even after Strauss's pioneering work. The most generally accepted theory at present is that *Bibium* is derived from the verb *bibo*, to imbibe, and *feltum*, a copyist's error that should have read *feltrum*, meaning felt. Thus the title would be derived from the alchemical attempt to turn felt into gold by lining a silver cup with felt and then filling it with beer. (Remember that the cult is German in origin.) If the attempt failed, one could always drink the beer. At the time of Peristalsis, considered by some the "second founder" of the Anophilists, by others the perverter of the essence of Anophilism, drinking beer from felt-lined cups seems to have become part of this cult's ritual observance.

Whatever its origin, the *Bibium feltum* remained a vital part of Anophilist theology down to the time of Strauss and, as we shall see presently, beyond. Although it was, as we have observed, originally a steno symbol, *Bibium feltum* was used in the nineteenth century as a tensive symbol by the Anophilists of that time. This was due no doubt to its greater existential adequacy in the context of the emerging modernity. It was this usage that allowed its application to the historical Franz, as it appears in the German form (rather than the Latin), *Bibfeldt*.

Although in the absence of an adequate monographic literature any account of the development must remain tentative, what happened was apparently this: Franz's theology, teaching, work, and above all, his life appealed to the Anophilists in Tübingen as the incarnation of all they had ever imagined. Franz became directly acquainted with them during his stay in Tübingen. It is said that he instantly recognized his affinity with the sect, and therefore rejected membership. Nevertheless, his later involvement with the Curia during his stay in Rome proved the final factor in his qualification as *Bibfeldt:* here was the means for fulfilling the eschatological hope of having Joan canonized. Franz, in the hope of getting a greater circulation for his forthcoming *Magnum Opus*, readily agreed, and even allowed the addition of the title "Bibfeldt" to appear on the title page of this work.

In retrospect, all that Franz ever wrote can be seen as Anophilist: his syncretism in particular, as well as his incomparable ability to take a stand on almost nothing. His *Numerologiegeschichte* was the result of his hermeneutical method applied to his alchemical sources — and it realized about as much success.

There remains for future research to distinguish the kernel of the historical Franz from the historic Anophilist Bibfeldt, for the latter is but the expression of the perspectival or faith-image of the former, seen through the expectation of the *Bibium feltum.* I must leave such questions to future scholarship. Foremost among these great theological questions, like Franz's own perennial preoccupation with the question of whether Adam had a navel, is the crucial question of whether Franz ever had a last name.

The Quest for the Historical Bibfeldt

JOSEPH L. PRICE

These days, after the invention of "faction," which blends facts and fiction, and after books like Joseph McGinnis's on Senator Edward Kennedy, which imagines incidents and conversations, it is easier to understand why not all details of all lives of Bibfeldt match. But the absence of reliable sources has never deterred any writers of factional biographies, so why should it slow down Professor Joseph L. Price of Whittier College in California? With the eye of a sleuth and long familiarity with the subject, he tracks down hitherto unimagined aspects of Bibfeldt's career. — ED.

Introduction and Method

Until recently, most of the readily accessible resources on the life and works of Franz Bibfeldt were the secondary compilations or complications conveniently labeled as the *M* and *G* sources, named after the proto-Evangelists (and perhaps even Protestant evangelists) Marty and Grant. Although the two sources are useful to this study, the quest for the historical Bibfeldt cannot and will not be bound by the dated and insufficient method of source criticism. In addition, since we lack a third queue of pericopes that might corroborate or obliterate some of the more miraculous portions of the two proto-Evangelical traditions, it is questionable whether or not an adequate narrative foundation could be established merely by appealing to the competing claims of the myopic *M* and gratuitous *G* sources.

Recognizing the swift slide into ambiguity that would follow

26

upon the juggling of the secondary *M* and *G*, I have focused instead on Bibfeldt's primary works, and I have employed the methods of most postmodern scholarly analyses: linguistic analysis, structural criticism, redaction and reduction criticism, as well as the more adventuresome approaches of Ouija board projections and visual sociology analyses of the photographs in the *National Enquirer*. Additionally, I have drawn upon letters and other sources supplied by Bibfeldt's wife, Hilda Braunschweiger-Bibfeldt. And using the most dignified scholarly style of writing in my quest to recover the historical Bibfeldt, I maintain the spirit of Franz by avoiding referential footnotes, thus tempting me to plagiarize freely.

Scholarly Context

The quest for the historical Bibfeldt gained national recognition and scholarly sanction in the autumn of 1975 when Joseph Kitagawa, then dean of the Divinity School of the University of Chicago, wrote the following letter to Attorney General Edward Levi, who had recently served as the university's president.

Dear Mr. Levi:

I am sure — at least I hope — that you remember that I am dean of the Divinity School at the University of Chicago. The Divinity School, you will recall, is housed in Swift Hall.

Now that you are our nation's Attorney General, I, and all concerned theologians, need your help in resolving a problem. Some years ago Franz Bibfeldt, the German theologian, is reported to have come to Swift Hall during midsummer. (In Swift's inverted fashion, you may well recall, the summer days are the dark and lonely ones.) Since none of our research faculty were here then — as is their custom every summer — there is no documentary evidence that he was indeed here, although two university police officers and a janitor claim to have seen his shadow.

The problem is this: some new theological students here, by adapting modern theories of steno and tensive symbols, have proposed that Franz Bibfeldt is (or was) *merely* a symbol, and they have begun to debate his character as either steno or tensive. Of course, you can realize the gravity of the situation. The future of constructive theology rests on our ability to prove that Bibfeldt is indeed — or rather was certainly — a historical person, not a symbol, either steno or tensive.

Since the Bibfeldt Foundation itself is located in Swift Hall, I request that you send it a copy of the FBI and CIA files on Bibfeldt himself. Revealing the contents of the files, I am sure, will squelch the symbolic Bibfeldt theories.

Thank you in advance for your assistance.

> Dean Joseph Kitagawa
> *(signed)*

The reply from the attorney general also is revealing:

> Yes, there is a Bibfeldt. He is as real as J. Edgar Hoover was. And regarding your request for copies of investigative files on Bibfeldt, I have personally made certain that they have been sent to you.
>
> Sincerely yours,
> Edward Levi, Attorney General
> *(not signed)*
>
> P.S. Please remit 20 cents for the xeroxing charge for the Bibfeldt files.

These two letters provide the serious context for the postmodern quest for the historical Bibfeldt.

The Early Years

Of the early years of Bibfeldt's life, we know very little from the *M* and *G* sources, which fact probably does more than anything else to affirm their credibility. What we do know or can reconstruct is this: Franz Joseph Haydn Martin Luther Bibfeldt, so named in order to provide a variety of stage names for anticipated musical and theological careers, was born in the trundle seat of an 1892 Fiat[1] on November 1, 1897. His father, a Protestant bishop with revivalistic inclinations, and his mother, a Roman Catholic with charismatic tendencies, were on their way to a Bavarian camp meeting when their Fiat broke down two miles from Sage-Hast bei Groszenkneten, Oldenburg, Niedersachsen, Germany.[2]

A few minutes after the car's radiator overflowed on that fateful All Saints' Day, so did Mrs. Bibfeldt. Her water broke. According to the *M* source, Franz's birthday was a day early, since he had been conceived on February 2 of that year after a Candlemas party. In later years, Herr Bibfeldt would joke that Franz had been like the Enlightenment — an unanticipated conception that came while a candle flickered in the darkness of a Candlemas midnight.

Although the two extant sources tell us little about the birth and infancy of Bibfeldt, we can reconstruct *Q* (or Queer source, which is nothing more than the first letters of Franz's given names applied anagrammatically to a Ouija board), and thus we can determine that Franz did have an Oedipal complex. And from a deconstructive analysis (the phrase itself appears to be an oxymoron) of his first-grade self-portrait, we can conclude with great certainty that Franz fantasized that his mother was a virgin. In contrast to this maternal obsession, Franz has never mentioned his father in his later teaching and writing; and this omission has led many scholars to speculate that perhaps the Oedipal complex was not merely a fantasy with Franz.

Of the adolescent years of Bibfeldt, we know even less from *M* and *G*, which may be quite revealing in itself. What we do know about this period in his life, however, comes from the sensationalist work of 1961 entitled *Lurid Stories from a Confessional Booth, or Everything You Always Suspected about Confessionals but Didn't Know for Sure*, by Father X. In the second chapter of Father X's account, he reports that he often heard "Franz Bibfel—'s" confessions during the boy's pubescent years because Franz's Catholic mother had required that he make confession before receiving his allowance. For obvious reasons, Franz chose to make his confessions to Father X rather than his own father.

---

1. Some years after the event, Franz's father recalled with certainty that the Fiat had been involved, even though Franz's birth preceded Henry Ford's first ride by more than a decade. Hearing that pointed out, however, Franz's father was undeterred in telling the story, asserting in fact that the name of the car was a divine sign that referred to its manner of creation and operation.

2. The Protestant-Catholic marriage of his mother and father early modeled a kind of tolerance that Franz was later to find vital to his "Both/And" philosophical, theological stance.

Father X recalls that Franz would sow his wild oats during the week, and then on Sundays he would go to mass and pray for crop failure.

Our knowledge of Bibfeldt during the next decade is even scantier than that of his adolescent years. But we do know that in 1929 Bibfeldt graduated from the University of Worms with a D.D.T. degree, or Doctorate in Digressive Theology. His first scholarly article appeared later that year, and it was inspired by his fiancée, Hilda Braunschweiger. The essay, entitled "How to Get More Out of Speaking in Tongues," was an unessential analysis of New Testament references to *glossolalia*, which Bibfeldt regarded as a French method of performing the Pauline injunction to "greet the brethren [or sisters] with a holy kiss." The article received such notoriety that Bibfeldt was immediately invited to teach New Testament theology at the University of Graustark.

The Adult Years

The bulk of our knowledge about the adult Bibfeldt comes from his own teachings and writings, most of which were published either pseudonymously or anonymously. The one book that has borne Bibfeldt's own name as author is his *tour de farce*, as he called it, *The Relieved Paradox*, which was published by Howard Press in 1951. In the book Bibfeldt sets forth the basis for his great theology of "Both/And," a position deduced from his desire for absolute adaptability and relevance; in it he also states his belief that theology is "the art of making things come out right." And as the *M* source also notes, "his motto is *respondeo ergo sum*, 'I respond, therefore I am.'"

The fact that most of Bibfeldt's works were published *either* anonymously *or* pseudonymously (an ironic, unrelieved paradox with his "Both/And" philosophy) presents us with the problem of having to determine what are genuine Bibfeldt writings. There are several criteria that we have used to ascertain which writings are indeed authentic Bibfeldt works.

First of all, there is the criterion of multiple attestation: if several critics and reviewers have attributed a particular work to several different theologians and/or televangelists, then the state of confusion surely points to Bibfeldt as the only logical author. The second test is that of uniqueness and difficulty: if the work in question is abstruse and absurd and unlike anything that would seem reasonable to the theological enterprise, then surely the work is that of Bibfeldt. This criterion is closely related to the third: if anything in print is too ridiculous to be believed, then surely it must be the work of Bibfeldt. For instance, the proclamation of the "wasness of God," as the G source points out, is indeed a statement too ridiculous to be attributed to anyone but Bibfeldt.

The criterion of contradiction, which is the fourth one that can be applied to the process of distinguishing authentic from pseudo-Bibfeldtian works, also indicates that a work is probably Bibfeldt's if a statement on one page is contradicted a few pages later. The principle of proximity applies here in particular, because the closer the contradiction to the initial affirmation, the more likely it is that the statements belong to Bibfeldt.

The final test for determining Bibfeldtian authenticity is that of characteristic linguistic usage. Here we cite Bibfeldt's unique formula with which he often introduces his most profound sayings: "Perhaps, perhaps . . . ," or as the phrase has been rendered in the paraphrastic perversion known as *The Living Bibfeldt*, "Yes and no! Yes and no!"

Primary Works

Applying these criteria to various pseudonymous and anonymous works of significant merit, we can prove beyond a reasonable doubt that several of the works are Bibfeldt's. The most significant book in this group is the massive commentary on the Epistle to Philemon. Published in 1933, *Philemerbrief*, as it has often been cited, flipped like a tiddlywink into the gloomy world of European fascism and the American Depression and created the playground for modern theology. In *Philemerbrief*, Bibfeldt refines his hermeneutical method of *Numerologiegeschichte*. His goals in writing the commentary were *both* brief (in number) *and* comprehensive (in scope), thus manifesting his philosophical predisposition toward relieving paradoxes. His goals were (1) to devote one full paragraph to each letter of each word in the German translation of the Greek text, (2) to write at least one chapter on each verse in the epistle, and (3) to complete a chapter a day in order to keep the devil away. As a result, he was able to produce a massive missive in a fleet fortnight.

In *Philemerbrief*, the most incisive chapter by far is the twelfth one, which Bibfeldt wrote on the twelfth night of his project. The verse makes reference to one whom Paul identifies as Onesimus, "whom I have sent again." Paul goes on to urge Philemon to "receive him [Onesimus], that is, mine own bowels. . . ." The primary insight that Bibfeldt offers here is that Paul used the phrase "mine own bowels" as a euphemism for "mine own chitlins."

With this perceived Pauline substitution of "bowels" for "chitlins," Bibfeldt initiates a redaction of his *Numerologiegeschichte* method with which he had begun the work. From the more quantifiable approach of *Numerologiegeschichte*, Bibfeldt shifts to a more qualified hermeneutic, one that he calls *Bullsgeschichte*, since he thinks that the name of the method should reflect the content of the interpretation that it facilitates. (Here we might note that the *Bullsgeschichte* hermeneutic has become the most influential method of reasoning and interpretation in the American academy today because of its popularity among undergraduates.)

Another New Testament theology book that can be attributed with great certainty to Bibfeldt is *A Pragmatist's Paraphrase of Selected Sayings of Jesus*.[3] Published in 1948, the book represents Bibfeldt's first attempt to say something useful. He decided to write the book in order to balance the one-sided, radical nature of many of the sayings of Jesus as they have been preserved by tradition. In an effort to deal with the impracticality of many of Jesus' teachings, Bibfeldt subdeveloped his *Bullsgeschichte* method by proposing a hermeneutic of reversism, which can be explained most succinctly by quoting from his preface to the book.

> Reversism operates as follows: Any saying that is too hard to understand or to follow is to be understood to mean the opposite of what it literally says. My rationale for this lies in the recognition that Jesus was a pragmatist.

The following selections from his chapter on the Sermon on the Mount are representative of Bibfeldt's experiment with reversism.

---

3. Although I have indicated that referential footnotes are to be avoided in this essay — even at the temptation of committing the unforgivable sin of academics (which is blaspheming the spirit of research by plagiarizing) — I must acknowledge my absolute indebtedness and ability to copy here from an essay by friend and mentor E. Glenn Hinson, who originally came up with this list of pragmatic paraphrases in a satire entitled, I believe, "Basil the Manly." (N.B.: Basil Manly had been president of the Southern Baptist Theological Seminary around the turn of the twentieth century.)

5:3 Blessed are the rich in money, for they can build bigger and better churches. Who cares about the Kingdom of God?

5:4 Blessed are those who are always happy, having everything they need, for they don't need to be comforted.

5:5 Blessed are the ambitious, for they shall eventually own the earth.

5:6 Blessed are those who are in charge of dispensing righteousness, for they won't have to go to jail unless they tamper with income tax laws.

5:7 Blessed are those who show no mercy to those who owe them money, for they shall build bigger and better bank accounts.

5:8 Blessed are those whose external appearance and behavior are impeccable, for they shall look nice when they see God.

From the uniform appeal to capitalistic sensibilities (if that phrase itself is not an oxymoron, even if it is a pun) in these selected verses, it is also possible to see why William James is reputed to have called Jesus "the Prince of Pragmatists."

Several other works published anonymously but as yet untranslated — except for my translation of the titles — are also presumably the products of Bibfeldt. (In keeping with the style of scholarship that Bibfeldt encourages, we must wait until the translations of his works appear before attempting to determine the possibility of his having written them. For one of Bibfeldt's most eagerly received teachings — at least by graduate students — is that critical research should never be done in a foreign language.) Some of the titles of books whose translations we fervently await are his classic about the Reformation, *There I Sit*; his speculation about God's preferential option for the rich, *Philanthropic Privilege as the "Imago Dei"*; and his scatological eschatology, *Raping the Whirlwind*.

Conclusion

For the past two decades, Bibfeldt has, like Elvis, manifested pervasive presence through absence. One of the last occasions that he was seen in the flesh,[4] so to speak, was the time that he visited Swift Hall at the University of Chicago in early July 1970. Although Bibfeldt found no faculty members present on that occasion — a fact that caused him to wonder whether it was a religious holiday — he was able to get into Swift Library, which was consolidated shortly thereafter with the University's main library. It was Bibfeldt who is thought to have first suggested that the space formerly occupied by the Swift Hall library would make an excellent greenhouse (or lecture hall, which itself might be an academic mutation caused by the greenhouse effect). Bibfeldt noted that with the frequent use of his own *Bullsgeschichte* method in theological analysis and explication, the Divinity School library space would be a fertile place for an indoor garden.

The shock of finding Swift Hall almost vacant caused serious complications. Since none of the Divinity School's faculty or administration were present to welcome him, Bibfeldt felt unjustifiably ignored and chose to withdraw from the public eye. Hilda, however, urges that letters, cards, and flowers — as well as reports of Elvis's return — can be sent to Franz in care of the Black Forest Home for Wayside Theologians, Brandenburg, Germany. And she also encourages Bibfeldt's mentees to remember Franz by contributing to the fund established at the University of Graustark, where several of his former colleagues have endowed the Bibfeldt Stool of Deconstructive Theology.

In keeping with the spirit of inclusiveness that Franz Bibfeldt appreciated, it is appropriate that we conclude the quest for the historical Bibfeldt with his favorite benediction, one that he first used when he shared a dais with Paul Tillich and Billy Graham in 1961. *Both* adapting *and* combining their emphases, Bibfeldt pronounced: "Perhaps, perhaps. May the ground of all being bless you all real good."

---

4. It is appropriate here to note that this appearance of Bibfeldt was not actually a fleshly encounter, for, as noted in the 1993 spring issue of *Criterion*, one of Swift Hall's janitors saw Bibfeldt's "shadow," which is hardly the kind of hard evidence of a fleshly appearance.

II. Bibfeldt's Postmodern Theology

There can be no great age for the Church until the Church comes of age. It must give up playing in its back yard and learn to work full time in the community.

FRANZ BIBFELDT,
Magnum Opus

Portrait of Franz Bibfeldt by Siegfried Reinhardt

Franz Bibfeldt:
The Breakdown of Consciousness and the Origins of the Quadrilateral Mind

ROBIN W. LOVIN

Robin W. Lovin, now the dean of Perkins School of Theology, is recognized as the most systematic and influential scholar who has devoted himself to the substance of Bibfeldt's work. We shall meet him three times in this book, once dealing with theology and psychology, once treating theology and politics, and a third time surveying Bibfeldt scholarship. — ED.

The quasi-annual gatherings of the Franz Bibfeldt Society have become occasions to explore the unexplored dimensions of the great Bibfeldt's work. Indeed, so much of Bibfeldt's otherwise unknown work has been presented that the file of past lectures maintained in the Foundation's archives gives new meaning to the phrase "better left unsaid."

In keeping with this tradition, exemplified in Landon's "The Quest for the Historical Bibfeldt" and in Dreydoppel's essay on Bibfeldt's innovative methods of pastoral care for the dead (see both, later in this book), I too have endeavored to find an area of scholarship into which Bibfeldt has — shall we say — not yet intruded.

Given even a very low standard of academic quality, this was not difficult to do. Indeed, it took only a few minutes' reflection to spot the gaping hole in the literature. Though Franz Bibfeldt has been studied in the lectures biographically, historically, text critically, and even in terms of his implications for pastoral theology, no attention has been given to Bibfeldt's own psychological development. Indeed, apart from that unfortunate episode in the early 1930s, when Bibfeldt was — shall we say, not to put too fine a point on it — *in residence* at a little sanitarium near Basel, very little attention has been given to the dynamics of this unique mind.

Why this should be so is something of a mystery, for we have no shortage of authors in search of a project today, and psychobiography is — as we say in the technical language of academic publishing — selling like hotcakes. Erik Erikson's monumental study *Gandhi's Truth* fairly begs for a sequel titled *Bibfeldt's Uncertainty*. Bruce Mazlish interpreted the historical role of the leaders of great political movements in a thoughtful book titled *The Revolutionary Ascetic*. Surely the career of Franz Bibfeldt invites exploration in a companion volume titled *The Hesitant Hedonist*.

Lawrence Kohlberg has a method for studying moral development that relies heavily on test interviews that record a subject's response to a moral dilemma. Certainly Kohlberg should have something to say about the theologian of "Both/And," about a man whose major work is *The Relieved Paradox*.

Consider one element of Kohlberg's interview protocol, the so-called Heinz dilemma. In this item, a subject is asked whether a character in a story should steal a drug from a selfish chemist in order to save his own wife from death. Bibfeldt's response to *that* would give new meaning to the word "equivocation."

I have uncovered one attempt to prepare a psychological study of Bibfeldt's development, however. Unfortunately, it failed due to what we may call "technical difficulties." Earlier this month I reproached my erstwhile teacher, colleague, and sometime collaborator, Jim Fowler, for failing to include Bibfeldt among the subjects for his faith development interviews. Fowler was properly chagrined over the omission, but he complained to me that he had tried to secure a record of Bibfeldt's faith development and failed. The problem was this: Fowler's faith development studies are based on a semi-clinical interview which records a subject's response to a set of questions and which may last up to two hours. Fowler has at various times sent six interviewers to meet with Bibfeldt, but all of them fell asleep during the interview after conversations ranging from a maximum of 38 minutes to a minimum of four minutes and 27 seconds. The last interviewer was severely injured when he fell off his chair after 12 1/2 minutes, and further efforts to interview Professor Bibfeldt have been suspended.

The root cause of all these failures should be apparent to anyone who has studied modern theology. Previous students of Bibfeldt's psychology have failed not from lack of will nor from want of persistence. They have failed because they lacked a *method*. Before we can begin a proper study of Bibfeldt's consciousness, we require a methodological prologue, a historico-hermeneutic propaedeutic, a preface to any future scientific system of understanding the mind of this master of modern theological reflection.

Now before you all rush out and submit dissertation proposals on this topic to the committee on degrees, let me warn you that I've already done it. In this publish or perish world, assistant professors are careful not to talk about problems that they haven't already solved — and, I might add, careful not to solve a problem without talking about it. As one astute poet has put it:

> The codfish lays 10,000 eggs,
> The humble hen but one . . .
> The codfish never cackles,
> To show you what she's done.
> And so we loathe the codfish,
> While the humble hen we prize;
> Which only goes to show you,
> That it pays to advertise.

Now with that wise counsel firmly in mind, let us proceed. I found the key to a psychological understanding of the work of Franz Bibfeldt while browsing in the writings of Julian Jaynes. Jaynes is a Princeton psychologist who recently wrote a book called *The Origins of Consciousness and the Breakdown of the Bicameral Mind*. Most of you know from some undergraduate psychology course or whatever that the human brain consists of two more or less discrete halves, which in ordinary consciousness function in tandem. The right brain, somewhat oddly, controls the left side of the body, and seems to handle the affective, intuitive, conceptual part of our thinking, while the left brain controls the right side, and busies itself with calculations, systems, logic, and problem-solving functions. Crudely put, each of us has in his or her head a poet and an IBM executive, and somehow or other they get along well enough to keep us functioning.

All that is a psychological commonplace. Jaynes, however, makes it the center of a startling thesis. If ordinary consciousness results from the coordination of left- and right-brain functions, then human beings in fact *were not conscious* until quite recently. Right down into early historic times, Jaynes argues, the left and right brains functioned more or less independently, and the kind of coordination that today we achieve by intuition and imagination happened then much more directly and dramatically. The right brain would "speak" to the left. People in times of stress, crisis, and decision did not think their way through problems. They heard voices telling them what to do.

Now you see what Jaynes thinks he's done here. In one bold swoop he's explained the origins of religion and the voices of the gods. And he's explained why the gods stopped speaking and secularization set in. At some point in time — Jaynes dates it precisely between the composition of the *Iliad* and the *Odyssey* — the left and right brains got hooked together like they are hooked for us; people started to think like we think, the two-sided mind became unified in one consciousness, and the voices stopped. Hence "the origins of consciousness and the breakdown of the bicameral mind."   -

Now that was the clue that launched my study of the psychology of Franz Bibfeldt. Unlike the Freudian theories of Erikson or the Piagetian theories used by Fowler and Kohlberg, this was a formula that matched the data. Those who know Bibfeldt have often remarked that he seems to be barely conscious. Jaynes's theory leads to the exciting speculation that perhaps he isn't conscious at all. Might it not be the case that in the author of *The Relieved Paradox* and the theologian of "Both/And," the left-brain/right-brain coordination that characterizes us ordinary mortals has broken down?

Perhaps. But there is one problem with that hypothesis. When the gods speak, they tend to be pretty definite about their opinions and quite demanding about what they want. When Bibfeldt speaks, he equivocates. How could we use a theory that Jaynes uses to explain Socrates' demanding, commanding *daimon* to explain the theologian who answered Barth's thunderous *Nein!* with a little pamphlet called *Vielleicht?*

The answer, I think, lies in a proper appreciation of the psychological and physiological foundations of Bibfeldt's theology. This man who has tried so hard to please everybody and who has attempted throughout his career as author and teacher to affirm *all* propositions simultaneously, in the hope that some of them might be true, and a few of them might even be popular — this man has obviously developed a specialized brain function that allows him to affirm a proposition with one part of his mind and deny it with another. Following the usual observation of his students and critics that Bibfeldt does all of his theologizing off the top of his head, we may identify the affirmation and negation functions of Bibfeldt's mind with the upper and lower brain, respectively.

Now you see how we arrive at an explanation of the theology of "Both/And." When Bibfeldt's unique functional separation of upper and lower brain is combined with the usual specialization of left and right brain, we get a fourfold division of labor in the head. The poet and the IBM executive are joined by a composer of TV jingles and a cardsharp.

When the coordination between that little team breaks down, we get a return to the preconscious condition that Jaynes describes: the breakdown of consciousness and the origins of the quadrilateral mind. And we get a reappearance of the oracular voices that Jaynes describes. But with an important difference: when, as in Bibfeldt's case, that oracular right brain is further divided into upper and lower functions, a new phenomenon emerges. In Bibfeldt's case, the gods not only speak, they bicker with each other.

It is evident, I trust, that the theological world must feel deep gratitude to Professor Jaynes (and, of course, to me) for providing the clue that enables us to understand Bibfeldt's work. Those who have long stood in awe of the theologian's ability to hold two contradictory opinions in perfect unity, without distinction and yet without confusion, have compared the workings of his mind to that of a great ecumenical council. This, of course, is superstitious hyperbole — well meant, but inaccurate. Scientifically considered, Bibfeldt's mind more closely resembles the workings of a small but fractious pastor-parish relations committee I once observed in the First United Methodist Church in Compton, Illinois.

Let us, then, push on to a further analysis of Bibfeldt's life and work according to the quadrilaterial model I have proposed.

One of the most important features of the quadrilateral model is that it not only helps us to understand the polarities, dualities, and paradoxes in Bibfeldt's systematic theology, but it brings order to the apparent chaos in his personal life as well. We all know about Barth's fondness for the music of Mozart, and some of you may have heard of Bonhoeffer's penchant for nineteenth-century Romantic German novels. Several investigators of the left-brain/right-brain hypothesis have suggested that interests like these, apparently unrelated to the professional work of the theologians, in fact provides a special sort of right-brain activity that lays an intuitive foundation for the systematic work of the left brain.

This is a fruitful suggestion for Bibfeldt's work, too. But remember that with Bibfeldt we have to divide that right-brain activity into upper right and lower right — and we have to expect a certain conflict between them. For example, Bibfeldt is a philatelist, a stamp collector, in his spare time. He has, in fact, amassed one of Europe's finest collections of postage stamps featuring religious art. This collection would perhaps be more widely displayed at philatelic conferences, except for the unfortunate fact that the stamps in question are attached to one of Europe's largest and most complete collections of obscene postcards. It is not known whether Bibfeldt intended to collect the stamps and acquired the postcards as an afterthought, or vice versa, but the theology of "Both/And" has clearly crept into his leisure life as well.

I'm sure you wish, as I do, that we could explore these aspects of Bibfeldt's personal life at greater length — but I see that our time is coming to an end. I suppose it is true that theologically our time is always coming to an end, but at a Bibfeldt lecture that circumstance gives new meaning to the phrase "not a minute too soon."

I suppose that the overall effect of this exploration of Franz Bibfeldt's psychology is, as always, to tell us something about ourselves — a circumstance that gives new meaning to the phrase "I'd rather not know."

But it is true nonetheless. If in Christ we see ourselves reflected as it were in a glass, darkly, then in Franz Bibfeldt we have an image of ourselves that is plain. When we look at Bibfeldt, the glass is perfectly clear, and we can see that it is we ourselves who are fuzzy around the edges.

Letters from the Front: The Hilda Braunschweiger-Bibfeldt Correspondence

JILL RAITT

The following correspondence suggests a sort of shift in genre and tone: if the men who wrote and spoke about Bibfeldt were befuddled and good-natured, the women he neglected or, worse, with whom he had dealings, had reason for resentment and outrage. In 1966, in the earlier years of feminism in theology and religious studies, some feminists took over the Bibfeldt observance and introduced a range of previously neglected themes. We are reproducing as we have come across it in the archives the exchange between the beleaguered and beleaguering spouse of the good doctor, Hilda Braunschweiger-Bibfeldt, and Professor Jill Raitt, who teaches at the University of Missouri at Columbia. A few allusions may be lost on readers today, but it seemed better to leave them in the letters than to try to update them and possibly lose some nuances. — ED.

AUTHOR'S NOTE: Hilda Braunschweiger-Bibfeldt's correspondence is one of the more surprising collections of letters from the wives of Protestant theologians gathered in the twentieth century. This author has gathered them, together with Hilda's responses, wherever they might be found, and is working on the whole collection. The first letter, written nearly thirty years ago on yellow scratch paper and now well faded, is in the Bibfeldt archive. It is estimated that, given the pace of collecting and editing, the three volumes should appear beginning 2001.

The editors of this volume are fortunate, therefore, to have this sample of the Hilda Braunschweiger-Bibfeldt correspondence. Franz Bibfeldt's permission has not been and will not be sought, but Hilda Braunschweiger-Bibfeldt is so happy about the entire enterprise that she has endowed a chair which for now I occupy. The funds are Hilda Braunschweiger-Bibfeldt's inheritance from the family Braunschweiger wurst business. The chair itself is therefore well-padded and supplied with a tray upon which the author places either her computer or her lunch of braunschweiger; a lifetime supply of the fine wurst is a major perquisite of the well-endowed chair.

J.R.

*   *   *

Hyde Park
May 1, 1966

Dear Jill,

It is a bright sunny spring morning, Franz is away on a lecture tour, and your note which arrived yesterday is before me. I must admit that many thoughts, over many years, have begun to crystallize around our brief conversation last fall after Franz's lecture.

You asked, only for the sake of conversation, I'm sure, what my life was like as the wife of so noted and sought-after a theologian. My perfunctory answer sparked a playful push from you: "But Hilda, what do *you* think about theologically? Are you weary at all of the men discussing theology and the women talking about babies and school board problems? Don't you ever wish you could join the circle around your husband as a participant and not just as a provider of cheese dip?"

You hit upon a sore point. Yes, I had wished I could express myself. I tried to say something to Franz. He took me in his arms and said, "After so many years of being so good a wife, where do such ideas come from? Do I not try out all my new ideas by talking to you about them first?"

I subsided, of course, remembering my role as echo and occasionally as critic. Anyway, I began reflecting further. I picked up one of Franz's favorite little volumes, Karl Barth's *The Faith of the Church*, and turned to page 45 and read a bit. Then I tried substituting all feminine words for the masculine ones. Try it. See what it does to you! At first I laughed at myself. Then a spark of long-suppressed anger began to catch fire. *Why* am I laughing? *Why* is everything male? How did women get pushed so far behind and below?

I thought back to Genesis, the very first verses. What is masculine/feminine here? In that dark, formless void, was not the matrix present? In those waters over which the Spirit moved, was there not potent life? I tried to think of a new way to say it, drawing heavily on readings and conversations with Mircea [Eliade], but letting my woman's experience and imagination work as well as my memory and mind. I am a mother, my womb a matrix for life. My husband is a father, a husbandman of my fertile soil. Let us go behind creation once again. In the beginning was the all-encompassing Matrix who felt compassion grow powerfully within her. Order, yet unenlivened, descended in search of being. Matrix called Order to her and embraced him. Of her compassion and order's need, life stirred.

There, I thought, why not? Why should not the feminine engenderer be called Matrix rather than chaos? Why should not Matrix be God rather than Sky-Father? What, after all, is order all by its lonesome self? What poems were written by law? Why should anyone aspire for greatness unless a potency yearns for expression and allows itself to be stirred? Are the shaping hands of this world male or female?

I then warmed to my theme and conceived of order as a perfect square. There it lay, perfect, and perfectly uninspired and uninspiring. Poor order. Poor male principle. What you need, my little block, is a dose of chaos! What you need, little Father-in-potency, is a Mother to make you swell out of your closed mind. I shall call you out and up. You shall lose your upright control and enter the ecstasy of dream of becoming and so together we shall find life and new life shall grow in me from us!

In the beginning was Matrix and the Ordering Word was with her and in her, daughter Wisdom grew to birth, sprang to earth to play among us, creating, calling into being and into responsibility, offering the fruit of knowledge and the glory of growing into women and men who know themselves as images of the procreators Matrix and Logos, who together are the Godhead breathing love.

My pen has run away with me. Franz would be shocked. But I am strangely elated. Why not such a myth instead of the Marduk-dominated *Enuma Elish*? But, for the sake of sanity and peace of our household and to protect the world that supports Franz, I beg of you to keep this letter to yourself until such a time and occasion as it may be appreciated.

As you know, Franz and I are beginning a series of lectures around Europe which will make correspondence difficult. I shall, however, be delighted to have your response to my outpouring.

>Best wishes always,
>Hilda Bibfeldt

P.S. Excuse this paper. My thoughts were too large for my linen bond note-paper. And the yellow fits the bright sunshine this May morning!

*   *   *

>Hyde Park
>May 15, 1966

Dear Hilda,

I loved your letter! Did you know that you wrote it on my birthday? I'll take it as a special birthday gift, if I may. I can't write at length: I've got two papers to finish and exams to study for, but I had to take a few moments of pure pleasure to let you know how much I enjoyed your letter. Is there any chance that you might enlarge on those themes? I'll keep your secret, but you are a really good theologian! I especially liked the idea of *Matrix* . . . and *Sophia* too. In fact your retelling of Genesis is certainly an improvement over Marduk, the mother-splitter! It certainly makes me realize how male-dominated our own tradition is. Maybe the water is Matrix and Mother was there, but as usual, when the story is written up, the female disappears, "embraced by the male," as some old fuddy-duddy said when I objected to his sexist language. He put his arm around me to illustrate his meaning, expecting me to enjoy his paternalism. Ridiculous, isn't it? Please do write more — I'll come over as soon as my papers are done.

>With respectful appreciation,
>Jill

*   *   *

Chicago
June 10, 1966

Dear Jill,

I'm sorry to be so long answering your letter. It's the end of spring quarter, and Franz has been grading term papers and assisting with a seminar at the university. You know that whatever he does involves me. In fact, I am "grader" and a proofreader, and he always gives his lectures to me first, so I have been as busy as Franz, maybe busier.

Thank you for your phone call. I wish we could have managed a good long visit, but surely we will soon.

When I read your letter and your reaction to my first attempt at understanding Genesis in a slightly different manner, I was both touched and encouraged. I had to laugh at your description of the "old duffer." My dear, the stories I could tell you now that I look at my relatively long life in the light of your remarks! When Franz and I were living in Basel, we were friends with the Barths. During dinner, the men would sometimes begin a theological conversation which would become intense, of course, and they would forget we were there! It didn't occur to them that we might have anything to contribute, or even the faintest desire to do so. Once I objected to something Karl was saying about the female being completely passive and thereby serving as a model for the human relation to God, who was male and active. I tried to say, as modestly as I could, that my experience as a woman was not so passive. Both men looked at me briefly with a slightly quizzical expression as much as to say, "How could your experience be relevant to our conversation?" Franz actually said, "Now Hilda, that's not quite the point that Karl and I were discussing, is it?" "I suppose not," I said, somewhat shamefacedly.

Karl and Franz returned to their conversation as though our little exchange had not taken place. I wonder, sometimes, what world they live in — it seems so divorced from the reality I experience. Frau Professor Doktor Barth and I took our coffee cups and retired to the parlor to talk about our planned visit to the Basel Zoo the next day. But that night, after Franz had gone to sleep, I lay awake thinking about the dinner party. Do men consult their own experience and if so, is it so different from women's experience? I suppose it is. But when they extrapolate from their experience, why are they uninterested in ours? We are half the human race, after all. If God made male and female in his image, then is not the female experience also a way of understanding God better? Why did I write "his image"? Don't I mean his/her image?

Jill, I have begun to think about these matters and it seems there will be no end to it. It seems that we have to rethink our language as well as what the human, rather than just the male, experience is, if it is to provide a basis for theology.

I can see Franz coming up from the walk, so I must stop. He will expect his tea.

As ever,
Hilda

*   *   *

Hyde Park
June 20, 1966

Dear Hilda,

What a shame that I missed seeing you before you left for Switzerland! I could not control my exam schedule. Anyway, I loved your letter and, as usual, it sent my mind spinning off in new directions. Happily, I have a little time for thinking about anything I like since exams are over and I have a week before I start teaching summer school at St. Mary's in Scranton. I agree with you about language. It is especially clear that language both frees us to think and prevents us from thinking freely. We couldn't formulate thoughts without it, but the direction our thoughts take is shaped by the words that express those very ideas. Professor Charles Long said something like that about language about blacks. And it is true also about the word "primitive." Professor Long said that even if you change the word, the context of the sentence or the paragraph still confines the thought expressed to certain patterns that express our prejudices, our pre-judgments. You found that out when you read the passage from Barth (I followed your advice, and tried the same experiment with the same results). How do we escape from the language trap?

Your letter started me off in a related direction, namely, the relation of experience to theology. I hadn't thought of that before, but you're right. And where in the world did the idea come from that women are passive and men active? When one stops to think about it, it's quite silly. And yet Barth did build his idea of God and man [sic] on that notion. I don't think any relation consists of purely active and purely passive. Even inanimate objects that a human works upon, like wood or stone, contribute something to what is manufactured. The nature of the wood or stone may not be active in the sense of *doing* anything, but to be wood or to be stone is its act. Do you know Aristotle or Thomas Aquinas? It seems to me that the notion of act and potency in those systems is truer to the nature of things. At least it allows for things to be both active and passive according to their natures. How would such a theory help us? I hardly know where to turn to escape from the male interpretation of everything! And they have laid traps, because those systems allow for more and less, and, of course, men are more active and women are more passive, according to those "guys." (A little disrespect is good for the soul!) In fact, as you hinted at your dinner party, a hint the men were astonished you could utter, the notion of passive and active comes primarily from intercourse, but let us not introduce anything so mundane, so ordinary and so ordinarily hidden into theological discourse. Or rather, let us not uncover the fact that such a fundamental animal reality underlies that discourse, in fact, is embedded in it!

I'll be teaching in a women's college: New Testament and Aquinas on the sacraments. How will I be able to do it with all of this in my head? Please write when you have time; I look forward to your letters.

As ever,
Jill

*   *   *

Geneva
July 25, 1966

Dear Jill,

Last time I wrote, Franz was finishing a semester, and now we are once again finishing up a series of lectures before August vacations send western Europeans rushing to spas and mountains, to Paris and London. Franz and I will be staying here, enjoying this lovely city on Lake Léman. We can take such lovely walks into the mountains or take the steamer around the lake or stroll through the magnificent rose gardens, still beautiful even in August. Franz will be working on a new book, but he is more relaxed than usual since he is playing with ideas, as he puts it, and so likes to walk, and seems to have more time. I enjoy this time as well. Only Americans knock on library doors and expect to get in to work in them in August!

Yes, Jill, I know something about Aristotle, although not much about Thomas Aquinas. Franz is a dedicated Protestant, and so, while he has read some Aquinas, he prefers to use a more modern base for his theology. Kant is certainly influential. I wonder sometimes if Franz hasn't lost all sense of the noumenal and the phenomenal as well. I'm never sure where he is grounded or if he is grounded at all. His work is so theoretical that I don't know to what reality it may refer. At least Kant began with phenomena. Poor Franz always begins with a theoretical statement. His thesis for his new book is "Theology as the Unsought Answer to the Unasked Question." It seems terribly abstract to me!

[Hilda breaks off here and picks this idea up later, I think.]

*   *   *

Scranton
August 1, 1966

Dear Hilda,

Summer School is over and I am about to leave St. Mary's to go home to see my parents. I'll be driving my little bug back to Chicago and then on to California. I wish you could go with me; think of the conversations we would have! I loved your last letter: it was so spry I could see you skipping up an alp and then running back down to the lake for a swim. I am delighted to be your confidante as you are mine. Of course, here in the states I don't run into so much sexism. In fact, I seem to be getting along with everyone pretty well.

But I must tell you about what happened here in Scranton! I can scarcely believe it happened, but it did. I went down the hill to the parish church for mass, and after the service I went back to the sacristy to introduce myself and to compliment the priest on his sermon: it was philosophical, but I've already forgotten on which subject. We chatted a bit and he said that I should come up to the rectory to talk some more about philosophy. So a little later I made an appointment and walked the nearly two miles to the rectory. It was a lovely summer evening and not yet dark.

The rectory was as stiff and uninviting as it could be. A housekeeper opened the door and showed me into the parlor — also stiff, and so brown! Father McKnight came down and we had a lively enough discussion until about 10 P.M. Father McKnight walked me to the door and held it open for me. I looked out into the dark and thought of those two miles on foot through none-too-safe streets and up a dark hill. "Father," I said, "would you please drive me to the college? I don't think it's safe for me to walk back." He looked a bit taken aback and decidedly uncomfortable. I was surprised as well that he had no thought at all for my safety and was willing to see me walk off alone into the night. "Wait," he said, "I'll ask the rector." He went upstairs and stayed at least ten minutes. When he came down, he apologized and said that he had permission to drive me home. When I got into the car, I looked at Father McKnight and he seemed very agitated. Forthright soul that I am, I said, "Are you afraid of me, Father?" "Yes," said he. And he looked it. "Why?" said I, *"Non solus cum sola?"* "Yes," he answered.

So we drove back in a rather tense silence. Can you imagine that? Was he afraid that I would attack him, throw myself into his arms? Rape him? But what distressed me most was that a rather decent man had been so twisted by his seminary training that he would prefer to send a woman out into the night to walk alone without a thought for her safety rather than risk being alone in a car with her. And this woman is me, Hilda! We had been talking philosophy and theology most earnestly. Where did he get the idea that he could possibly be in danger, except that priests are taught that all women are *femmes fatales?* And with that attitude, maybe we are!

I look forward to your next letter. It's so helpful and even fun to exchange these new perceptions of who we are and who men think we are — or should be!

With love,
Jill

*   *   *

Geneva
October 4, 1966

Dear Jill,

I must apologize for not responding sooner to your good letter of last
August. Franz is writing furiously because of our pending trip around
the world. He demands all the free time I have. Today I am declaring
a holiday for myself. I told Franz that I am not at his disposal today. It
always surprises him when I declare a day of independence, but he has
learned not to say anything. The last time he insisted that I give up my
plans and proofread some pages with him, I took off two days instead
of one. He no longer protests my single days off. Today is my day, so
I am trying to pick up my neglected correspondence.

Your description of the priest's behavior is appalling. It makes one
wonder how men like that think! But then we shouldn't be so surprised
given the number of women who have been raped throughout history.
It is as though the ambivalence men feel toward women includes
genuine hatred. I have to ask myself if I harbor similar, if hidden,
feelings toward men; my personal answer is "No." But then neither am
I as accepting as I once was. Only a few years ago I would never have
dreamed of declaring occasional independence days, and now I do so
regularly. It's been good for our marriage since I am happier and Franz
has learned to respect me more as a person who is not just his wife,
but my own self.

Having said that much, I have to confess that I have given in and
consented to accompany Franz on a trip around the world with stops
in all sorts of exotic and not so exotic places. I don't think I'll have time
to write much, but I will send you postcards. If we stop long enough
for me to send you a letter and receive an answer from you, I'll let you
know. It looks as though our correspondence will have to be put on
hold for a while. You will be busy with classes anyway. This is your
second year at the Divinity School, is it not? And did you not tell me
that you have a part-time job teaching at St. Xavier's College on the
south side? How will you manage classes and teaching? How I admire
modern women! By the way, we will be in Geneva until the end of
October — time enough for a letter to reach me if you have time to drop
me a line.

Love,
Hilda

*   *   *

Hyde Park
October 15, 1966

Dear Hilda,

Of course, I have time for a last letter before you and Franz leave to go around the world. I wish I could go with you — wouldn't we have a wonderful time!

Yes, I am teaching at St. Xavier. I like it, but it does make it hard to meet class deadlines in both places, as you can imagine. Last year I had an NDEA loan. This year I have to find ways to support myself. I've moved out of International House into an apartment. No more cereal and dried milk on the window sill and no more hours at the switchboard for minimum wages! This is really much better. Besides, St. Xavier's is a women's college, and there is something to be said for spending time where one's own sex is in the majority! The only men are fellow professors and they are good guys as far as I can tell.

I will sorely miss our correspondence; I am never too busy to read your letters and respond to them. What a good time we will have when you get back! I hope you will continue to think about your reinterpretation of Genesis. Perhaps you could work on that while you travel. How would you reinterpret the Fall? Eve is always blamed for it. One wonders where Adam was while the serpent was conversing with Eve. Where are men when you need them? Or did Eve need Adam at that point? What if the story were originally quite other and misogynists altered it to read as it does? Let's restore it to a more humane (does that always mean from a woman's point of view?) interpretation. You write and I'll write and when you get back, we'll compare our stories! How's that for an assignment!

I see that this letter is full of exclamation points and question marks. I suppose that means that I should put my nose back in my books and become the serious Ph.D. student I'm supposed to be. Writing to you is much more fun — an outlet for my imagination.

Love to you and maybe just a
little to Franz,
Jill

Chicago
October 28, 1968

Dear Hilda,

What a challenge! I've been racking my brains to think of how the Fall might have been told before the "Fathers" got hold of it. How about this? Adam and Eve were wandering hand-in-hand in the garden when they decided to picnic under the beautiful forbidden tree. The shade was deep, the grass green, and the view of the garden superb. Eve opened the basket and Adam spread the tablecloth and set out plates and napkins. [Before the Fall, there was no problem about men helping in the kitchen.] As they sat down to eat, the serpent wandered by.

"Hi, Eve. Hi, Adam. Lovely day, isn't it? Whatcha got to eat?"

"Hi, Serp," said Adam. "We're just having a bit of bread and cheese and wine. Want some?"

The serpent sidled over and had a bit of wine. "You know what goes best with cheese? Apples," he said.

"What are apples?" asked Eve.

"You're sitting under an apple tree, Eve," replied Serp. "Just reach up and pick one and you can have apples and cheese."

"But serpent," protested Eve, "you know we're not supposed to touch the fruit of this tree! What can you be thinking of?"

"Why, I'm just tasting a bit of apple and cheese — it's even better if you make the apples into pie first. Here, let me pick one for you."

"Did God say *you* could pick fruit from this tree? If you, why not us, I wonder," mused Eve.

"Come on, Eve. God's just pulling your leg. God wants to see how dumb you can be — she's just teasing you! Here, take a bite."

Eve hesitated and looked to Adam to see what he had to say, but Adam had slipped away. Apparently, he didn't want to get involved.

"Okay," said Eve, taking the apple. "I bet you're right. God wouldn't pull such a trick on us, I'm sure."

Eve bit the apple and was pleased at the taste and texture. She called to Adam who appeared from the other end of the garden. Adam was as easily persuaded as was Eve and enjoyed the apple as much as Eve had. They picked a few more and Eve thought how she could make a pie of them. She reached for her kitchen apron and suggested Adam put on an apron and help her.

"What," said Adam, "me wear an apron? No way, Eve. Cooking is woman's work."

Astonished, Eve stared at Adam. "What's come over you, Adam?

Since when did cooking become my job? What are you going to be doing in the meantime?"

Adam sat down with a can of beer. "Who, me? I'm going to enjoy the sunset while you make a pie."

Eve knew something serious had happened. Adam had never behaved like this before. Maybe the serpent was wrong and God meant what she said, thought Eve.

Just then thunder crashed and Adam, never before afraid of thunder, cowered. Eve ran to him and together they realized that the relationship between them and God had changed and that their own relationship had changed: something bitter had entered the garden. A heavy male voice called out, "Adam, Eve, where are you two? What have you done?"

You know the rest of the story. Adam and Eve had to leave the garden and from then on God spoke only in a male voice, so men took over and began ordering women around; it's been that way ever since.

Well, Hilda, even if this fantasy is mostly play, it gets the point across that God didn't intend to be understood as a male and that only sin could have produced the impression that she is a father rather than a mother.

Tell me your story!

Love,
Jill

*   *   *

The Island of Maniluku
February 10, 1970

Dear Jill,

I'm so sorry I have been unable to respond to your letter of October 28, 1968. You may find it hard to believe the adventures Franz and I have had since we left Geneva in November 1968. We intended to vacation in Hawaii, and indeed we began a lovely stay on the big island, where we rented a sailboat. A storm arose and we were driven far out to sea, where we eventually found ourselves coasting off the island of Maniluku. The people here came out to rescue us, gave us a feast and a little house to sleep in, and here we have been ever since. I don't know when this letter will reach you. There is no communication between these islanders and the rest of the world. When they heard what happened to Hawaii and New Zealand and the Cook Islands after being "discovered" by whalers and missionaries, the Manilukans decided to remain *un*discovered by anyone but themselves. No one, therefore, will help us back to Hawaii. We are prisoners in a sense, as the Manilukans are afraid we will tell the world about them. And so we would!

Franz has been trying to teach the people here about Christianity, but they are determined not to listen, since the results for the other Polynesians have been so destructive of their culture, language and self-respect. So Franz has been listening to them tell him of their religion, and . . . I think he may be converting! It is rather amazing, but he finds that Bané, their primary manifestation of the ultimate God, is quite convincing. He has been learning to surf, since that is part of the worship of Bané. I wish you could see him, bony knees, fanatic expression, grass skirt flying!

In the meantime, I've been thinking about your story of the Fall. Living here has given me some new ideas. Let's say that Maniluku is the Garden of Eden — and indeed it has many of the characteristics!

Everything is here in abundance, the weather is continually temperate, the people friendly. They love to swim, surf, dance, play and worship. So along comes a missionary who tells them their lives are sinful. At first they don't believe him. But slowly they become convinced that sin is a reality and they must be "saved" from it. They begin to see sin in each other and start arguments over who first offended. Since the missionary told them woman was responsible for the first sin, the men begin to blame the women and to order them around, slapping them into submission if they resist. The men argue about who owns which woman, which leads to a murder when the argument becomes bitter. The people break into two camps, one defending the murderer, the other demanding vengeance for the victim. The groups pull apart, one moving to the north, the other to the southern part of the island. From these fortresses they engage in warfare. Captives are enslaved, women raped and paradise is lost. Neither a serpent nor God had a thing to do with it! A basic error on the part of the missionary followed by intensifying misunderstandings accounts for the whole state of affairs.

In short, I'd rather have Franz surfing than trying to convert the people of Maniluku.

I hope you receive this letter sometime!

Love,
Hilda

*   *   *

Chicago
May 1, 1978

Dear Jill,

Our adventure is over. A ship passed by and Franz managed to flag it down. I am concerned about the Manilukans, who have now been "discovered." Franz is in a strange state. He keeps his surfboard in the living room and looks longingly out the window at the lake where, alas, no waves roll in to tempt him into its cold waters. When Franz was asked to preach at the chapel and to recount something of his stay on Maniluku, he declined. It's the first time Franz has said no to a prestigious lecture in all the time I've known him. He wants to eat coconuts and mangos and a vegetable called *paru*, which I can't find. I don't know what Franz will write next. He seems to have lost all interest in abstract thought. He's even talking about writing up the religious practices of Maniluku. But then, he is torn between honoring the desire of the Manilukans to remain unknown and his real admiration for their religion. Poor Franz, he tosses and turns and I can't help him. He has to make this decision himself. Sometimes he even thinks seriously of returning to Maniluku.

I'm enclosing a letter I wrote eight years ago.

My best to you,
Hilda

*   *   *

Durham, North Carolina
June 12, 1978

Dear Hilda,

I love your letter, even if it is eight years overdue! Thank you for sending it. I'm so glad you got home and are now safely back in Chicago. I wish I could visit you and Franz. It's hard to picture Franz as a sort of anthropologist. And how I would love to hear more about your years on Maniluku!

My life has been full. I got my Ph.D. and for four years helped to build a program in religious studies in California. I've been at Duke since 1973 and find it incredibly sexist. Some of the women students asked me to teach a course on women and religion. It was quite an experience, mainly because the students were so fine, intelligent and determined. The high point of the class was the reaction of Laine to the visit of an Episcopalian bishop who tried to persuade us that women should not be ordained by asking us to imagine a crucified woman. At the next class, Laine brought her own oil painting of a crucified woman and the painting took my seat as the head of the class. There is nothing more horrible about a woman on the cross than a man on the cross. Both are unspeakable. Anyway, women are often crucified. Every battered woman is on a cross.

While you have been in the south seas, women have been making progress, as you must have discovered on your return. We still have a long way to go, of course. For example, I am still the only woman on this thirty-man faculty — and it is no picnic! Nevertheless, women bond and work together, quietly and anonymously managing to persuade the president of the university to make changes in hiring practices. But I have to tell you this story. A group of us meet every two weeks; those meetings keep me sane, I can tell you! We have lunch in the faculty dining room and, would you believe, the men circle around and sidle up to us and ask, "What are you girls up to?" It makes men so nervous to see women talking together, especially when it is clear that they are talking about serious issues. I wish I had the nerve to go up to one of their many all-male tables and ask, "What are you boys up to?"

The most appealing move on the part of women theologians, I think, is an emphasis on relationality and equality instead of on macho individualism and hierarchy. In line with that is my dream of collegiality instead of the competitiveness that sours the milk at this university.

How much further we could get in academia if we pulled together instead of endlessly playing "king of the mountain"! I won't play that game, and, if I ever have a chance to build a department, it will be based on cooperation and sharing — what a lovely dream![1]

Let's stay in touch. I look forward to your next letter.

Love,
Jill

*   *   *

1. EDITOR'S NOTE. The dream was fulfilled when Professor Raitt established the World Center for the Study of Missouri Religions in 1981.

Chicago
July 4, 1978

Dear Jill,

We are preparing to celebrate the Fourth of July. It is a special joy for us to join in your celebrations. Switzerland has long been proud of its freedoms, and so we rejoice in freedom wherever it is found. I pray that women find the freedom we seek and deserve. Your tribulations on an all-male faculty are not that rare, but that is not less, but even more to be lamented. I quietly continue to assert my personhood with Franz. He looks bewildered most of the time, and unable to understand the issues. But he is basically a good man, and so he "suffers" what he terms my "idiosyncrasies."

Speaking of idiosyncrasies, what do you think of this? Franz has been praying more lately. In fact, he sometimes stops in the middle of what he is doing and prays, hands clasped, head bowed and mouth slightly open. He stays that way for over an hour sometimes. Since a visit to his doctor, he is trying to keep his mouth closed. It turns out that a marked increase in flatulence occurred about the same time as his increased prayer. His doctor diagnosed the problem as "air-eating" (aerophagy, I think it is called). The doctor said that air enters the stomach through the mouth in only two ways: bean-eating and air-eating. Since we eat beans very rarely, it has to be air-eating.

As Franz reflected upon this fact, he was inspired to work out a new sermon based on appropriate biblical texts which he now understands in an entirely new context, Job 39:4: "I put my finger to my lips," and Isaiah, I think, about kings shutting their mouths. It is Franz's contention that Job and the kings were aerophages and so covered their mouths in God's presence lest, as the Scriptures say, "worse befall thee" as a result of their open-mouthed awe. It seems far-fetched to me, but Franz is so excited about his new understanding that he forgets to close his mouth, even when he isn't praying. The results are such that I remind him to imitate Job and the kings morning, noon and night.

Well, my dear Jill, I must hang red, white and blue bunting on our front porch and pack a light picnic for the fireworks display at the university — you remember how grand it is — fireworks, Handel's celebratory music, and the carillon going full tilt! We do enjoy it. Happy Fourth of July!

Love,
Hilda

JILL RAITT

*   *   *

EDITOR'S NOTE: The Hilda/Jill letters ended here. The two friends began using the telephone rather than writing — one of the perils of the modern world. No longer will historians be able to reconstruct an age on the basis of a healthy correspondence, providently saved by appreciative recipients. Perhaps future historians will be able to tap into past telephone conversations through some kind of time eliminator. But barring such an event, the further exchanges of Hilda and Jill must remain unavailable to the reading public. — J.R.

The Braunschweiger-Bibfeldts:
The Metaphysical Incarnation of Wo/man

MARK TOULOUSE AND REBEKAH MILES

> Professors Mark Toulouse and Rebekah Miles of Brite Divinity
> School at Texas Christian University in Fort Worth have co-taught
> a seminar on Bibfeldtian post-postmodernism. (They describe it in
> the article, using various "posts" to do so.) But rather than get lost
> in the intricacies of the theologian's theology, they get lost in a
> theme in his biography: gender relations, spousal connections, and
> a "fateful January evening." For detective work about detective
> work, read on. — ED.

For the last several years, Franz Bibfeldt has rarely surfaced. He did
show up in Paris a few years ago to attend the twenty-fifth anniversary
celebration of the Society of St. Fiacre held at the Notre Dame Cathedral
in November 1991.[1]

But few other Bibfeldt sightings have been reported during the
past several years. Some have argued that the Bibfeldts have kept pretty
much to themselves in the old family home just a few blocks east of

---

1. Bibfeldt had founded the society in 1967 after his second hemorrhoid
surgery. St. Fiacre is the patron saint of hemorrhoid sufferers and, for the past thirty
years or so, St. Fiacre has had special meaning for Bibfeldt. From all reports, Bibfeldt
made but a brief appearance to accept a special honor commemorating his historic
contribution to the life of the society. The current board of directors presented him
with a "Founder's Stool." Cushioned all the way around, the stool had the name
of Franz Bibfeldt embroidered on the top half and, on the bottom half, the name of
St. Fiacre provided a kind of balance to the design.

downtown Oldenburg, Germany. But no one has been able to catch them at home, or they have simply not answered the door. A short notice in the newspaper in late 1991 mentioned that Dr. Jack Kevorkian had attempted to visit. Kevorkian was evidently interested in discussing the ongoing work of Bibfeldt's dead-consciousness movement, something to which Bibfeldt has dedicated an increasing amount of his time of late.

Rumor circulating throughout the theological circles of Europe had recently claimed that the Bibfeldts were having a rough time of it. Everyone has known for years that Hilda Braunschweiger-Bibfeldt had been greatly influenced by feminist theology. In fact, she has written rather extensively on the topic over the last decade but has refrained from presenting any public papers. Recently she has become more openly strident in her rejection of Professor Bibfeldt's correlation method. Her latest work, *Vielleicht Nicht!* (Perhaps Not!), she wrote as her answer to Bibfeldt's *Vielleicht?* (Perhaps?). Needless to say, its appearance did not offer much promise that things were getting better for their marriage. Franz Bibfeldt's own pamphlet, *Vielleicht und/oder Vielleicht Nicht,* appeared shortly thereafter; and Hilda Braunschweiger-Bibfeldt's published review of it was entitled "You Still Don't Get It, Do You?" (We are eagerly awaiting Frau Bibfeldt's forthcoming work, *Both/And and/or either/or, No More!*)

As he does with the work of all articulate theologians, Franz has affirmed Hilda's work wholeheartedly. But he really *didn't* get it. No one could say for sure just how bad things were until recently. All that changed on May 31, 1993. On that day some incredible materials fell into our hands. We write to inform the scholarly community of a most exciting discovery that will turn Bibfeldt scholarship upside down and relieve the academy once and for all. Religion scholars have been straining for some time now toward the accomplishment of a movement beyond both relativism and objectivism. This entire scholarly generation has been pushing, even bearing down, to overcome the stoppage in this crucial area. Now is the time for this collective logjam to pass, in order to make way for a whole new flow of religious material. Who is a major harbinger of this movement? None other than Franz Bibfeldt. He has help, but we will say more about that later.

How can Bibfeldt be the solution to our present darkness when we know not where he is or when he will next appear? We may fail fully to comprehend the mystery of his random appearances, but it always seems that Bibfeldt has been everywhere recently and will be somewhere soon. What Charles Dickens wrote of Mr. Bucket in *Bleak House* seems most appropriate as a description of Bibfeldt: "Time and place cannot bind Mr. Bucket. Like man in the abstract he is here today and gone tomorrow — but very unlike man indeed, he is here again the next day." We readily admit that our eyes have not rested upon his transient person, but our eyes have seen the next best thing. On May 31 we found a typed transcript containing nearly ninety days of Franz Bibfeldt's daily journal. The circumstances of this unlikely occurrence are nearly as strange as the events of Bibfeldt's experiences recorded by the journal itself.

The two of us had just completed the first week of our five-week, co-taught seminar (Post-Postmodern Modernism: The Relationship between Foundationalism and Relativity in Public Life). Around 4 P.M. on a Sunday, we drove out to Dallas/Fort Worth Airport to pick up Ellis Regenstein, a graduate student in theology who was returning from a year's research sabbatical (taken between the fifteenth and sixteenth year of his doctoral program) in Amsterdam, where he had undertaken extensive field work for his dissertation, "The Erotic as the Religious: A Case Study of Postmodern Culture in the Streets of Amsterdam." Contacts had informed us that Regenstein would be passing through the Dallas/Fort Worth Airport on his way back to Chicago and suggested that we take the opportunity to meet him. We extended a written invitation to him to spend the weekend and lecture to our seminar during Monday's class session.

Tragically, Regenstein never gave that lecture. A few hours after we picked him up, we took him to Jimmy Don's, "the world's largest honky-tonk," to enjoy a little live country music. Enthralled by the atmosphere, he wanted to try his hand at bull riding. (On occasional nights, Jimmy Don's allows its more sober customers to ride a very old bull under highly controlled conditions. This was one of those nights.) But as Regenstein attempted to mount the bull, he slipped and fell; the bull bucked away from its handlers and trampled him. Ellis Regenstein died at 11:35 P.M. on May 30, 1993.

Early the next morning, we gathered his personal effects from the seminary's guest room. In the pure interest of scholarship, we looked through his notes from the Amsterdam research on the erotic as the religious. To our amazement, we discovered in Regenstein's notes the fact that he had spent much of November through January with Franz Bibfeldt in Amsterdam. His research repeatedly referred to Bibfeldt as his "mentor" and noted Regenstein's claim to have translated nearly three months' worth of Bibfeldt's personal journal. Though Regenstein had obviously read the entire journal, he had evidently developed the regimen of reading one of the daily entries in Bibfeldt's journal each day as his morning devotional. At this point in his life, he confessed in his notes, he found the journal "more inspirational than the New Testament." We quickly realized that somewhere in his personal belongings lay a copy of Bibfeldt's journal; indeed, we found it on the bedside table. The first entry both shocked and depressed us:

All Saints' Eve, 1992. My dear Hilda has left me. How can I go on living without my beloved? Early this morning, I thought I heard a tapping on my bedroom door, but had decided it was a dream. When I awoke and opened my door, I saw a small piece of parchment nailed there entitled "I Only Need One Thesis." This title was followed by the words: "Mein Franz: You are a sick, Eurocentric, male chauvinist. I give up. Get some help and we will see. Check your stool. Your loving Hilda B.-B."

Before Hilda Braunschweiger-Bibfeldt left, she had taped an advertisement across the "Founder's Stool." The slick brochure, taped into the second page of Bibfeldt's journal, described a twelve-step program designed especially for men like Bibfeldt. The pamphlet announced the formation in Amsterdam of the new group, Male Euro-Centric Chauvinists Anonymous (MECCA). Across the top of the ad, in Frau Bibfeldt's hand, were penned the words: "HEAL THYSELF." The next entry to the journal is dated two days later.

Nov. 1, 1992. My 95th birthday (or is it my 96th? 95 or 96? Yes . . . that's it).

Hilda is right. I must change! I must go to MECCA to find my true self. I will leave for Amsterdam on the morrow. God help me. Here I stand, and I must stand someplace else.

Bibfeldt made the one hundred-mile trek to Amsterdam on November 2. He described the city as one of "openness and tolerance." He saw Amsterdam as "refuge to the outcast, the drug dealer, the pimp, the prostitute, and even to sick males like me." In the early Amsterdam entries Bibfeldt mostly described his bouts with loneliness and despair. But the entry for November 12 records his experiences at his first MECCA meeting.

Nov. 12, 1992. I was welcomed warmly by my fellow chauvies as a sinner among sinners. I sat in the circle and, when it came my turn, stood up and said: "My name is Franz and I am a Male Eurocentric Chauvinist."

Bibfeldt described the good feeling he had after finally admitting that, though he could talk the talk, and even, to some degree, walk the walk, he had never really gotten it. The first night was quite emotional for him. He confessed that he had cooked less than five percent of the meals he had consumed during his married life, even though Hilda had worked as hard at her scholarship as he had worked at his. This admission he understood to be a profound and painful demythologization of his lifelong rationalization that he had held up his end of the cooking duties by charcoaling every third Saturday or so. Fellow chauvies prompted further confessions from him. No, he had never held an iron in his life. But neither had Hilda, he told them in his self-defense. What about washing the clothes? He had tried that once, but had mixed the whites with the colors and concluded that Hilda was, naturally, more proficient than he in this area. Besides, he mowed the lawn (twelve foot by thirteen foot, though he noted in his journal that he did not mention its dimensions to the group).

He began to see that such habits, and his lifelong rationalizations concerning them, were symptomatic of far more damning attitudes and convictions. That evening, as experienced leaders and repentant chauvies exploded myth after sacred myth, Bibfeldt began to experience a cognitive dissonance threatening enough to begin to break through his Enlightenment-dependent male rationalizations to reveal his own personal and devastating addiction to inappropriate gender dependencies that lay beneath the self-protected surface of his life.

During this first meeting, Bibfeldt had discovered that twelve out of the thirteen members of this new group were theologians; the thirteenth was a sitting United States senator from Oregon whose attendance was part of a congressionally mandated recovery program. One of the theologians present had been Ellis Regenstein. Bibfeldt's journal indicates that the two of them went out for drinks afterwards. Regenstein, of course, knew Bibfeldt by reputation. Though nearly fifty years in age stood between them, the two men hit it off immediately.

Over drinks, Regenstein informed Bibfeldt that he had copies of several past Bibfeldt lectures (held annually at the University of Chicago Divinity School) with him in Amsterdam. Bibfeldt asked if he might borrow them for a while. Regenstein agreed. During the course of their conversation, Bibfeldt also discovered that the two of them shared a love of country music, from Willie Nelson to Wynona Judd to Garth Brooks. Bibfeldt offered to exchange a few CDs for the loan of the Bibfeldt lectures. When they arrived at Regenstein's apartment, Bibfeldt also decided to borrow a few cassette tapes from the 1992 American Academy of Religion meeting held in San Francisco. Several days later, the following entry appeared in the journal:

Nov. 19, 1992. This afternoon I listened to the most intriguing set of lectures from the AAR Bisexual, Transsexual, Homosexual, Heterosexual, and Asexual Working Group on Human Sexuality. The session was entitled "Postmodern Reflections on Particularity and Identity." These papers stirred me deeply. The first paper, "Beyond Monotheism and Monogamous Coupling from a Straight, Polytheistic, Multi-Partnered Perspective: Four or More or I'm Out the Door," presented a most interesting analysis of the postmodern tendencies to create new forms of community and religious life. The second paper, "Toward a Lesbian Feminist, Post-Episcopalian, Faulkner County, Arkansas Quilter's Theology," contained a fascinating critique of high-church styles of sexuality and worship and offered a patchwork model of Southern American religiosity and trans-male family life for the twenty-first century.

The third lecture struck a different chord altogether. A Methodist professor, rumored to be the founder of the American branch of MECCA, from a university in the Southeast, presented a paper entitled "There May Not Be Much Truth, But Damn it to Hell, What Truth There Is, I Have." When a member of the audience asked if an appropriate subtitle for the paper might be, "Towards a Post-Christian Male Eurocentric Ethic," the lecturer replied, "Towards? Hell, honey, I've already arrived." I saw a poster today announcing that this particular professor would be in Amsterdam during the third week of January to speak on the subject "After Christendom: Let the Church be the Church." Yes, I agree, that is a very good thing for the church to be. A protest group has formed in response to this meeting and has invited a philosopher from the University of Chicago to speak on the general theme, "The Autonomy of the Academy: Let Reason Be Reason." Yes, that seems to me to be a very good thing for reason to be. I look forward to these lectures with great anticipation.

Sometime in the next week, Bibfeldt turned to a reading of some of the Bibfeldt lectures loaned him by Regenstein. He found Robin Lovin's 1980 examination of the psychological foundation of his work fascinating. Finally, with this analysis of the quadrilateral mind, he had a fairly convincing explanation of those incessant voices in his head. And all this time he thought he had been cursed with four consciences instead of just one. "Too bad at least one of those voices could not have been feminine," he confided to his journal. Nonetheless, Bibfeldt indicated he had always appreciated the way his mind worked. It had, after all, helped him to gain his tremendous reputation as a conciliatory voice in the often conflicting world of theological discourse.

Over the next month, Bibfeldt faithfully attended MECCA meetings. He learned a new mantra, which he repeated faithfully every day: "Even though my dear Hilda left me, even though I am an addict to chauvinism, I must remember that I am on my way to recovery. Every day in every way, I am getting better and better." Bibfeldt came to understand that his recognition of his own chauvinism had to be a continual aspect of his life from now on. He assigned the need for continual accountability of it to the upper right and upper left quadrants of his mind. Day by day, the voices emanating from those quadrants took on new characteristics and tone. By December, they had a definite feminine sound to them, and had begun to speak with increasing forcefulness to the remaining quadrants of his mind.

Bibfeldt spent his days writing and his afternoons with his MECCA acquaintances. Most of them he spent with Regenstein discussing theological issues of great importance and helping him analyze the results of his fieldwork. His journal shows that, three evenings a week, following the recommendation of a Swedish member of the group, he frequented the local "isolation tank" franchise. Upon entering the doors of the franchise, one is met by a "birthing guide" who leads the customer back into one of many darkened rooms in the rear of the building. After stripping naked, the customer is placed in a shallow pool of saline solution, maintained at the approximate temperature of the human womb. A lid of sorts is placed on the tank to replicate as nearly as possible a fetal environment. Once the person is in the tank, the room becomes totally dark. The saline temperature provides a kind of floating sensation. Heartbeat kinds of sounds, and other sounds reflective of internal bodily functions, begin to fill the tank. Bibfeldt found the relaxing environment of the isolation tank to be the only place in Amsterdam where he did not feel alone.

Dec. 15, 1992. With each trip to the isolation tank, I appear to be regressing further into my youth. It is as if I am actually being reborn. The mystical dimensions of my experience are approaching a peak I do not know how to describe. I am beginning to feel like I am a part of a much greater whole, like one who is at peace with the many, one who is both one and many at the same time. I do not know any other words to describe it. . . .

On the days between his visits to the isolation tank, Bibfeldt liked to take long walks late in the evenings. These walks helped him to reflect on his developing sense of self. Part of his walk took him through the red light district of Amsterdam. Flesh for sale: all ages, all sizes, all preferences. An open marketplace of drugs, a pharmaceutical circus with no generics in sight. Another segment of his walk took him past some of the oldest churches in the city. Tolerance of two kinds, both with their own kind of sacrality and sinfulness. And, in the midst of it all, he felt a profound sense of both happiness and sadness.

Dec. 17, 1992. I feel "born again." My "Both/And" method is taking on new meaning, transcending all known gender, racial, even sexual differences. Yet I remain exceedingly lonely. If only my Hilda B.-B. were here with me.

On New Year's Eve, the following entry appeared in the journal.

Dec. 31, 1992. I wrote what I consider to be one of my more important theological treatises today. It is entitled "From Right Brain to Left Brain and Back Again: Theological Foundations for the Mind-Altering Process of Gender Equalization in the Heterosexual Male."

[Unfortunately, this essay was not discovered among Regenstein's papers.]

In mid-January, Bibfeldt finally took the time to listen to the last of the AAR tapes loaned to him by Regenstein. The resulting journal entry is worth quoting in abbreviated form:

Jan. 15, 1993. This session was sponsored by the Working Group for the Promotion and Adoration of the Theology of Dead White European Males (Affectionately known as DWEMS). . . . During the business meeting the chair urged his members to join the fight against the encroaching postmodern, multicultural chaos threatening the extinction of all reverence for DWEM theologians. . . . Because of my commitment to the dead-consciousness movement, and as well to my concern for pastoral care to the dead, I find this cause most compelling. Besides, some of my best friends are Dead White European Males. And there, but for the grace of God and the longevity encoded in my genetic pool of origins, go I.

In a passing reference in his journal, Bibfeldt noted the titles of these scholarly papers: "Universal Human Experience as DWEM Experience"; "Uncovering the Multiculturist, Postmodern Plot to Exorcise the Ghosts of All DWEMS"; and "A Standard for Us All: Normativity of White Eurocentric Male Experience for All Theology and All Morality Forever and Ever, Amen." Bibfeldt acknowledged that this explicit focus on male experience helped him to begin to get in touch with his repressed primal masculinity. After listening to the final lecture, "Men's Groups and Man-Church: Robert Bly as the High Priest of DWEMS and their Undead Disciples," Bibfeldt resolved, anticipating his next trip to America, to attend one of Bly's Men's Groups. In his words:

If only I could sit at Bly's feet and hear the stories of the wild, primal masculinity. "In the company of men," bonding in fraternal oneness through the wearing of a tiger pelt and a sharing in the growling and drumming, I believe I might rediscover some heretofore underdeveloped part of myself.

Between January 15 and January 21, Bibfeldt expressed his increasing experience of at-one-ment resulting from his emerging feminist consciousness. But he sorely missed Hilda. He decided that, though he did not know of her current location, he would chance sending her a letter to the address of their home in Oldenburg. Perhaps, he reasoned, she would stop by the house to pick up some of her belongings. For days, he anguished over how he should phrase the letter. He wanted to tell her of his great longing for her, but was fearful that anything he might write could unconsciously betray the ever-remaining traces of his addiction. He would always need MECCA. He realized that, but he also longed for the return of their loving relationship. He gave the matter a great deal of thought and finally settled on sending her the lyrics of one of his favorite country music songs, "Walking After Midnight." It expressed so well what he was feeling, and, since both Patsy Cline and Garth Brooks had recorded it, it stood as good a possibility of being gender neutral as most anything he could write on his own. On January 19, his journal recorded the following entry.

> *Jan. 19, 1993.* I sent my Hilda the following missive:
> My dearest Beloved: I am faithfully attending MECCA meetings. With the help of many new friends, some even sicker than I am, I have recognized fully my addiction to the MECCA mindset. I am trying to change. My journey to discover the new Franz has led me to frequent an isolation tank here in Amsterdam. As I immerse myself into the warm fluid, I yearn for the renewal of my true self and a revival of our love. I am beginning to realize how I have misunderstood you and taken you for granted all these years. Perhaps I am finally beginning to "get it." I have completed the legal paperwork to have my name legally changed from Bibfeldt to Braunschweiger-Bibfeldt to reflect my commitment to the fulfillment of our equal partnership. I have been told that the change will be official January 23, 1993. I miss you so much. Please know that the lyrics of the old Patsy Cline/Garth Brooks country song, "Walking after Midnight," which I have enclosed, represent my deepest feelings.
>
> All my love,
>
> Your Franz (Braunschweiger-Bibfeldt), Ecclesiastes 4:9-12

On January 21, Bibfeldt skipped his MECCA meeting to attend the Amsterdam lectures on the church and on the academy that he had read advertisements about a few months earlier. He greatly enjoyed both of them. Recognizing that the two lecturers seemed to have great difficulty with one another's systems, Bibfeldt invited both of them to get together with him in an effort to work toward bringing them to some understanding of common ground. They met around 10 P.M. at Jimmy's Tavern. After their meeting, Bibfeldt reflected on the evening's conversation.

> *Jan. 22, 1993. 4:00 a.m.* I just returned from Jimmy's Tavern. My friends from the Midwest and Southeast and I had many hours of interesting conversation, but my attempts at correlating their work eventually came to naught. My Methodist friend from the Southeast spoke passionately about the post-Christian age in which he claims we live. He expressed his belief that the search for universal moral rationality can only wind up undermining the

more important search for a Christian identity. "Concern for universal rationality leads nowhere but straight to hell," he said with a wink of his eye as he looked in my direction.

Our philosopher friend from Chicago spoke calmly and in measured even tones. He spoke confidently of the modes of reasoning shared by agents in many diverse cultures, at least those who think about moral values. Where the Methodist conversationalist had claimed the only true morality was Christian, the philosopher intoned that morality needed no religion to insure its normative standing. "Metaethics," he said, "is a matter of moral precepts, basic human rights in possession of a degree of oughtness applicable in any cultural or ethnic context." "Hell," replied the Methodist, "one man's oughtness is always another man's pile of prized fertilizer; you'd know that if you ever attended a national denominational meeting."

At one point, after long and heated discussion of the meanings of post-Christian, post-Enlightenment, and postmodern, the two turned to me and asked where I stood on the polarity between foundationalism and relativism. I said: "Some of my friends are foundationalists. And some of my friends are relativists. As for me, I stand with my friends."

After these comments, Bibfeldt mostly just listened to their continuing discussion. He records that they did not ask him any more questions. Nor did they ever reach any kind of mutual understanding. As the early morning hours wore on, he made one last effort at achieving some kind of synthesis between them.

"Yes," I told them, "human beings are a universally reasonable people who are often particularly unreasonable. We are a universally sinful people who occasionally transcend our sinfulness and truly act beyond, or even in spite of, our own relative interests. We are a universally presumptuous people in possession of many erroneous and particular presumptions. We are one people; we are many people. We are both the one and the many."

With that said, Bibfeldt extended his hand to each of them and, when he left them, they were ordering another round of Chivas Regal scotch. His last comment in this entry to his journal was, "At least they had that in common."

Bibfeldt returned home and took a short nap. Around 10 A.M., he recorded in his journal as he ate his breakfast that he had tossed and turned most of the time he had spent in bed. He attended his MECCA session that morning and afterwards spent the remainder of the day with Regenstein. Finally, late into the evening, he set out on his nightly walk.

Jan. 22, 1993, 11 p.m. After leaving Regenstein, I walked the city streets, dwelling on the events of the night before. I had failed to show my new friends from the states a way toward unity that recognized and valued their differences. What contribution could I make that would reconcile those theologians across the world who love multicultural particularity and those who adore the DWEMS? Can there be both oneness and manyness? How can a city like Amsterdam retain its cherished values of tolerance and openness without falling into moral anarchy and perversion? Can the multiplicity of human cultural experiences be faithfully reconciled with any universality of human moral experience? I feel the weight of these difficult issues upon my shoulders. The task has fallen to me to bridge the gap between relativism and foundationalism. In order to think through these difficult issues, I have stopped at the Swift Kick coffee shop, just down the block from the isolation tank center, and now sit here with a cup of coffee in my hand as I write these words. This place has become a favorite spot of mine throughout this period of unrelenting struggle. . . .

At this point, Bibfeldt continued his narrative discourse on the apparent irreconcilable nature of the moral conflicts in modern culture as exemplified in the conversation of his friends the night before. He even wondered if his correlation method might have reached its limits. "Is the breach irreparable?" This haunting question only reminded him of the rend in his own marriage.

Are Hilda and I forever separated by irreconcilable differences? Is there no possibility of creating a union out of our difference? Can we never find ourselves as one? Are oneness and multiplicity forever at odds? I long for the uniting of our full selves together in a new and more perfect union. I dream of the moment when our lips meet together and that which is not one also becomes one. Neither one nor two. Yet both one and two and more than one. Woman and Man, yet more than the two. [Regenstein's note: "This is a Bibfeldtian revision of Luce Irigaray's essay against oneness."²] *Can it never be?* "*Oh lost and by the wind grieved, Ghost, come back again.*"³

Bibfeldt's musings are cut short nearly in mid-sentence. Then, across the bottom of the page is scrawled the following:

The isolation tank attendant just stopped in for coffee. She said that a woman was looking for me there earlier in the evening and had left a note that is now here before me. Oh Joy. Can it be? Is she searching for me as I search for her? I will both seek and be found.

These words constitute the last entry in Professor Bibfeldt's journal. Two additional documents were stapled onto the back of Regenstein's translation. The complete text of these documents is contained below.

Document 1

January 22

Dear Franz,

How I have missed you in these past months. I had come to depend too much on you as you had on me. And I was enraged at your inability to see and hear me as I was. I had to find my full self apart from you. And I know that you had to do the same. After leaving you I found a group of women who were able to "hear me into speech." [Regenstein's note: "This quotation is attributed to Nelle Morton, and is often used in feminist settings."] I too joined a twelve-step group to help me beyond my "stinkin' thinkin'." [Regenstein's note: "This is a common 12-step phraseology."] Through my meetings with Anonymous Women Against Men In Everything (A. WAMIE), I have come to find my identity in myself and not so much over and against the MECCAs of the world. I have even come to realize that not **all** DWEMS are without some good qualities, and that some "wannabe" DWEMS might even possess **minimal** virtues. Is there a way beyond our separateness within our separateness? Can we find oneness through a return to the womb? Can we be re-created through the

---

2. Luce Irigaray, "When our Lips Speak Together," *The Sex Which Is Not One*.
3. Thomas Wolfe, *Look Homeward, Angel*.

renewing power of the God/dess? I search for you as you search for me. We will enter the waters together.

Your loving Hilda B.-B.

Document 2

From the *Amsterdam Daily News*, January 23, 1993

"Police are investigating the bizarre disappearance of an elderly couple from an isolation tank business establishment. According to the tank attendants, the couple, Dr. and Dr. Bibfeldt, both renowned German theologians, entered the tank together shortly after midnight. Forty-five minutes later, when the attendant went to open the tank, she found the door ajar and the room empty. The attendant claims that a strange figure clothed in a gown of fluorescent white stood before her at the door and said, "Fear not, for I know that you seek the Braunschweiger-Bibfeldts. Come, see the place where they were floating. They are not here. They have gone before you, for they are the many and the one." The figure, said the attendant, then left in the blink of an eye.

Several employees of the business also claim to have seen a note written on the steam of the mirror in the tank room. According to the attendant who first saw the note, it read, from the top of the mirror down to the bottom, as follows:

> I am both She who is
> And was
> And He who was
> and is
> — the Many and the One.

Others who saw the writings a few moments later claim that they read only:

> She who
> was
> And He who
> is

According to unidentified sources in the police department, investigators have taken this second more widely affirmed reading as a clue in their investigation of this disappearance.

Recently come to light is the fact that these two Drs. Bibfeldt were estranged from one another and had been living apart for several months. Investigators are convinced that the steam-written note points to Herr Bibfeldt as the perpetrator of the disappearance and perhaps even the murder of his spouse. Because the only evidence in this mysterious case faded so quickly, they must await further evidence before they will be able to file a warrant for his arrest.

Our sources tell us that regardless of the police decision, a warrant will serve little purpose because the couple seems to have disappeared without a trace. Only their clothes and miscellaneous personal effects remained in the room. An unidentified source at the isolation tank claims that another customer, often seen in the company of Herr Bibfeldt, was observed slipping from the room with a bundle of papers under his arm about the time of discovery of this disappearance. Police hope to recover these papers as evidence in an eventual case against Herr Bibfeldt. No new leads are forthcoming.

*   *   *

As faithful followers of Bibfeldtian theology as well as the truth, we have a different interpretation of the events of that fateful January evening that will both exonerate Ellis Regenstein and Franz Braunschweiger-Bibfeldt and also shed new light on the nature of our true human existence. First of all, we are convinced that Ellis Regenstein took Bibfeldt's journals not to cover up a crime or even, as some crass academics might claim, to secretly incorporate Bibfeldt's reflection into his dissertation. No, Regenstein appropriated Bibfeldt's papers for the more mundane purpose of carrying them home to their proper resting place, the Bibfeldt Archives at the University of Chicago.

Second, it is our contention that Regenstein was not an accomplice in a crime, for the simple reason that there was no crime. The police failed to arrive at a coherent interpretation of the note on the mirror. The correct mirror message was the one the first attendant saw. The message as it is printed above makes clear that the later witnesses who came into the room saw only a fragment of the original after the door had been open for a time and the message had faded around the edges. The message in its original form does not suggest that Hilda Braunschweiger-Bibfeldt is dead or missing at the hands of her spouse. On the contrary, the message in full suggests not death but union in many-ness: "I am She who is and was and He who was and is — the Many and the One."

We contend that neither Hilda nor Franz Braunschweiger-Bibfeldt lost herself/himself in the isolation tank. On the contrary, they were mysteriously joined unto a united yet multifaceted new being for a new age, the incarnation of the true God/dess. They became not simply a man and a woman, or even Man and Woman, but Wo/man — the archetype of a new race, a new way of being that both overcomes and contains the conflicts and dualisms of their psyches and of our culture. Correlation and Anti-Correlation, Yes and No come together in one diverse being that is one and yet more than one, united in the present and yet moving us beyond relativism and foundationalism. They became together, in the flesh, the manifestation of both/and and/or either/or *and/or* both/and and/or either/or, no more! In them the tensions of our age are made one and yet more than one. They became not one mind but two; together, their minds are more than quadrilateral. In this mystical event, the octagonal mind has been born. Two become one and one becomes eight. And through the eight we may find our authentic selves. It is through this new Wo/man that we can come to our true selves, which contain both the oneness and multiplicity of the God/dess and of all existence. They are at once the same and different, the one and the many, the ever-present and never-present.

Where is this new creation? Where have all the Braunschweiger-Bibfeldts gone? *Si monumentum requiris, circumspice* (If you seek their monument, look around you).

The Politically Correct
Fundamentalism of Franz Bibfeldt

R. SCOTT APPLEBY

For six years the American Academy of Arts and Sciences put energies into the Fundamentalism Project, a comparative study of intense religious movements around the world. One would think that Bibfeldt would have nothing to do with any movement implying religious intensity. However, R. Scott Appleby, associate director of the Fundamentalism Project, who knows more about the project, and, for that matter, about fundamentalisms around the world, than anyone else, did find implications. Note his concentration on Bibfeldt's alternative to *The Fundamentals*. — ED.

Many will recall, from the details of Franz Bibfeldt's narrated life, the emergence in his early childhood of a need to please and appease, but also to withhold final commitment. Bibfeldt was born on All Saints' Day and baptized the same day so as not to offend any of the saints; and even as a small child he exhibited a probing, if not to say prurient, intellectual curiosity, scrutinizing all things physical — meta- and otherwise.

It was not until well after the publication of his groundbreaking dissertation "The Problem of the Year Zero," however, and following a number of reversals in his personal and professional lives, that Bibfeldt perfected his now-famous theological method of creating very little out of absolutely nothing but calling it scholarship anyway — a widely imitated methodology that was coined *Horsgeschichte* by Professor Robert Grant and further refined to *Bullsgeschichte* by Bibfeldt historian Joseph Price. Following that triumph in theological innovation, Bibfeldt, displaying a resourcefulness that would serve him in good stead when he was able to secure two academic appointments at the same time in two different German universities, managed to slip an ersatz scroll containing hallucinatory references to events of the year zero into a clay jar in Qumran, thereby throwing a generation of Dead Sea Scrolls scholars into a tizzy from which they have yet to recover.

Bibfeldt came under heavy criticism for his simultaneous academic appointments, which he had received on the basis of the confused notices that his study of the year zero had earned. But he was redeemed, at least for the moment, when a mentor and colleague came to his defense in *The Chronicle of Higher Education*, where he wrote: "Bibfeldt is a martyr on the altar of self-hatred. His sin was to reveal academe's dirty little secret."

Buoyed by that indiscriminate advocacy, Bibfeldt was able to turn the scrutiny and universal revulsion to his benefit, and he enjoyed a modest string of successes. He quickly established his reputation as a jack-of-all-trends, devotee of none, a characteristic celebrated in his family coat of arms, which features the god Proteus rampant atop a weathervane, surrounded by the Spanish words for "I dance to the tune that is played."

But, as happens all too often with a great figure in mid-career, Bibfeldt peaked too early: his reputation took control, and he became a prisoner of his own successes, his legacy fought over by lesser scholars, each of whom claimed to be the true Bibfeldt standard bearer. Meanwhile the real Bibfeldt lived on, impoverished of new ideas, forced to repeat himself in a string of repetitive publications released by a humility press. Thus, following his last original work of theology, *The Relieved Paradox* (1950), he issued a series of sequels: *Paradoxes Observed* (1958), *Paradox Lost* (1959), *Paradox Regained* (1960), *The Relieved Paradox and the State* (1961), *The Relieved Paradox and Society* (1962), and so on — bigger and bigger books, each with essentially the same content. Even the dust-jacket photo, a close-up of the young, bold Bibfeldt holding his finger to the wind, remained the same. From time to time, Bibfeldt would briefly return to form, as he did in his inscrutable yet highly praised 1966 Society of Biblical Literature essay entitled "Outline for a Future Examination of New Testament Envoys in the Context of Greco-Roman Diplomatic and Epistolary Conventions: The Example of Timothy, Titus, and Anaïs Nin." But these achievements were few and far between indeed.

As with other seminal figures now dried up, Bibfeldt became the subject of seminars and pretentious lectures. Encomia to him, which replaced the coma-like state he induced himself, were reflections on the past glory and meteoric rise of a scholar who was, after all, only in his mid-fifties when he burst on the American theological scene, and who had kept himself in tip-top shape by his principled refusal to do an honest day's work and by living a lifestyle that gave new resonance to the phrase "casual hedonism."

In these years Bibfeldt's intellect and work received careful scholarly attention. For example, Robin Lovin masterfully diagnosed Bibfeldt's quadrilateral mind as one-fourth poet, one-fourth IBM executive, one-fourth TV jingle writer, and one-fourth cardsharp. Otto Drey-doppel reviewed Bibfeldt's innovative theory of pastoral care for the dead, summarized in his formula, "I'm OK, you're DOA." Yet these were, in truth, retrospectives on a career in eclipse. Indeed, the signs were unmistakable and unthinkable: Bibfeldt had fallen from favor with his public, as evidenced most dramatically in an erstwhile fan's one-word response to a National Public Radio discussion of the great theologian (on file with the Foundation): "Disgusting!"

Not long thereafter, references to "the late Franz Bibfeldt" began to appear in the previously favorable tabloid press, which Bibfeldt had always cultivated and favored with scoops of his forthcoming books. This premature consignment to the tomb, coming at a time when Bibfeldt was already on the lam, was a devastating blow. In any event, Bibfeldt went underground. There are some clues to the kind of event that precipitated his withdrawal, but the larger background of ennui has been sketched. Indeed, the actual whereabouts of our subject, especially in the last decade or so, have been unknown, shrouded less in a veil of secrecy than in a fog of apathy about his comings and goings. There have been sightings, of course, but more of that anon.

Clearly, Bibfeldt was in crisis. (It would be generous to the point of sentimentality to describe this as a mid-life crisis.) But even the setback of seeing his star fall so precipitously could not stifle the indomitable spirit of appeasement that imbued Bibfeldt's work. In his very first year of exile, 1979, he began searching for a new trend upon which to latch. When he first heard the phrase "culture wars," referring to the widening chasm between "fundamentalists" and "libertarians," he was intrigued, for it struck a distant, mystic chord of memory. He was transported to the local *bierstube* in Sage-Hast bei Groszenkneten, Oldenburg, Niedersachsen, Germany, to an image of his *Vati* reminiscing blithely with friends about someone named "Uncle Otto" and his

Kulturkampf. Thereafter, his *Vati* repaired to a cabinet filled with canned tuna and, weeping quietly, would gather his children in his arms and sob, "You are all my children." Bibfeldt was transfixed by this memory, his weathervane spinning wildly now, the tune indiscernible above the din, but gradually coming into key: he, Franz Bibfeldt, would be the arbiter of these new culture wars.

It would seem natural for Bibfeldt to easily present himself as a tried-and-true Christian fundamentalist. As Hilda Braunschweiger-Bibfeldt's long-ignored correspondence attests, he was nothing if not pluperfect patriarchal. And at heart he was an inerrantist, if an inveterately adaptive one, preferring to use a sliding scale of inerrancy, granting ultimate authority to the particular text that suited him best in any given situation — another method widely adopted by both sides of the culture wars.

And yet, for all that, there was the unfortunate matter of Bibfeldt's record. He had always been uncomfortable with any absolutist stance, especially one that refused to shift direction with the prevailing winds. Thus, after the conservative Southern California Christian and oil millionaire Lyman Stewart published twelve paperback volumes entitled *The Fundamentals* between 1910 and 1915, a young, brash Bibfeldt had responded in the early 1920s with his own series, entitled *The Variables.* The Stewart brothers immediately denounced Bibfeldt as the "the most dangerous man in Europe."

The Variables was one of the young Bibfeldt's least realized works, yet a cursory reading — and it deserves nothing if not a cursory reading — reveals that when the Stewarts and the Princetonians insisted on affirming the absolute inerrancy of the Bible, Bibfeldt's response had been: "Yes, the Holy Scriptures are without error, but the inerrant text is found only in the original autographs, which have long since vanished. Thus we are forced to develop a *neue* hermeneutic based on the primary assumptions of *Bullsgeschichte* by posing a central situational question to each text." When Curtis Lee Laws coined the term "fundamentalist" for any Christian willing to do "battle royal" for the fundamentals, Bibfeldt responded with the now widely adopted maxim: "When defining the fundamentals, always consider the royalties."

As the century wore on, Bibfeldt's reputation with the fundamentalists deteriorated further, especially when it became known that he was President Eisenhower's ghost speechwriter when Ike uttered the memorable line, "I believe that Americans should have a deeply felt religious faith, and I don't care what it is." Nor did Bibfeldt ever develop much of a political backbone, much prized by the fundamentalists. His political hero, after all, was Senator Everett Dirksen, because as far back as anyone could remember, the senator had never taken a principled or consistent stand on any issue. Such character traits weighed heavily on the minds of televangelists and fundamentalists to whose fund-raisers Bibfeldt would migrate annually, arriving of course a year late but in his own way right on time. Bibfeldt's bid for acceptance by the fundamentalists became increasingly desperate. His development of a political theology that trumpeted God's "preferential option for the rich," a last-ditch effort to woo the Prosperity Theology crowd among them, failed to impress.

These were dark days indeed for the Bibfeldts. In a letter from the recently unearthed Hilda Braunschweiger-Bibfeldt correspondence, Bibfeldt's spouse laments:

> Franz has hit rock bottom. His letters and constant self-promotions go unanswered and our phone has stopped ringing. He is a broken man; he just sits there stroking the dog absently and staring dully into the distance. His speech is that of a little lost boy, a babbling idiot. You may well ask, how can I tell that he's changed? Well, one rainy afternoon in Salzburg, after making his annual appearance in the production of *Jedermann* (playing, as usual, the role of Niemand), he returned home and in a burst of existential angst descended into *fiction* writing.
>
> From what I can make out of Franz's ravings, the gist of his fiction goes like this. In order to mildly satirize American religious society, whose favor he had sought but who so decisively rejected him, he invented an extraordinarily industrious and peripatetic American church historian for his fiction. In the belief that Americans would only understand satire if it were couched in hyperbole, Franz wildly exaggerated the professional output of this character, playing obvious if not sophomoric numerological and symbolic games in the process. I believe he had his character writing some forty books and 4,000 articles during his forty years of wandering the American wasteland of higher education.
>
> "To poke gentle fun at American fecundity — gentle fun which became quite bitter bile to Franz after the unfortunate skiing accident — he wrote of his fictional theologian-historian that he fathered four sons, eleven foster children, and — intellectually at least — something like eighty doctoral *studenten*. This character wore a pedometer on his belt so that he could finish five miles of walking

at midnight if he had not done so during the day. He camped with his family in every one of the forty-eight contiguous states. He perfected — and of course wrote articles about — a special method of sleeping for only ten minutes at a time, roughly the time allotted for student appointments, so as not to lose a minute of peak-time energy. In creating this character, Franz has even had a bit of self-deprecating fun at his own expense: long criticized for being a year late to everything, Franz made his American theological character a year ahead of everyone.

But now Franz's foray into fiction has apparently backfired. People in America appear to believe that this scholar whom Franz has made up actually exists! Franz seems particularly embittered by the amazing success of his own fictional character. Just the other day I heard him ranting to himself: "The Americans are unbelievably gullible. Even as my public has forgotten me, the real genius, I see this hyperbolic character quoted everywhere — *Time, Newsweek, Reader's Digest, Hustler* — on every topic imaginable. It's enough to make me doubt my own existence. *Gott sei Dank* for the Foundation."

Thus, cast out by what he had considered his own kind, Bibfeldt searched furtively for an identity and an angle in the 1970s and '80s. Drawing heroically on his *Bullsgeschichte* methodology, which had saved him so many times before, he sought new trends that few reputable scholars would dare embrace, movements at which he could become an instant expert, attracting appearances on broadcasts of *Nightline* and *Crossfire*. Slowly — a year late, in fact — it dawned on him what the answer was: *Global fundamentalism*. "Eureka!" Bibfeldt exulted. "I'll go in search of patriarchy, aggression, and the fashionable, politically rewarding use of religion wherever it is found. I'll denounce it if that's what plays, or sympathize with it when it suits me."

Of course, Bibfeldt was only beginning to sense the enormity of this challenge, for at the same time that he was attempting to play both sides of the fence on fundamentalism, he was also concerned with mollifying the politically correct deconstructionist-multicultural-radical feminist group. And at least a couple of problems confronted the now-renewed Bibfeldt almost immediately. First, in the age of the woman, in the era of liberation from all forms of oppression, not the least of which was patriarchy, he found himself in the most unenviable of ontological situations: he was a white European male. In fact, as noted above, many assumed the worst of him: that he was a *dead* white

European male. Second, regarding his ambition to become an expert on world fundamentalisms, Bibfeldt had to admit to himself that he didn't know a Shi'ite from a Levite, a rig-Veda from a Chevy Vega, the Koran from Koresh.

So he turned to the media; the mesmerizing beam from the television and silver screen guided him. He studied its wisdom about modern culture, absorbing all the cues and reverencing all the icons. In that arena he found reassurance that fundamentalists and anti-fundamentalists were not that different: after all, each had an assertive, exclusionary, alternately self-righteous and charming ideology, and, most important, each spoke of the language of the marketplace and the modern lingo of privilege, rights, and power. Bibfeldt was beginning to feel at home.

He made a full-bore assault on the airwaves. His first step was to carve a niche for himself in the politically correct, multicultural landscape; and in so doing he shrewdly embarked on a study of victimology. He hoped to cast himself and his kind — namely, the dead white European males — as the oppressed of the contemporary world, something the men's movement had gotten around to a year earlier. Assuming that there would be more sympathy for this strategy in what in better days had been called *Das Vaterland*, Bibfeldt introduced a measure before the *Bundestag* and German television cameras, entitled "A Declaration of Human Rights for the Ethnically Impaired." When the measure failed, though not by much, Bibfeldt was badly shaken.

He had too slowly come to realize the two great commandments of multicultural politics: (1) Thou shalt not comment upon the distinctive traits of any race or ethnic group, (2) unless and until the race or group in question decides to exaggerate and market those stereotypes, at which point thou shalt indulge, nay celebrate, the practice thereof. Thus Bibfeldt learned his lesson and took notes for his forthcoming book, *Multiculturalism Today: The Unrelieved Paradox*.

Turning in some despair to the world fundamentalist scene, Bibfeldt approached a major foundation to fund his comprehensive fundamentalist project, only to find, to his chagrin, that an observant group from an unassuming midwestern university had been there years ahead of him and was already reaping the benefits. Confused and reeling from this final indignity, Bibfeldt became a chameleon — he even pronounced the word *shameleon* after the 1992 presidential debates — and bounced around the globe posing, utterly unconvincingly, as a modern fundamentalist. He had heard on television — though it was a theory put forth at the highest levels of scholarship — that fundamentalists are very modern indeed.

But if one is not a fundamentalist, it is very difficult to blend the stubbornly traditional and the late or postmodern. Bibfeldt tried to do this in a much-anticipated international lecture tour, and failed. Finally, his spirit of greed and exploitation undaunted, he returned to the United States, where he appeared in an interview in the pages of *Christianity and Crisis*, in which he attempted to establish his politically correct deconstructionist credentials. The Americans were much more receptive to his message, and he was installed in an endowed chair at a major midwestern university.

That did not, however, put an end to Bibfeldt's cultural contributions, as it has done to so many in the past. Finding the literature on fundamentalism and feminism and the debate on multiculturalism far more expansive than he cared to tackle, Bibfeldt took his usual shortcut by scanning the most prominently displayed paperbacks at his university bookstore: *Woman on Top; My Mother, My Self; The Woman's Room; Backlash*, etc. He then concocted a treatise that was a melding of fundamentalism and feminism which suited his deeply rooted but unacknowledged male chauvinism quite well. Entitled *Whiplash*, it described Bibfeldt's image of the perfect woman for the schizophrenic, *kulturkampf* 1990s: she was an English professor, a literary and art critic dressed in leather carrying a coiled whip and declaring that true liberation lay in exploiting women's power to dominate men sexually as well as intellectually. Bibfeldt was excited by this concept — in more ways than can be elaborated in this brief essay. Alas, his problem with the year zero once again reared its ugly head: the idea was by now at least a year old. But Camille Paglia did send him a self-portrait, inscribed: "To Franz — the real intellectual pinup of the '90s."

In the last report to date, Bibfeldt, now wearing a saxophone in his lapel and frequently seen loitering around the McDonald's in Sage-Hast bei Groszenkneten, Oldenburg, Niedersachsen, Germany, whence he has recently returned in retirement, is placing his remaining hopes on the latest politically correct trend. He carried with him a signed publicity photograph of the president of the United States, inscribed with the words: "To my fave p.c. fundie: I'm proud to be an FOB [friend of Bibfeldt], Bill." The quixotic theologian has also taken to including his wife's name in all of his writings and signatures, so that his card catalog entries must all now be refiled under Franz Braunschweiger-Bibfeldt.

Franz Bibfeldt and Dispensationalism

STEPHEN R. SPENCER

"Dispensationalism" is a word that will be very familiar to American premillennialists in the fundamentalist camps. The term has to do with an interpretation of the Bible which sees God acting toward earth through differing dispensations. Dallas Theological Seminary has been a theological center for the development and propagation of this viewpoint, and Stephen R. Spencer of that seminary's faculty has stayed alert to Bibfeldt scholarship. Keeping one's eye out for both the second coming of Christ, which is serious business, and the appearance of some year/some time/some place by the elusive, calendrically impaired Bibfeldt is a full-time job. Here is Dr. Spencer reporting in.

Franz Bibfeldt has attracted significant scholarly attention (and of a quality that has been all that his work deserves). Although the investigations have been wide-ranging, they have focused, without exception it seems, on his later thought, which has been primarily Lutheran in orientation. Undeservedly overlooked has been an earlier phase of Bibfeldt's theology, his brief but significant dispensational period.

Dispensationalism, of course, began with John Nelson Darby (1800-1882), a member of the Brethren assembly at Plymouth, England, after leaving his ministry in the Church of Ireland. The Irish Darby (not to be confused with the Irish Derby) traveled widely on the Continent as well as in North America preaching his distinctive ecclesiological and eschatological views. Among his continental contacts were Swiss and German groups of Brethren.

It was through these contacts that adherents were won, through whose later ministry young Bibfeldt was first exposed to Darby's teaching, which was modified subsequently in a variety of ways. (For instance, his view that four-leaf clovers were a perversion of Trinitarianism by an heretical Irish sect found few adherents.) Darby typically held eight-day conferences, one for each of his eight dispensations. (It is unclear whether Scofield's later discovery that seven-day conferences were easier to book had anything to do with his adopting the now familiar seven dispensations.) Darby's teaching was in the familiar "Bible-reading" style of the Brethren, which would take a word or topic and trace it through the canon, concordance-like, reading each passage in succession. The association of this method with his dispensational period later would lead Bibfeldt to eschew word study in particular (and biblical study generally) as a theological method. It must be stressed, however, that there is no reliable evidence to substantiate the claim that Bibfeldt's description of this method while visiting friends in Vienna in the 1930s gave rise to Ludwig Wittgenstein's notion of "language games." The continued repetition of this baseless charge has unjustly sullied the dispensational tradition.

Bibfeldt embraced dispensationalism with alacrity. Despite his youthfulness, he devoted his energy to this new approach to the Bible. Soon his creativity yielded developments in the dispensational tradition. At first startled by the sight of this child producing notable theological scholarship, the elder Brethren soon were convinced of the value of Bibfeldt's innovations. They in turn spread them everywhere they traveled, gladly sharing with others "things both old (Darby) and new (Bibfeldt)."

It was not long before C. I. Scofield heard of these developments. He too embraced Bibfeldt's contributions and would pay lasting tribute to the German prodigy in his *Scofield Reference Bible* (1907, 1909, 1919). There he states, "The Editor's acknowledgments are also due to a very wide circle of learned and spiritual brethren in Europe and America to whose labours he is indebted for suggestions of inestimable value" (Introduction, p. iv).

Bibfeldt's contributed to others in the movement as well. The intricate charts of Clarence Larkin (1850-1924) are a well-known feature of early and mid-twentieth-century dispensationalism, whether in Larkin's several books (the best known of which is *Dispensational Truth* [1920]) or on the large murals hung across classrooms and church sanctuaries. Although the evidence does not permit us to be certain, it is likely that these graphic illustrations of Bible prophecy are in fact adaptations of originals composed by Bibfeldt himself while listening to Brethren preaching. Young Franz, short of paper on one occasion, used the back of his father's stationery. Due to a mix-up, the elder Bibfeldt wrote to W. E. Blackstone (1841-1935) on those very sheets. "W.E.B.," as he signed his books [note the Quinian epistemological anticipations], took the inclusion of the drawings as intentional, and was so impressed with their power and profundity that he passed them on to Larkin. The rest, as they say, is history.

This early dispensational period contrasts sharply with Bibfeldt's later, though no less influential, eschatological views. Perhaps in reaction to the futurist, apocalyptic dispensational teachings, Bibfeldt for "a time, times, and half a time" espoused an "already and then some" or "*over*-realized" eschatology. C. H. Dodd later adopted this perspective, though, in typical British fashion, he moderated the extremism of Bibfeldt's version. It is important to distinguish Bibfeldt's "already and then some" view from the then current "already and done with" (or *past* eschatology). This latter view was soon out of fashion, though it would reappear in somewhat altered form in J. Barton Payne's "past tribulationism" (see his chapter in *When is Jesus Coming Again?* by Hal Lindsey et al., Creation House, 1974). After a brief flirtation with a view he called "not already and yet. . . ," he eventually proposed an "already not yet *and* not yet, already," in keeping with his mediating "Both/And," "all things to all people at all times" theological method. He combined this with his "semi--millenialism," resulting in a most original and provocative contribution to eschatological scholarship.

In view of the Lutheranism of Bibfeldt's parents and of his own adult convictions, Franz's dispensational period must be seen as an intercalation (or at least a parenthesis) in his theological pilgrimage. This much is clear. What remains unclear, however, is the reason for the break with dispensationalism. Several proposals have been made.

Fundamental to some of these proposals is the rash of deaths of theologians in 1920 and 1921: James Orr, B. B. Warfield, Herman Bavinck, A. H. Strong, C. I. Scofield. It will be noted that all of these men were associated with the Reformed tradition by denomination and theology. Some have conjectured that Franz was frightened into abandoning Reformed theology, of whatever sort (including the dispensational form) by this rash of fatalities at just the period he was reaching full manhood. Lutherans seemed safe from this plague, whatever it was, and thus Lutheranism (nondispensational, of course) offered a safer prospect, or at least Franz hoped — perhaps an early precursor of

Moltmann's later "theology of hope" (a Lutheran theologian, perhaps not so coincidentally — or is he Reformed?).

A more unpleasant suggestion is that these deaths came *after* Bibfeldt's reversion to Lutheranism and result from a campaign of terror, a seeking of revenge for the wasted years in the dead-end street of Reformed theology generally and dispensationalism in particular. There is little hard evidence to support this horrifying theory, thankfully, and current research focuses on other possibilities.

I would like to propose a new solution to the puzzle of Bibfeldt's sudden departure from the dispensational ranks. It is common knowledge that his doctoral dissertation was entitled "The Problem of the Year Zero." His continuing struggles with this chronological conundrum are evident in his propensity to miss speaking engagements, etc., always being a year too late or a year too early. (We all regret his unfortunate absence from the 1988 AAR session which addressed his theological contribution.)

It is also widely known that chronological calculations are central to dispensationalism's prophetic interpretations (see, for example, the treatment of Daniel's seventy "weeks" [Dan. 9:24-27]). Such calculations require a chronological dexterity and sure-footedness that Bibfeldt was doomed to lack. This proved to be a crippling weakness and thus he was forced to abandon dispensationalism. Larkin, armed with Bibfeldt's drawings, and spared the chronological perplexity of Bibfeldt, went on to achieve fame for his illustrative prophetic charts. Bibfeldt would later develop his *Numerologiegeschichte* but forsook dispensationalism for amillennialism, which offered a less calendrical and thus less frustrating eschatology.

Franz Bibfeldt and the Future
of Political Theology

ROBIN W. LOVIN

Robin W. Lovin, having made his first contribution in 1980, was invited back seven years later for a second; he is the only person to have been thus honored. The text showed him assuming he was "stuck" in his present position, but he has since moved on to become a dean elsewhere. He reveals a deft approach to Bibfeldt's deft approach to relevance in political theology. — ED.

It is indeed a singular honor to appear for the second time, charged with the awesome — if unenviable — task of bringing this community of scholarship up to date on the latest work of this master of modern theological reflection. Indeed, this occasion is so — how shall I put it? — overwhelming that I am somehow reminded of Mark Twain's remark, "I would not want to join any club that would ask me to be a member." To which Bibfeldt reportedly added, "But if the food was good enough, I would join anyway."

There is, however, one important difference between this appearance and my last Bibfeldt lecture in 1980. In 1980, I was an unknown, impoverished assistant professor, without tenure. This is what people in the business school call a "career trajectory." And it is that career trajectory, really, that brings me back before you again today for this second appearance as a Bibfeldt lecturer. You see, once you have tenure at an institution like this, you are, not to put too fine a point on it, *stuck*. M.A. students come and go; even Ph.D. students eventually finish their degrees and move on; but once you are a tenured member of a faculty, you're *stuck,* sentenced to an eternity of cheeseburgers and beer at the local tavern, waiting in line at the bank, and running around the field-house track like lost souls in some lower circle of Dante's hell.

To be sure, other institutions may try from time to time to lure you away, but by the time you get tenure, you're addicted to the odd combination of high-level intellectual discussion and devastating peer pressure that characterizes a university like this. This is the only kind of place I know that has a book-of-the-month club where the members write the books.

So sooner or later it occurs to you that once you've got tenure, the only way you're going to get out of here alive is somehow to get rid of it. And according to the university statutes and the AAUP standards, the only way to get rid of tenure is to be found guilty of gross incompetence and/or moral turpitude. That is where the Bibfeldt lectures and essays present a unique opportunity.

You see, most forms of moral turpitude require considerable competence to pull them off. So if you try to get out of here by committing moral turpitude alone, the authorities will probably just say, "Aha, that proves it! We can't fire you. You're too competent." And if you try to get out by displaying gross incompetence, they'll just pat you on the shoulder and say, "That's OK. At least you haven't committed moral turpitude." This is what is known as "Catch-22."

In that context, an invitation to deliver the Bibfeldt lecture is a singular opportunity, because a Bibfeldt lecture is one of the few human activities in which you can display *both* gross incompetence *and* moral turpitude at the same time.

With that prefatory statement of purpose, then, I proceed to our subject for the day, "Franz Bibfeldt and the Future of Political Theology."

Things have been remarkably quiet in Bibfeldt studies since 1980. It is as though this great master of modern European thought were exhausted by the labors that gave us his seminal dissertation on the problem of the year zero, the epochal theology of "Both/And," and the innovative methods of pastoral care for the dead. Perhaps, some of you had thought, the time has come at last for Bibfeldt's retirement, a well-deserved rest in his little chalet at the foot of the Swiss Alps, surrounded only by his books, the memorabilia of his distinguished career, and his world-famous collection of pornographic postcards.

But if you had thought that, you would be wrong. The elusive Bibfeldt has not been retired. He has been extending his work into yet new areas of study. This master of history, biblical studies, systematic theology, practical theology, and religion and psychological studies has been traversing the globe, looking for a new orientation for his theology — and, of course, for a good stein of beer.

Bibfeldt's research methods for defining a new area of theological studies may be of interest to those of you who are looking for a dissertation topic, or for the large number of you who happen to be methodology junkies. Whatever your purposes may be, it's worth my taking a few moments to describe it. Here I borrow heavily from a recent treatise on the subject by Kent Dorsey, who has done extensive research applying the Bibfeldt method to the definition of dissertation topics in ethics and society. The method, known as the method of "cognitive integration through randomized deflection," is subtle and difficult to grasp on first hearing; but it will help if you will try for a moment to visualize the intellectual universe as a very large pinball machine. What happens next is best expressed in Dorsey's own words, from which I quote:

> The thought of a graduate student bouncing about from book to book, lecture to lecture, and conversation to conversation may sound unfortunate unless you remember that the value of the bumpers and targets and holes and passageways increases each time the steel ball runs into them. In other words, a random search for a viable dissertation topic can be fruitful if you listen for the bells and pay attention when you occasionally hit something with some substance.

Using this sophisticated research method in hopes of pinpointing a new area for his own theological reflections, Bibfeldt has himself been doing some bouncing recently, not only from lecture to lecture and book to book, but indeed from continent to continent, and, some would say, from bar to bar. He has, of course, made the obligatory trip to China, although his work there has not received the publicity it deserves. Owing to the poorly trained translators employed by the major wire services, no one recognized that among the Western bourgeoisie heresies that the discredited Chinese leaders were recently forced to recant was the theology of "Both/And."

Bibfeldt's real breakthrough, however, came after the trip to the Orient, in a visit to the Third World. Or, to locate it more precisely, on a two-week package holiday in Cancun. That two weeks concluded with one long evening at a tequila factory and two days in bed watching the intellectual universe flash "tilt" in bright red letters. But Bibfeldt returned home with the realization that what had been missing in his theology up to this point was politics. He had spent his career doing the kind of theology that Segundo has called "traditional academic theology," though when Segundo was asked about Bibfeldt's theology in particular, he called it something quite different. What Bibfeldt knew he needed, after his close encounter with the Third World, was a theology of political *praxis*.

The transition to political theology was not easy for Bibfeldt, for political theology, as we all know, requires fundamental choices and cannot remain neutral about the social conditions and ideological conflicts that divide persons in today's world. Bibfeldt, by contrast, had always been neutral to the point of blandness. Other theologians have built their careers on John 3:16: *Sic enim Deus dilexit mundum,* "For God so loved the world." Bibfeldt's theological motto, by contrast, is Revelation 3:16: *Sed quia tepidus es, et nec frigidus, nec caldus, incipiam te evomere ex ore meo,* "Because thou art neither hot nor cold, I will spew thee out of my mouth." Bibfeldt is the theologian of "Both/And"; and his hermeneutical method, as I suggested in the Bibfeldt lecture of 1980, had always been to affirm all propositions simultaneously in the hope that some of them might be true, and a few of them might even be popular. Choice, particularly controversial choice, runs against the grain of Bibfeldt's theology.

But his Third World experience changed him profoundly, and after several weeks of reading the major works of the Latin American theologians, he discovered his own angle of vision on the problems of political theology. Bibfeldt surveyed the possibilities, made his choice, and affirmed it boldly. He announced a new theology, based on God's fundamental option — for the rich.

The "fundamental option for the rich" did not initially inspire the level of interest for which Bibfeldt had hoped. It did get him roughed up a bit by four angry priests who had previously had reputations as pacifists, but who have subsequently taken to writing essays in favor of revolutionary violence. Nevertheless, Bibfeldt pressed on, against the criticisms of the skeptics, to clarify the basic premises of the fundamental option for the rich.

These premises have now been made clear in a brief article that has not received the attention it deserves, partly because it was rejected by most of the major journals and finally appeared in print in the March 1987 issue of *Penthouse*, where, for reasons that will suggest themselves, it was largely overlooked.

On the supposition that most of you will not have seen it, I will venture to summarize the main points. Bibfeldt's "fundamental option for the rich" begins, like much political theology, with social theory, in particular with Max Weber's analysis of the role of religion in the shaping of modern capitalism. Bibfeldt, however, goes beyond Weber, for Weber simply noted an "elective affinity" between capitalist acquisitiveness and Protestant religion. Bibfeldt turns this elective affinity into a normative theological position. Unlike the classical Calvinists, who, according to Weber, believed that material success was a coincidental mark of divine favor, Bibfeldt offers us a more Arminian theology that leaves room for human action in the divine plan. For Calvin, those whom God loves are apt to become rich. For Bibfeldt, those who become rich God is apt to love.

In place of the austere Calvinist deity who inexplicably allocates election and damnation to a helpless humanity, Bibfeldt offers us a God who, not to put too fine a point on it, toadies up to the wealthy. In place of a God who sides with the poor and the peasants, Bibfeldt offers us a God who likes to hang out around the yacht club. This theology has the immense practical advantage that it eliminates almost all of the inconvenient discrepancies between Euro-American popular culture and the requirements of Christian faith. Once this is clearly understood, it is certain to catch on.

Bibfeldt, never shy about his own innovations, quickly moved to put the "fundamental option for the rich" into practice by opening a neoconservative think tank in Washington, D.C. It is, of course, important for those who advise major political figures to keep themselves out of the limelight; thus few people have been aware of the importance of the work that has gone on at the Wahlverwandschaft Institute in recent years. But Bibfeldt's impact in administration circles has been widely felt. It is a little known fact that Lt. Col. Oliver North was once a student at Yale Divinity School, and you can be sure that when he had to mastermind the secret approaches to the Iranian moderates, he knew whom to ask for advice on the proper theological overtures to make to Muslim fundamentalists. When the full story is told, one of the great moments in twentieth-century theology will be Bibfeldt's secret trip to a remote airport hangar, where he thrust a cake and an inscribed Bible into the hands of a startled Robert MacFarlane just before the latter set out on his momentous trip to Teheran. Even the Senate doesn't know about this meeting yet.

I could go on. I could describe Bibfeldt's efforts in domestic policy areas, including his little-understood part in the preparation of the first version of the W-4 withholding form. I could speculate on the allegations that during his government service, he was also moonlighting as a fundraising consultant to Oral Roberts, but you get the idea. Bibfeldt is far from retired. And given his new practical political turn, the influence of his theology is bound to be a political presence among us for some time to come.

More could be said, but that is a research project for another day. For the moment, my purposes have been served. Bibfeldt's fundamental option for the rich is now available to you for study and for further discussion, and I am at least halfway to a solution of my tenure problem.

Some of you are aware that I have recently received a grant which is intended to allow me, as the announcement states, to pursue my research for the next year "under the freest possible conditions." I conclude that with this presentation today, I have taken care of gross incompetence, and I now have a full year to work on moral turpitude.

A Faith for Franz

SAM PORTARO

In an address in 1992, the Episcopal chaplain to the University of Chicago, Sam Portaro, looked back on other essays (some of which appear later in the book) and then looked around at the Germano-centrism of so much Bibfeldt research. In an era of multiculturalism, Portaro connects Bibfeldt with Anglicanism, one of the smaller and put-upon minorities in pluralist America. — ED.

In this Columbian year we are reminded that the importation of Western European characters and cultures to these shores has been a dubious achievement. As we gather here on this occasion, we commemorate yet another of those questionable extensions of Europe, namely the work of Franz Bibfeldt. Born November 1, 1899, Herr Bibfeldt would be 92 years of age on April 1, 1992 (I note that Richard Rosengarten places the birthdate in 1897, an unfortunate error in his otherwise admirable summary of the Bibfeldt scholarly output).[1] The coincidence of age 92 and year '92 suggests a numerological phenomenon of singular significance, though I for one do not know what it might be. I can only share that the coincidence was sufficiently off-putting to cause Shirley MacLaine to decline my invitation to be with us today. I had thought to ask Ms. MacLaine to channel Franz that we might make this event a bit more memorable. But I could not assure Ms. MacLaine that Franz is actually deceased. Then she reminded me that, as an Episcopalian, I

1. Richard Rosengarten, "Franz Bibfeldt: The Life, and Scholarship on the Life," March 30, 1988, pp. 170-175 below.

95

should recall that Bishop James Pike shares this distinction of status with Franz and that, unless I am prepared to share a like fate with each of them, I might reconsider the whole idea. I have.

I am aware, as I stand in this hallowed place and invoke the name Bibfeldt, that I hold something of a distinction. I speak of Bibfeldt from a different perspective than that of those who have preceded me at this podium. I am particularly grateful for this occasion since it marks a significant anniversary for me. I have been among you for ten years now. And since I hold no hope of either a degree or tenure, I consider this anniversary a measure of sheer love of God. There are those uncharitable sorts who consider the concept of campus ministry at a modern university a classic oxymoron. That we have all persevered and even thrived is a tribute worthy of celebration on this day when we commemorate the person of Franz Bibfeldt, the most lavish perennial in this garden of academic delights.

If you will indulge my extension of the herbivorous metaphor, my earliest investigations into Bibfeldt confirmed my premonitions that Bibfeldt is the kudzu of the theological community. Like the tenacious vine that grows in abundance throughout the southern regions of this country, Bibfeldt and his influences cling to every untended place in the otherwise tidy and methodically methodological minds associated with this school. And like the vegetative kudzu, Bibfeldt's abundant presence is not nearly so lamentable as his seeming uselessness. I say "seeming," for there are many things of God's creating whose value is not readily apparent. Like the hemorrhoid. I have divined at least one salutary property of that humble tumor. I have it on good authority that in order to be elevated to the rank of bishop in my own Episcopal Church, one must have gray hair in order to look distinguished; and one must have hemorrhoids in order to look always deeply concerned. But I digress.

I was addressing the merits of kudzu. While kudzu vines are not edible, they do prevent the erosion of soil from roadside embankments. I suppose we might be grateful that, in similar fashion, Bibfeldt's signal contribution to our life here prevents the erosion of such sense of humor as remains after the rigors of theological inquiry have completed their excavations into our souls, like, say, rigor mortis.

It is my purpose today to do two things. First, I wish to add a note to the corpus of Bibfeldt scholarship. Not a mere footnote, mind you, but a genuine milestone. Indeed, I propose to share with you momentarily what I believe to be the very cornerstone of a promising new direction for Bibfeldtian biographical research. Secondly, I wish to advance a proposition — or indulge a fantasy, which is what many gathered here today do all day long, some for a good wage.

Let me attend to the first of these purposes by building upon the work of my friend and colleague Robert Grant. It was Professor Grant who some years ago shared his own findings in "The Quest for the Historical Bibfeldt." Having only lately completed my reading of John Dominic Crossan's *The Historical Jesus: The Life of a Mediterranean Jewish Peasant*, I well appreciate the laborious task of such historical exploration. I can neither reinforce nor refute Professor Grant's findings. But I do come today prepared to make a substantive contribution to the important and ongoing quest for the historical Bibfeldt.

I begin with the confession that my own doctoral studies were in ministry. Nevertheless, I am informed that in order to secure some scholarly respect, I must share with you my method. Trained in ministry and honed in the school of experience, I drew upon the most practical of practical theology and adhered to the bulwark of my discipline, which is the inexorable truth that it is not *what* one knows but *whom* one knows that matters in this life. My method was simple. I called the Reverend JoAnn Leach, a dear friend who serves as Episcopal chaplain to the University of Utah. I asked her to hie herself over to the Mormon archives and dig up anything she could on the name Bibfeldt. Enlisting the aid of another Episcopalian in the employ of the Latter-day Saints, JoAnn searched the computer records. What I am about to share is, unlike much of the Bibfeldt corpus, verifiable. We can now put to rest any and all claims that Franz Bibfeldt is nothing more than an extensive figment of an expansive imagination aided by expensive education.

The Mormon archives record that a Henry and a Margaret Bibfeldt did reside in Prussia, in the town of Bosseborn, in the region of Westfalen. Henry and Margaret baptized five children in the local Catholic church, from whose baptismal records in the original Latin these facts are derived. The eldest of their children, Catherine, was baptized in 1652. Then followed John, Gertrude, and Margaret. Young Fredrick, baptized in 1665, was the last born. This much of the family, we are assured, has been baptized and sealed by the Mormons in the Salt Lake City temple.

There exists, then, a considerable gap from the records of this family to the notation in the Foundation's archival papers that trace Franz Bibfeldt's origins to a baptismal record in Niedersachsen, Oldenburg, Germany.[2] I shall leave the genealogical task to future historians,

---

2. Martin E. Marty, "About Franz Bibfeldt," a memo circulated to a limited audience.

but I am happy to be able to offer a landmark for future research into the fascinating matter of the Bibfeldt family tree. I am devoting my honorarium to further research, since I am told that the Mormons will want more money for further investigation. Should the honorarium prove insufficient, I suggest that several of us band together and request suitable funding from the Lilly Endowment, or a similarly high-minded benefactor. I detect the beginnings of a new institute.

In the interest of time, I move to my second purpose, namely the advancement of a proposition. It seems to me that Bibfeldt scholarship has been too long silent on the matter of the theologian's personal faith and worship. I realize that confessional theology is not the strong suit of modern schools of theology or religious studies. After ten years as a denominational chaplain at this university, I can personally attest that objectivity can be carried to extremes. One can be so open-minded that one's brain falls out. One can also be so religiously diffuse that the soul evaporates. Sad to say, both conditions can be met on this and many other campuses. It's a particularly lamentable occasion when both conditions are met in a single person. But I digress again.

We have been told that Franz Bibfeldt is, by virtue of his baptism at Niedersachsen, a Lutheran. I have proven with hard evidence that the Bibfeldt progenitors were actually Catholic. That a Franz Bibfeldt may have been baptized at a Lutheran font in Germany at the turn of the century indicates a liberal tendency in the family. Still, this assertion, while it may tell us everything about the faith of Franz Bibfeldt's parents, reveals nothing of Franz Bibfeldt himself. Another suggestion, that Franz was conceived in the backseat of an 1892 Volkswagen following a Candlemas party, is simultaneously questionable and revealing.[3] We must reject the Volkswagen, that vehicle having been invented some forty or so years later. The Candlemas party theory, however, has much to commend it, suggesting as it does both the liberality and the high-church leanings of the parents.

It is my thesis that Franz Bibfeldt continued the liberal leanings of the family. An exhaustive consideration of his work suggests that Bibfeldt was, by faith, an Anglican. And who better to advance this proposition than an Episcopal priest of Sicilian and Swiss ancestry? If I can be an Anglican, why not Franz?

That Franz resisted the Anglicanization of the family name may be attributed to a mixture of pride and prudence. The Oxford Dictionary of English Etymology indicates that the prefix *Bib* is from the Latin

3. Rosengarten, p. 171.

bibere, meaning "to drink." The suffix *feldt* is, of course, the German word for "field." No nation whose geographical nomenclature includes a place called "Spitalfields" could be trusted to render a felicitous equivalent to the rich cadences of Bibfeldt. Thus did pride intervene to prevent a most unhappy alteration. Moreover, no theologian desirous of living off publication royalties could want for a more impressively brooding Germanic moniker than *Bibfeldt.* Thus did Prudence make her contribution.

Bibfeldt was likely drawn to the Anglican tradition for the same reason that the Church of England has proven a haven for successive generations. The Church of England is, as one member of the faith put it, "all that stands between us and Christianity."[4] That Franz Bibfeldt emerges as one of the premier exponents of the Anglican tradition is evinced by a simple review of his life and impressive output.

According to the *Ur*-essay, "Bibfeldt is . . . the compleat theologian because he is capable of engaging in complete reversals of positions depending upon the *Zeitgeist.*" This facility for reversal must surely have come early to Bibfeldt and may have been derived from his experience with the English educational system. My dear friend Caroline Cracraft, of the British Consulate General in this city and product of the English educational system, recently shared a scholarly technique often employed for survival in the English academy. For all children of imagination, of which number we must surely count Franz Bibfeldt, daydreaming is a classroom liability. One must early learn defense or perish. My English friend offered that students can survive handily if they have mastered a time-honored device. When caught off guard by a professorial question, the student must be primed to respond with a question, and preferably one that matches the countenance of one too quickly snatched from reverie. It was likely in just such a setting that Franz learned the very British technique of tilting the head winsomely and answering any professorial inquiry with the palpably engaged retort, "But couldn't it be the other way around?" From this beginning we trace Bibfeldt's penchant for reversals.

Bibfeldt's first American appearance, we have been told, was in a published book review in 1951. It was an auspicious beginning, this review of Bibfeldt's work entitled *The Relieved Paradox.* The title alone suggests those Anglican tendencies that shun conflict and seek a middle way. Those tendencies are further evident in his dissertation, "The Problem of the Year Zero," wherein Bibfeldt explored the missing year

4. George Plimpton, "Off My Father's Cuff," *Esquire,* February 1992, p. 57.

between 1 B.C. and 1 A.D., an exploration that took him quite literally into the temporal *via media* and thus established his lasting fascination for the middle way.

But it was Bibfeldt's response to Kierkegaard's *Either/Or* that truly established his central place in Anglican theology. Bibfeldt's *Both/And* and its sequel, *Both/And and/or Either/Or* remain, in my mind, the quintessence of Anglican thought. Evidently, the present archbishop of Canterbury agrees and offers his portrait on this occasion in token of his esteem for Bibfeldt's rightful claim to the title Defender of the Faith.

Joseph Price, in a lecture that appears as an essay in this collection, generously shared the discovery of a rare manuscript entitled "A Pragmatist's Paraphrase of the Sayings of Jesus." Employing what was identified as a "hermeneutic of reversism," Bibfeldt offered that "any saying [of Jesus] which is too hard to follow is to be understood to mean the opposite of what it literally says."[5] This work has obviously exercised far-reaching influence. One need only study the history of Anglican homiletics to see the practical application of this principle at work. Or just drop in next Sunday to any Episcopal parish. Odds are good you won't be disappointed. Of course, there is evidence that the influence has spread beyond the Anglican communion, but ours is an ancient and hallowed experience, and I doubt that one could find earlier evidence than is posited in our history. Indeed, there are hints that Bibfeldt may have arrived at his own thoroughgoing reversism from a close study of Henry VIII's application of these principles to Roman canon law, a process undertaken six times, obviously to satisfy the demands of the empirical method.

It was this hermeneutic of reversism that gave rise to Bibfeldt's foundational translations of sacred Scripture. He rendered Matthew 5:3 as "Blessed are the rich in money, for they can build bigger and better churches. Who cares about the Kingdom of God?"[6] Anglican architecture, though rivaled in this city by Catholic structures, still claims the Cathedral Church of St. John the Divine in New York City and the Washington National Cathedral in the nation's capital as stunning exemplars of this beatitude in action. Bibfeldt's reading of Matthew 5:8 yielded "Blessed are those whose external appearance and behavior are impeccable, for they shall look nice when they see God."[7] Need I say more?

5. See Price's essay in this volume, pp. 26-34.
6. Price, p. 33.
7. Price, p. 33.

Robin Lovin, for his part, traced the course that led to Bibfeldt's political theology which propounds God's preferential option for the rich.[8] This theological bent, of particular interest to Anglicans, enjoyed notorious popularity in the Reagan administration and perseveres in the mind and legislative agenda of President Bush. Bibfeldt's contribution, however, was the backbone of Mrs. Thatcher's administration, an indebtedness acknowledged in the contribution of her photograph to our precious archival collection of Bibfeldtiana.

It was also Professor Robin Lovin who contributed a paper entitled "Franz Bibfeldt: The Breakdown of Consciousness and the Origins of the Quadrilateral Mind." While Professor Lovin aimed to explore the cerebral composition of Bibfeldt, I wish to note here the remarkable coincidence that there exists in the archive of Anglican history a most important ecumenical document called *The Chicago-Lambeth Quadrilateral 1886, 1888*. This document sets forth the fourfold principles which this communion holds essential to the unity of the divided branches of Christendom. I suggest that Mr. Lovin revise his earlier treatise. Given the dates of the document's composition in Chicago in 1886 and its ratification at Lambeth in 1888, we must entertain an earlier source and date for the breakdown of consciousness and the origins of the quadrilateral mind, or attribute to Franz Bibfeldt a precocity normally reserved only for the persons of the Trinity. Of course, it may well be that Professor Lovin's thesis was sound, but his information insufficient. Could it be that the Bibfeldt whose influence shaped this important Anglican document was father or grandfather, mother or grandmother to the man we revere today?

In 1979, Otto Dreydoppel offered important insight into Franz Bibfeldt's theory of the pastoral care of the dead. Bibfeldt advanced the "insight that the dead are the truly silent majority and thus the definitively oppressed group."[9] One cannot fully appreciate this insight, nor its incarnation, until one leads worship in an Episcopal congregation. I shall be forever indebted to Bibfeldt's definitive work in this area, his magnificent book *The Minister as Mortician*. It has guided me on many occasions and made me a far more effective pastor, especially upon those occasions when I have been invited to visit congregations in the suburbs.

In one regard, however, Franz Bibfeldt distinguishes himself even amongst Anglican theologians. It is not characteristic of our tradition

8. See Lovin's essay in this section, pp. 89-94.
9. See Dreydoppel's essay later in this volume, pp. 107-113.

to write much down. That we have such rich resources by which to trace the trajectory of Bibfeldt's ascendancy (or, one may maintain, his descendency) into Anglican theological history is not due to the abundance of primary resources but rather to an extensive catalogue of secondary materials. That so much theology could be derived from so little actual script is a distinctly Anglican characteristic. Still, Franz Bibfeldt remains the perfect antidote to those Anglicans who seem to have maintained for centuries that the only guarantee of safe theology is to do no theology.

Indeed, in researching this paper today, I found among the archives, scribbled on the back of a scrap of paper, some random notes in the unmistakable hand of Franz Bibfeldt. The script is unmistakable because, in a characteristic act of solidarity with adolescent women for whom he held abiding respect and morbid fascination, Herr Bibfeldt always dotted his "i's" with a small open circle. The notes were scrawled on what appeared to be a matchbook cover from a pub named The Trojan, or perhaps a fragment from a box of prophylactics. It is difficult to tell. In either case, our hero was obviously smitten by the theological muse even in such unlikely circumstances as the evidence suggests. He seems to have been pondering the terrifyingly modern challenge of doing "safe theology." The notes sketch a campaign for safe theology, with posters, placards, television spots and music videos featuring comely scholars demonstrating the proper use of conundrums. The campaign slogan is worthy of even an august university and reflects something of its scholarly philosophy. It reads, rather fetchingly I think, "Practice Safe Theology: Put a Propaedeutic on your Hermeneutic."

In conclusion, let me remind you that, as has been suggested elsewhere, "In the world of Bibfeldt, not what actually happened but what everyone believes happened, matters."[10] Dear friends, dare I suggest that this truth extends beyond the world of Bibfeldt and is the basis of most, if not all, religion? Bibfeldt, then, invites us into the world of faith. In these times such invitation is seldom taken. Though those of us who confess faith offer open invitation to this wonderful world, few accept. Could it be that we fail in our evangelical task because we have it backward, or if I might borrow from Franz Bibfeldt, because we do not have it backward enough? Could it be that we need to apply that unerring Bibfeldtian reversism even to evangelism itself?

If so, then we are mistaken to begin our evangel with the pre-

10. Martin E. Marty, *By Way of Response* (Nashville: Abingdon, 1981), p. 36.

sumption that others must in the first necessity love our God. Instead, our evangel begins with the proclamation of our God's abiding respect and love for every person. Thus, in a true reversal of evangelical mission, I do not demand that Franz Bibfeldt embrace Anglicanism, but rather affirm Anglicanism's affectionate embrace of Franz Bibfeldt. While I cannot know if Franz loves my God, I can and do affirm that my God loves Franz, and me, and you, and all who struggle to get it right.

I may not have succeeded in convincing you of my thesis that there is a faith for Franz, that faith being my own tradition of Anglicanism and the Episcopal Church in particular. I have had my chance and taken my chances. I thank you for allowing me this special opportunity. Having thus used my time and yours, I conclude with the wisdom of W. C. Fields who — perhaps in an unattributed paraphrase of Bibfeldt himself — said, "If at first you don't succeed, try, try again, then quit. No use being a damn fool about it."[11]

11. Plimpton, p. 57.

III. The Pastoral Theology of Franz Bibfeldt

What I gave, I have; what I spent, I had; what I kept, I lost . . . philanthropy is a ministry.

FRANZ BIBFELDT,
The Relieved Paradox

Portrait of Franz Bibfeldt by Siegfried Reinhardt

Ministry to and with the Dead:
The Pastoral Theology of Franz Bibfeldt

OTTO DREYDOPPEL, JR.

Bibfeldt is not only a systematic theologian; he also makes contributions to practical and pastoral theology. In 1978 Otto Dreydoppel visited a major Bibfeldtian theme in an essay that demonstrates once again that good taste in matters delicate has never been an affliction of contributors to this volume. A few of the references in this essay, as in so many others, may be lost on some younger readers or on those who, like Bibfeldt, now have poor memories. But the flavor remains fresh and the point remains vivid. Dreydoppel now teaches at Moravian Theological Seminary in Pennsylvania. — ED.

Christian theology has in recent years accepted the responsibility for responding to the situation of those who are oppressed: blacks, people in the Third World, gays, women, George Steinbrenner. Alongside all these discriminated-against minorities stands — or perhaps I should say lies — a group that has in the past had few advocates. I refer, of course, to the dead, that true "silent majority" in Christendom.

Most of us became aware of the crying problem of the dead only late in 1975 when reports of the ongoing terminal mortality of Generalissimo Francisco Franco began to be widely circulated. With that, the dead-consciousness movement was born.[1] The movement has been concerned recently not only with trying to arouse its constituency but also

1. See M. M. Lazarus, "Raising the Dead Consciousness: Up from the Grave and Out of the Coffin," *Archives of Psychiatric Thanatology* 7 (1976): 246-63.

with gaining passage of anti-discrimination ordinances in several large
American cities. Alas, the dead-rights opponents have carried the day in
Miami, St. Paul, and Wichita, where electorates were swayed by their
emotional campaigns. In those cities the pro-life forces saturated the
media with such slogans as "Would you want your child taught by a dead
person?" and "Dead people have an agenda that they're trying to impose
on America!" The issue has even found its way into the popular music
scene where an anti-dead-rights hymn called "Stayin' Alive" was for
several months at the top of the charts. Another recent song has sought to
make plain the groundlessness of prejudice against the dead by deliber-
ately exaggerating it. This is, of course, the pop short "Dead People":

> Dead people got no reason,
> Dead people got no reason,
> Dead people got no reason to live.
> They got clammy hands and glassy eyes,
> They lie around just drawin' flies.
> They don't boogie much and they lie so low
> You got to dig 'em up just to say hello.
> Don't want no dead people round here.

This truly sums up the existential crisis of the dead and points to the
need for a theology of ministry to and with the dead.

Long before the current dead-consciousness movement, however,
there *was* one man alive to the dead issue: Franz Bibfeldt. Professor
Bibfeldt has for some time been sympathetic to the problems of the
dead. His doctoral work, you will recall, treats "The Problem of the
Year Zero." This study of the radical contingency of temporal location
is a perfect theoretical basis for ministry to those who have entered
eternity. Furthermore, Bibfeldt has distinguished himself as the theologian of "Both/And," the insight that all things can be made to come
out right, that nothing should be excluded, and that the scholar's task
is to adapt so as to be relevant in every age and circumstance. According
to Bibfeldt, it is therefore wrong to exclude someone from our field of
concern merely because he or she happens to be dead. Dead people
have serious problems that deserve to be addressed. Moreover, dead
people themselves perfectly exemplify the Bibfeldtian method. Who,
asks Bibfeldt, is better able to adapt to new conditions and to do so
quietly and without fuss better than the dead? Out of his continuing
desire to please everyone, not just the living, and in gratitude to the
dead for their adaptability to his system, Franz Bibfeldt spent several

of his most creative years seeking to devise a pastoral theology suitable for ministry to the dead.

Bibfeldt first began the attempt to craft a system of pastoral care especially for the dead in the early 1950s when Rogerian counseling was in vogue. On the advice of colleagues at the University of Worms, he sought out Rogers and finally found the great nondirective counselor in a public television studio outside Pittsburgh. After several months of clinical training with Mister Rogers, Bibfeldt was ready to go public with his method of counseling the dead: "It's a beautiful day in the neighborhood . . . Hi neighbor! . . . Can you say 'thanatology?' . . . I thought you could!"[2]

Back at Worms, Bibfeldt learned that he had had the wrong Rogers. But he finally did meet the author of *Client-Centered Therapy* and eagerly began to adapt the concept of reflective listening to the problem of ministry among the dead. Nondirective counseling, however, proved to be ineffective with these clients. Bibfeldt discovered that while the dead make excellent Rogerian counselors, since their ability to listen patiently is unexcelled, they somehow lack the necessary facility to state their problems and provide the terms for meaningful counseling inter-changes. Besides, none of the dead with whom Bibfeldt had worked ever really felt threatened by a directive pastoral counselor. Bibfeldt's project on pastoral care for the dead was to lie moribund for another decade.

In April of 1966, *Time* magazine announced the death of God, and Bibfeldt's pastoral theology was given new life. How better to inspire a faith and practice ministry among the deceased, he thought, than by reference to a deity who was himself dead? The God-is-dead theologians were, of course, only trying to make the point that God is wholly immanent. According to the Bibfeldtian "Both/And," however, this implied that God was also wholly transcendent. Dead people were obviously well in touch with this wholly transcendent God, since they too transcended time and place. Bibfeldt briefly considered suicide in order to facilitate his ministry among the dead in the name of a dead God, but cowardice prevailed, and *der Alte* (as he was even then beginning to be called affectionately) cast about for better pastoral techniques.

At about that time, pastoral counseling was being influenced by what has come to be known as the human potential movement. These were the advocates of group-grope and encounter sessions, transactional analysis and transcendental meditation, Arica and est. This move-

2. Bibfeldt published an account of this experience as "Neighborhood Ministry in Forest Lawn," *Presbyterian Life . . . After Death* 20 (1953): 83-90.

ment seemed promising to Bibfeldt in helping the dead to get in touch with themselves. Dead people proved perfect clients for the Erhard seminars, since they were willing to sit still not for a mere twelve or sixteen hours, but for really *long* stretches of time. Unfortunately, few of the dead clients who participated in est "got it." Bibfeldt subsequently discovered that his dead clients were unable to repeat a mantra, and TM also had to be abandoned. At first, transactional analysis seemed to offer a most useful therapeutic technique. In all of his transactions with the dead, Bibfeldt never found a single one who was not OK, which was a hopeful sign.[3] But when it came to charting life scripts — or, in this case, *death* scripts — Bibfeldt found so little variety in the existence of his various clients that he gave up the effort and moved on in his quest for the perfect pastoral therapy for counseling with the dead.

There was the brief promise of a new pastoral theology in the early 1970s with the emerging theology of future hope. The eschatological theologians spoke of the creative possibilities of a "God who is in front of us." (This seemed to be the necessary Bibfeldtian corrective to Satan, who is behind us.) The theology of hope also discussed the "draw of the future." Dead people, of course, have nothing *but* future. And the idea of a "novum" which would break in seemed perfectly suited for providing a new meaning structure for the dead, since their chief problem was one of boredom: nothing new ever happened.[4] The promise of future theology for the dead died, however, when Bibfeldt confused future theologian Carl Braaten with rock star Johnny Rotten, and declared menacingly, "I won't listen to that punk!"

Professor Bibfeldt was much taken with the "life-after-life" movement of the mid-1970s. Life-after-lifers Elisabeth Kübler-Ross and Raymond Moody detailed the experiences of those who, having been clinically dead, were resuscitated and then were able to discuss the beauty of the afterlife: brilliant colors, a feeling of wholeness and peace, and the presence of a comforting "Being of Light." These people and their out-of-body experiences convinced Kübler-Ross and Moody that life after death existed "beyond a shadow of a doubt." If, reasoned the theologian of "Both/And," there is life after life, then there must also be death after life. His resolve to formulate a pastoral theology for the dead was renewed.

At this point Bibfeldt sat down and began to think carefully about the pastoral problems that ministry to the dead should meet. Beyond

3. See Bibfeldt's article, "I'm OK, You're DOA," *Journal for the Scientific Study of the Weird* 3 (1968): 127-43.
4. Bumper stickers even began to appear which said "Dead People Never Have a Nice Day!"

the previously mentioned problem of ennui, of the awful sameness of the day-in-and-day-out life of the dead, it occurred to Professor Bibfeldt that dead people were extraordinarily prone to depression. This is not only because of the loneliness and rejection they experience daily (dead people are usually allowed to associate only with their own kind), but also because the dead are condemned to sedentary lives and are denied meaningful work and, therefore, any sense of accomplishment.[5] This became abundantly clear to Professor Bibfeldt when he attempted to discuss with a late colleague what future work Bibfeldt could expect to see him produce. "   ," replied the dead friend. Professor Bibfeldt also discovered that the dead suffer from incredible housing discrimination. They are, for the most part, consigned to small, dark, subterranean one-room apartments.

The problem of inadequate housing launched Professor Bibfeldt on several months' worth of study of what should be done with the remains of the dead. Burial was aesthetically unacceptable, and, besides, cemetery space was becoming more and more scarce. Bibfeldt searched the pastoral care literature but found little of help there.[6] Then, while reading the *Dialogues* of Alfred North Whitehead, Bibfeldt came across the insight that "the English never abolish anything. They put it into cold storage."[7] This led Bibfeldt to consider dealing with the dead cryogenically, or by quick freezing. Empathy has always been the keystone of Bibfeldt's life and work, however, and since he shivered at the thought of being frozen himself, he could not stand the idea of freezing anybody else, living or dead. The cryogenic option turned out to be a big sleeper. Bibfeldt finally determined that cremation would be the best disposition for the remains of the dead, and he published the results of his work under the title *The Fire We Can Light*.

Bibfeldt's complete theology of ministry to the dead was finally set out in a book he wrote in 1976 with Paul Pruyser, *The Minister As Mortician*.[8] The authors asserted that dead people come to pastors for counseling intentionally and for religious reasons. They therefore expect to be addressed from the standpoint of faith, using religious language. Dead people come to their pastors, that is, to engage in "soul searching."

Gail Sheehy's book *Passages* on the predictable life crises gave Bibfeldt his final insight into the pastoral care and counseling of the

---

5. One notable exception is the late King Tutankhamen who, even in death, has proved to be an expert at fundraising.

6. Most of the books he read had terrible plots.

7. This is the obligatory Whitehead citation for this paper.

8. Recently released as a movie called *Looking for Mr. Good Bier*.

dead.[9] Since, according to Ms. Sheehy, one should develop coping mechanisms to face these crises, Bibfeldt sought ways for dead people to come to terms with the state of being dead. The professor then realized that the dead, merely by being dead, are in fact already coping with their condition. The best therapy for the dead, therefore, he saw to be the advice of the nursery rhyme, "leave them alone and they'll come home."[10]

After the overwhelmingly positive reception that his pastoral theology for the dead received, Bibfeldt threw himself with new vigor into the dead-rights movement. One of the churchly causes he became involved in was the demand for the ordination of the dead. Since Mormons baptize for the dead, he reasoned, why shouldn't the dead also be ordained? Not everyone agreed, however, and the ordination issue has threatened to split the Episcopal and Presbyterian communions, among others. Likewise, Roman Catholicism, though it has shown admirable willingness to keep the dead alive through hagiography, shows little sign that it will soon ordain dead Catholics.

The rise of dead-consciousness has, inevitably, found dead people in the evangelical wing of Christendom. They have, in fact, their own caucus without the church triumphant, usually referred to as "died again." Of this, Bibfeldt, the affirmer of everything, is a charter member. Dyed-in-the-wool died againers are not, of course, content with Professor Bibfeldt's *laissez faire* pastoral theology for the dead. Dead evangelicals find more comfort in the charismatic psychotherapy propounded by Ruth Carter Stapleton, usually referred to as *The Gift of Inert Healing*. Church growth has been spectacular among dead evangelicals, since their evangelism techniques are highly refined. People join the died again movement literally minute by minute. But even among the mainline churches the roll of dead members grows daily.[11] Franz Bibfeldt

9. From the foregoing, it will have become clear to the reader that Franz Bibfeldt's pastoral theology did not develop systematically: it just grew like "Thanatopsis."

10. Professor Bibfeldt is still trying to come to grips with the problem of those who may have been coerced into the ranks of the dead against their will. Many of these dead cult members, especially young people, can be seen mooning around on street corners selling flowers. Attempts at rescuing such unhappy dead have been, at this writing, inconclusive. One thinks, for example, of the recent incident in which Missouri fundamentalists sought to bring a deceased believer back to life. See Professor Bibfeldt's guide on deprogramming the dead, *Righteous Vampire*.

11. I call your attention to the book *Dying Churches Also Are Growing*, Franz Bibfeldt's answer to Dean Kelley's study on the decline of the mainline churches. Here Bibfeldt advances the "absolute value" theory of church growth: it doesn't matter whether your membership increases or decreases, as long as the numbers change.

leaves us finally with cautionary words about those leaders of the died again movement who have become larger than life. These dead evangelists are media celebrities, and they tend to draw money and vitality away from local congregations. Their vehicles are such TV shows as PTL (i.e., "Pushing up The Lilies") and the 666 Club. By using space-age electronics and technology, these died again superstars become powerful beyond the range of mere mortal dead preachers. Beware, Bibfeldt warns us, of the "Bionic Church."

During the late 1970s deadism has proved itself to be the most lively of issues. Franz Bibfeldt is now in his 82nd year, and thus he will soon be looking forward to joining the dead for whom he has been such a faithful theologian, therapist, and pastor. It is therefore fitting that *Newsweek* recently profiled him in a cover story. (Unfortunately, it was only the extraterrestrial edition of the magazine that actually had his name on the cover.) Franz Bibfeldt has finally begun to receive the recognition that he has long deserved as pastor and theologian of the dead.

The Bibfeldt Hustle,
or Saturday Night Plague:
Some Recent Theories of Pastoral Care

MARK MILLER-McLEMORE

If Bibfeldt has been relevant to anything and anything has been relevant to Bibfeldt in recent decades, it has to be in the context of the congeries of therapies, recovery movements, transactional analyses, self-esteem, and self-help advisements. Mark Miller-McLemore, pastor of First Christian Church in Chicago Heights, Illinois, tracked the Bibfeldtian influence in some of these zones, engaging in some scholarly cross-referencing and revisionism along the way. — ED.

The explication of the theories of pastoral care originated and espoused by our own Franz Bibfeldt leads us at the outset to a brief reexamination of the best recent semi-autobiographical data available. You will recall, I am sure, the colorful expositions of the G (Grant), B (Brauer), M (Marty), L (Landon), and P (Price) sources. While mighty contributions to the history and lore of Bibfeldtiana, each of these sources by itself cannot stand up to the careful and continuing scrutiny of scholars. In short, they are not the best exemplifications of the total spectrum of *Bibfeldttheologie* today.

If we are to examine the evolution of Bibfeldt's theory and practice of pastoral care, we must glance briefly at the life of this great man, a life he himself has humbly characterized, in a phrase reminiscent of

Socrates' "gadfly of Athens" statement, as "a pimple on the nose of modern theology." We shall thus turn to these sources and commence our brief sketch with them, confident that we have authority for so doing in the directive of the *L* source: to "look first to the *Sitz im Leben* — and then ignore it."

Bibfeldt, you will remember from the *M* and *P* sources, was born in the trundle seat of an 1892 *Ur*-auto on November 1, 1897.[1] His life has been sketchily attested; however, we know some reported incidents to be true. Bibfeldt, for example, did write his doctoral thesis on the problem of the year zero, a continuing problem that causes him to this very day to arrive either a year early or a year late — and sometimes both — for any appointment. He achieved some fame through the publishing of *The Relieved Paradox*, the masterwork that sets forth his theological method of "Both/And." This was Bibfeldt's way of achieving what he saw as the theological task: to reconcile all opposites and make things come out right.

But enough of a chronological account. We shall return to any significant details of Bibfeldt's life as the occasion arises while interpreting his thoughts on pastoral care. However, we must ask one final biographical question: What has become of Professor Bibfeldt today? The *M* source leaves Bibfeldt at Esalen sometime in the early 1970s. The *L* source claims that Bibfeldt comforted President Nixon over the telephone during his famous "prayer with Kissinger" episode, undoubtedly demonstrating Bibfeldt's involvement in the "dial-a-prayer" movement of that era. The *P* source — here spurious, one does not doubt — alludes to Bibfeldt's residence at an unlikely place called the Brandenburg Home for Indigents and Crazies, Brandenburg, West Germany. Obviously, nothing is clear. But at this point a serious question must be asked: *Is Bibfeldt still alive?*

Let us attempt an answer. A short two years past, Dennis Landon enunciated his theory of "Bibfeldt enjoying culture" and proposed his hermeneutic of "looking for the man who wasn't there" in order to join the quest for the historical Bibfeldt in culture. We affirm this principle: we have witnessed its fruitfulness in that short span of time and shall use it ourselves. Yet, as responsible Bibfeldt scholars, we are shocked

---

1. Scholars still debate Bibfeldt's birthdate. Was Bibfeldt born on All Saints' Day in prefiguration of his future theological stance? Or was he, in fact, born late in the evening of October 31, Halloween? The argument for the October 31 date has been largely discredited due to a film presentation of the Bibfeldt birth-drama, this a poorly conceived and produced, thinly disguised allegorical attempt entitled *Rosemary's Baby*. Happily, the public was not fooled.

in retrospect at the ease with which this one-sided hermeneutic was accepted. We must follow the Bibfeldtian program through to its conclusion; we must not allow ourselves to rest with either affirmation or negation. In short, if two years ago we sought the Bibfeldt who *wasn't* there, this year we must look for the Bibfeldt who is. And in so doing we assert: Bibfeldt is *both* here *and* not here. He is alive and yet, we must add, in some strange manner dead. And, even more important to today's topic, he is participating in the general theological discussion, and his participation is centered in the area of pastoral care.

Enough questions have been raised so far to satisfy the most skeptical Bibfeldtian; thus we will no longer question the facticity of his life. But, in order to balance the scale, we will now turn to the evidence of his life among us today. First, we must recall the motto of his recently released essay on the lack of creativity in theological titles. This essay is itself entitled, in a masterful piece of irony, "Beating the Whirlwind into the Ground." The motto, Bibfeldt's favorite scriptural citation, reads, "And, lo, I am with you alway, even unto the end of the world" (Matt. 28:20b, KJV). In this motto to his incisive essay Bibfeldt gives clear indication of his intent to haunt us for many years to come.[2]

Two further data — in this instance, two songs from popular culture — will be adduced as evidence of Bibfeldt's continuing life among us. Each of these tunes has topped the charts in the past six months; both are blatantly Bibfeldtian in form and content. The first is a bland and innocuous little number, "You Light Up My Life," performed by Debbie Boone. Though ostensibly dedicated to her father, Pat Boone, popularizer of white buck shoes, the song reveals itself under the analysis of the renowned Bibfeldtian hermeneutic of *Horsgeschichte*. In fact, it is a paean of praise to Ms. Boone's personal and musical mentor, Bibfeldt himself. For who else but this utter genius of adaptation and *coincidentia oppositorum* could put the word "light" — known to describe the combination of *all* colors — into the lyrics of a song sung by so color*less* a performer as Debbie Boone? Additionally, the presence of

---

2. This essay was published in *Idiot Wind, the Journal of Loquacious TV Meteorologists*, June 1977. Incidentally, it is worth noting that another reason Bibfeldt liked this scriptural text so well was that it precisely represented his theological positions in relation to the major philosophical and theological movements of the twentieth century. In keeping with his motto of *Respondeo Ergo Sum*, Bibfeldt felt the need to respond accommodatingly to any philosophical or theological position with which he came into contact over the years, no matter how contradictory. To them all — classical theological liberalism, neo-orthodoxy, social gospel, existentialism, process thought, liberation theology — he responded with cunning simplicity and foresight, "I am *with* you always . . ."

the word "life" also reveals Bibfeldt's handiwork in this cleverly serious joke. Surely he is aware of our quandary over his continuing existence and is making a statement of this quixotic sort in partial reply.

The second pop hit to which we point is a part of the soundtrack from the surprise movie hit of the year, *Saturday Night Fever*. It is obvious — one need not even be an experienced practitioner of *Horsgeschichte* to see this right off — that Bibfeldt is making as clear a statement as possible of his continuing productive theological existence in the song "Stayin' Alive." The context of this song is crucial to understanding the present-day Bibfeldt. But we shall return to that later.

We can now take it as conclusive that Bibfeldt is alive and "with us," as the Scripture says. But what of his work in pastoral care? We have ample evidence of Bibfeldt's contributions in this field, and here, obviously, is the place to give this great man his due.

Again, you will recall that Bibfeldt was "for some time a parish pastor." But his first serious work in pastoral care theory is surely represented by his attempt to come to grips with the nondirective, client-centered therapy of Carl Rogers. Bibfeldt's adaptation of Rogers, spelled out in his famous book *I Hear What You're Saying, but I Just Don't Care*, has come to be known as Self-Centered Therapy, or as some hostile reviewers have scornfully described it, the "new narcissism." In this work Bibfeldt presents his discovery that the phrase "I hear what you're saying" has a peculiarly soporific quality to it. Thus he advocated incessant repetition of that phrase, by client and therapist in turn, until the point at which both fall into a sound, trance-like sleep.

Bibfeldt, of course, was firmly convinced of the therapeutic value of sleep in "helping one forget one's troubles"; he has set forth further research into the historical antecedents of this technique in an unpublished essay entitled "Rip Van Winkle as the Father of Modern Psychotherapy." Case studies of his use of the self-centered method in pastoral care and its relations to his theological stance are presented in his classic *Theology after Van Winkle*, now unfortunately out of print. Bibfeldt, however, was forced to abandon this self-centered model of pastoral care due to a practical difficulty: being a sound sleeper himself, he found that he often awoke only after his clients had, and therefore was never able to collect his fees.

During a brief stint of pure academia, Bibfeldt read Don Browning's book *The Moral Context of Pastoral Care* and flirted briefly with a James-styled pragmatic approach. He left us with but one judgment concerning this school of thought: "Pragmatism is all right, as long as it works."

The *M* source tells us that Bibfeldt visited Esalen, and we learn from the *L* source that he was also drawn to the "human potential" or "self-actualization" movement and that he began to practice transactional analysis. But the *L* source does not tell us how Bibfeldt was also excited by his discovery of the multiple uses of the phrase "I'm OK" and its various permutations — "I'm not OK, you're OK"; "I'm OK, you're not OK"; "I'm OK but you're not so hot," and so on. The flexibility of the phrase "I'm OK" thrilled Bibfeldt at first because he suspected that its various forms might produce sleep-inducing qualities that were similar, even perhaps superior, to the phrase "I hear what you're saying." Furthermore, the possibilities of the phrase's permutations fit well into the methodological stance of "Both/And," for example, "I'm not OK and that's OK," and so forth. However, Bibfeldt became disillusioned with the possibilities of this method of care when he found that repetition of this phrase had a definite grating and unsettling effect on client and therapist alike, especially when spoken in Bibfeldt's own native tongue. I here quote Bibfeldt:

> Imagine, if you can, the auditory effect of these phrases: "Ich bin OK; du bist OK; er, sie, es ist OK; Ich bin nicht OK." It was *not* OK!! After several attempts with this therapeutic technique, I learned always to hold my sessions in a basement room, as both client and therapist were often driven to attempt to throw themselves from the office window. Not quite the desired effect![3]

Needless to say, Bibfeldt abandoned this model as well in some desperation.

The late 1970s saw the reporting in *Time, Newsweek,* and even the *Chicago Sun-Times* of May 2, 1978, of a new form of Bibfeldtian psychotherapy known as "paradoxical therapy." This therapeutic model represents the next stage on life's way for the Bibfeldtian in search of his/her mentor's influences on present-day pastoral care. I quote here from the *Sun-Times:*

> The paradoxical technique is a reverse psychology of sorts. The therapist agrees with a person's assessment of himself, or of his situation. Instead of telling the person that his assessment is nonsense, which usually makes him more angry and frustrated because he believes no

---

3. Franz Bibfeldt, *Gunfight at the OK Corral: A Brief Study in Transactional Marketing* (Oklahoma City, OK: Okey-Dokey Press, 1972).

one understands him, the therapist agrees with the assessment. Then the person sees how silly he is.

Psychiatrist Allen Fay wrote on paradoxical therapy in his book *Making Things Better by Making Them Worse* in 1978. But it was Bibfeldt who had pioneered the approach three years earlier as an early attempt to inject his theological method of "Both/And" directly into pastoral care technique. Since Bibfeldt has had frequent difficulty finding a publisher for his ground-breaking work, however, he must often work through semi-respectable ghost writers. The public is thus forced to wait several years to find out what Bibfeldt is really thinking and then only receives it in watered-down form. For example, Bibfeldt's seminal study on sadomasochism, whips, chains, and bondage as a form of "primal scream" therapy was first released as the widely read title *The Agony and the Ecstasy*. So it was also with his work on paradoxical therapy, released only in another's writings.

Bibfeldt soon moved on to even greener pastures than those opened by his brilliant exposition of paradoxical therapy. We know that he had suffered an unfortunate and embarrassing injury as a young man while attempting to acquire a dueling scar. He did acquire the scar, but since he had jumped nervously at just the wrong moment, it was in a place he could never expose. His dueling scar first led Bibfeldt to suspect he had an affinity with the "punk rock" movement, which itself affirms such acts of minor self-mutilation. His reluctance to expose his scar, however, caused him difficulty in relating to the punk rockers. The one time that he did expose his scar, he tells us, "left him cold." He also had difficulties in assuming the punk rock look. As Bibfeldt tersely put it in his typical self-effacing humor, "I used to have a crew cut, but the crew bailed out."

You will remember the earlier mention of the song "Stayin' Alive" from the movie *Saturday Night Fever* as evidence of Bibfeldt's ongoing presence and influence. Let us expand on that now. In the mid-1970s, Bibfeldt found himself called to get back to his earliest beginnings in order to confront the problems of an adequate theory of pastoral care. His first move in this direction was to reinvestigate his family tree, a fairly common preoccupation. The Bibfeldt family crest and coat of arms offered him a delightful surprise: the motto thereon was "I dance to the tune that is played." Bibfeldt reflected that this represented a thrillingly serendipitous beginning, and he decided to hang onto this precept as a part of his forthcoming investigations.

He next attempted to recapture his theological roots. To this end he returned to a study of Søren Kierkegaard, from whom Bibfeldt had derived his theory of "Both/And," which was his response to Kierkegaard's own stance of "Either/Or." Bibfeldt finally understood Kierkegaard's thoughts on "infinite reflection" when he visited the house of mirrors at a traveling carnival, and he determined to retain this aspect of Kierkegaard's thought as well. Finally, Bibfeldt found himself intrigued once again with trinitarian doctrine. Here he felt truly at home. Both three-in-one and one-in-three.[4]

Bibfeldt then faced up to his task. The problem was this: how to relate and accommodate these three foundational precepts — trinity, "infinite reflection," and "dancing to the tune that is played"? How does one put these principles together in a way that allows everything to "come out right"? Bibfeldt was led to one inescapable conclusion: that any true Bibfeldtian pastoral care *could only be performed in discotheques.* Only there, in the discos, did *everyone* "dance to the tune that is played." Only there, amidst the flashing of the strobe lights, the hissing of the fake fog machine, and the incessant droning of the beat, could be found enough mirrors for an infinity of infinite reflections. And there he would find *singles* — a clear representation of the unitary pole of a trinity necessary for any trinitarian theorist. And where he found couples, he, Bibfeldt, would make them a threesome! Everyone would then be providing infinite reflections of both three-in-oneness and one-in-threeness, all the while dancing to the tune that was played.

Bibfeldt was inspired by these possibilities. But his work "in the trenches" has left him precious little time in which to publish his findings. What we have concerning this necessary and loving labor are only hints. We know from other sources that Bibfeldt had difficulty relating to his dancing clients the possibilities of eternal punishment, and thus he resorted to the medium of popular music once again, turning out the hit disco single "Disco Inferno." And we have had strong indications that Bibfeldt is attempting to develop specific styles and modes of interaction with his clients that are correlative and consistent with his "Both/And" theological stance. He has characterized this style as "In/Out Interaction," but recent scholarship has shown that he has not had much success in refining his techniques clinically. Apparently, his dancing style, like his dueling, left much to be desired.

4. You will recall from the *L* source Bibfeldt's own transactional analysis, "where it was discovered that his parent, adult, and child were indistinguishable from each other and, what is more, formed three 'selves' of a multiple personality, calling themselves Moe, Larry, and Curly." Clearly, this shows the psychological grounding of Bibfeldt's fascination with trinitarian thinking.

This brings us to the end of our search for evidence of Bibfeldt's involvement in pastoral theology today. How, in the end, do we characterize our odyssey? We are tempted to agree with the Grateful Dead in a line from their classic song "Truckin'": "What a long, strange trip it's been!" However, when it comes to the esteemed Franz Bibfeldt, we never seem to get enough. We feel inclined to agree with the attitude of the Sufi mystic and teacher Nasrudin, who, soon after moving to a new address, was approached by his mailcarrier. The postman called and said: "I hope that you are satisfied with the mail deliveries." "More than satisfied," said Nasrudin, "and, in fact, from tomorrow you may double my order." Let us hope that we might ask of Bibfeldt the same.

An Exegesis of Franz Bibfeldt's
The Food Context of Pastoral Care

L. DALE RICHESIN

Speaking of practical theology, what could be more practical than food? A year after Dreydoppel's contribution, Dale Richesin, now instructor in Old Testament at Chicago Baptist Institute, presented a menu of Bibfeldtian options in respect to things gustatory. — ED.

The past year has been a busy one for Bibfeldt scholars. Scholars of this generation, the postmodern Bibfeldtian age, have not been content to explore just the important issues of the past: the existential problem of the year zero,[1] the interpretative dynamics of the "Both/And" theory, as well as the very important innovation in the hermeneutics of *Horsgeschichte*. These issues have certainly laid the basis for Bibfeldt research in the past. In this year we have seen many new advances in these areas, as well as the emergence of Bibfeldtian scholarship in new and challenging directions beyond those originally set down by the great founder of our movement.

Franz Bibfeldt has now broadened his theology into many new areas. His basic appeal at present is to a more secular audience. On the heels of Langdon Gilkey's latest work, *Reaping the Whirlwind*, we were

---

1. In researching the chronology of time, Bibfeldt discovered that ancient calendars skipped the year zero. In other words, 1 B.C. was immediately followed by 1 A.D. Bibfeldt waged a vigorous campaign to restore the year zero and to re-date all of Western history since the year zero accordingly. As a result, all scholarship related to Bibfeldt, particularly the publication dates of his works, have two dates noted.

quite pleased to see the epic film produced by Franz Bibfeldt and Associates, "Gone With The Whirlwind," which will be released this August. The hit musical single from that movie, "Blowing In The Whirlwind," is already receiving some airplay. The disco version, "Stayin' Alive In The Whirlwind," has garnered much acclaim as well.

But by far the most important development of the past year among the postmodern Bibfeldtians is the Bibfeldtian concept of pastoral care. Bibfeldt's writings on this subject have just recently been catalogued, although, regrettably, all are now out of print. As a dedicated scholar,[2] I searched the university research libraries only to find that all the volumes of this valuable collection had been checked out. Undaunted, I went to a nearby seminary, only to discover the same thing at their library. At this point I made a copy of the Bibfeldt bibliography on pastoral care and set about to apply the Bibfeldtian hermeneutic *(Horsgeschichte)* to a study of the titles of this newly discovered but as yet unread collection.

The first item in this bibliography that caught my eye was an article published in *The Rhinelander Quarterly* (April 1961/62), "Pastoral Care and the Problem Drinker." The article was two and two-thirds pages long and began on page 26. Since this was all the information I could gather from the bibliography, I began to work back from the title, as it were, to discover the article behind the title. I checked the index to that particular issue of *The Rhinelander Quarterly* and discovered that the article "behind the title" was an article published by a certain B. Brown entitled "Pastoral Care and the Problem Pizza." I was able to find a copy of this article about a week ago crumpled under my seat at a local restaurant. Fascinated by this find, I began to read it with anticipation. The article was essentially a condensed version of a longer paper entitled "The Problem Pizza and the High Church."[3]

This article contained little that was useful in the area of pastoral care, except for a footnote of another title that was in the Bibfeldt bibliography on pastoral care! This item was a book entitled *The Food*

2. In his epic work, *Definitions of Hermeneutics,* (New York: John Anduri Press, 1934/35), Bibfeldt defines scholarship as "anything that a scholar can do and get away with . . . providing that your research grant does not expressly forbid it" (p. 319). In a private conversation, Bibfeldt related to one of his scholars that his own method of scholarship was "to make up any quote or statistic that he couldn't locate, as long as it generally sounded true and didn't contradict the main thesis."

3. This is an ecclesiological study that partially meets the requirements for the D.Min. degree. This is not to be confused with the Catholic Study Report entitled "The Problem Pizza and the High Church in Human Sexuality," Vatican II, *venatae sensorium pizzarium,* 28 October 1965/66.

Context of Pastoral Care, a fragment of which follows. After glancing over the rest of the items in the Bibfeldt bibliography on pastoral care, I quickly realized that this book was central to the bibliography. Having discovered the actual existence of this valuable text, although not having yet read it, I set about to understand it through the Bibfeldtian hermeneutic of *Horsgeschichte.* According to this hermeneutic, Bibfeldt goes back to Scripture for an understanding of the true nature of the pastoral care of Jesus.

The Food Context of Pastoral Care [a fragment] by Franz Bibfeldt, edited by B. Mahan (Bangkok: Browning and Brown Publishing House, 1976/77).

The increasing doubt that the modern age has placed on the miracles of Jesus has demanded a new understanding of his true pastoral abilities. Modern medicine has cast questionable glances at the ethics of the healings of Jesus. So if you take away the validity of the healing miracles, what is left? A few clichés, which were the bulk of his teachings, and his food miracles! If one looks closely at the accounts of Jesus in relation to food, an understanding of the true nature of his pastoral activities becomes apparent. The first miracle occurs at the wedding feast at Cana.[4] Anyone who has run low on wine during a party or a sherry hour knows the danger of unsatisfied guests. Jesus' miracle at this point was a sincere act of pastoral care to the host of the feast.

Although most people cast serious doubt on the validity of the miracles of the feeding of the 4,000[5] and the feeding of the 5,000,[6] anyone who has cooked for more than five people (say a luncheon of some sort) knows what a miracle it is when everyone is finally fed, and how easy it is to have many baskets of food left over. Not only is food seen as important to the pastoral care context of the ministry of Jesus, but it reflects upon his personal life as well. When told of the illness of Lazarus[7] and the illness of the

---

4. Franz Bibfeldt used the little-known biblical manuscript, *Canon Bibfeldt, 346/7.* In this work, which was written in the Ethiopian dialect of Amharic, Bibfeldt abandons Jerome's chapter and verse numbering system for his own. The miracle at the wedding in Cana is found in the Gospel of Mary and Mary, chapter 3, verses 15-25.

5. Gospel of Mary and Mary 15:45-56.
6. Gospel of Mary and Mary 45:15-105.
7. Gospel of Lazarus 110:45-78.

magistrate's daughter[8], did he rush immediately to their side to heal them? No, he waited around to collect a few meals that people owed him. An early drawing[9] of Jesus that was recently unearthed in Samaria, which dates back to the first century, indicates that it was most probable that Jesus weighed from 180 to 240 pounds, was about 5'6", and contrary to tradition, did not sport a beard, but was clean shaven and slightly balding. Food was obviously very important to the ministry of Jesus.

In Jesus' command to his disciples concerning their mission activity, he instructed them "to stay at one house before you leave a village."[10] His reference, of course, was to the importance of adapting to the cuisine of a particular location rather than changing quickly from one type of food to another. If received poorly in any village, in other words, if the food was not adequate or the wine was bitter, "one should shake off the crumbs of that village."[11]

The food context of the pastoral care of Jesus draws upon a similar emphasis in Jewish tradition. The strict dietary laws of the Jewish people indicate the importance of this aspect of life. The ancient Semitic root for the word *rabbi* comes from the Amharic word *rabbitar*, which means great eater. The rabbinic school arose not, as usually understood, as a school of scholars and teachers of the old tradition, but as great hosts of the banquet. Their knowledge of all the particular details of the dietary laws gave them considerable authority in the Jewish community. Their stature in the community was later broadened to include more general authority over morality, history, and heritage. In the Jewish tradition, a great emphasis is placed on the feasts and banquets that mark various religious holidays. This is only natural since the authorities who preserved these traditions, the great eaters, placed much emphasis on the pastoral care aspect of food in the community.

At the time of Jesus, the Jewish rabbinic tradition had lost its *rabbitaric* emphasis. His general ministry was an attempt to recover this tradition of the *rabbitars*, the great eaters. His fame as a *rabbitar* was widespread. While dining with a famous publican,

8. Gospel of the Unknown Daughter 3:15-15z.
9. Published in *Playboy*, November, 1963.
10. Gospel of Missionaries 15:25-151.
11. Gospel of Missionaries 48:15.

he was anointed with oil and his feet were washed in ointment as a sign of his authority over the banquet. When he was not received with such acclaim, he rebuked his host for failing to acknowledge him as a great eater.[12]

The most original teachings of Jesus were those that reflected food imagery: the parable of the mustard seed, the leavened bread, the sower, the master of the vineyard, the great catch of fish, the fig tree, etc.[13]

Even metaphorically, images of food are common. Jesus speaks of himself as "opening my mouth in parables,"[14] indicating the relation of food to wisdom. He also speaks of himself as food: "I am the bread of life; he who comes to me shall not hunger, and he who believes in me shall never thirst."[15] This passage foreshadows the eucharist injunction to "eat of the flesh and drink of the blood of Christ."[16] The imagery of the church he also casts in terms of food: "I am the true vine, and my Father is the vinedresser. Every branch of mine that bears no fruit he takes away, and every branch that does bear fruit he prunes, that it may bear more fruit."[17] Even Christian believers are referred to as "salt of the earth and light of the world."[18]

The feast of the Last Supper has always been regarded as a central and important point in the Christian tradition. The service of the Last Supper is one of the few elements of worship that is incorporated in almost all churches of the Christian tradition. The love feasts of the first century show how important the early church regarded the celebration of this feast. Jesus' command to "eat of my body and drink of my blood"[19] was taken very seriously.

We have seen how important food was to the whole ministry of Jesus. In the post-resurrection appearances, food took on a critical role. It became a paradigmatic motif of grace. In the Luke account[20] Jesus appears to the disciples outside of the town of

12. Gospel of Mary Magdalene 15:15-25.
13. Gospel of Food, Parables, and Great Sayings 15:32f.
14. Gospel of Matthew 333:30-43.
15. Gospel of John 4:488-491.
16. Gospel of John 36:62.
17. Gospel of Mary and Mary 1:1-5.
18. Salty Parables 33:1.
19. Gospel of Mary and Mary 3:15f.
20. See also Gospel of Mary and Mary 45:15-40.

Emmaus. He walks with them into town, but they do not recognize him. He finally reveals himself to them and they touch his wounds, but they still do not believe. In desperation, he asks them for a piece of broiled fish and begins to eat with them. They finally recognize him as their Lord, and bow down to praise him.

In the Gospel of John[21] Jesus appears on the shore while the disciples are fishing in a boat on the lake. He tells them where to cast their nets and they haul in a great catch. As they come to shore, Jesus is cooking breakfast for them, and their eyes are opened and they recognize him. He gives them the missionary charge to go into the world with the simple phrase, "feed my sheep."[22] [fragment ends]

We see, according to Bibfeldt, the importance of food in the pastoral care context of the ministry of Jesus, theologically, a discovery of profound importance. The food context of Jesus' ministry reflects both a scriptural and a common human experience basis for faith. Separated for centuries, these two sides of the Christian tradition have finally been brought together in the thought of Franz Bibfeldt. For Bibfeldt, this *rabbitaric* tradition has been preserved in the modern church through a matriarchal tradition of church suppers, picnics, food baskets to the needy, and bake sales. The patriarchal structure of the church has preferred to think of the message of reconciliation and grace in broad, symbolic terms. The matriarchal tradition of the church, however, has preserved the true *rabbitaric* teachings of Jesus.

The implications of this important fragment from the Bibfeldtian bibliography on pastoral care are quite significant. Pastoral counseling and pastoral psychotherapy can receive important new directions from this study. The implications for theology are also quite exciting. The conclusions that Bibfeldt draws which relate to the matriarchal tradition in preserving the *rabbitaric* emphasis are of key importance to modern feminist theology. The implications that can be drawn from this fragment are really quite staggering and offer much food for thought.

21. See also Gospel of Thomas 4:45-54.
22. Gospel of Missionaries 25:25-125.

The Protoecological Theology
of Franz Bibfeldt
and/or
The Massive Derailment
of Twentieth-Century Thought

ROBIN PETERSON AND
STEVEN BOUMA-PREDIGER

While readers have learned with what degree of seriousness to take all the authentic essays on Bibfeldt contributions, there should be room for one exception. Steven Bouma-Prediger, who teaches at Hope College, and Robin Peterson, whose career will take him back to South Africa, depart from the authentic lore and, if we read them right, make up something. They engage in an experiment in wordplay that involves the mix between "beans" and "beings." Those who like puns will appreciate their achievement. Those who do not are advised to move on quickly to the essays that depend not on wordplay but on simple, unadorned, unaffected, bedrock prose about truth. — ED.

In the course of our independent research — Mr. Peterson's on the early life of Paul Tillich and Mr. Bouma-Prediger's on the roots of ecological theology — we have unearthed astonishing historical and theological evidence that compels us to conclude that in the early writings of Franz Bibfeldt are to be found not only the groundings of a revolutionary, provocative, and comprehensive eco-theology, but, perhaps more significantly, evidence of the systematic derailment and distortion of twentieth-century thought as a result of the misapprehension and even loss of the early Bibfeldt *oeuvre*. We wish to correct this travesty of scholarly justice and hail Franz Bibfeldt as the rightful progenitor of eco-theology and the real father of twentieth-century thought.

This is indeed a bold, not to say reckless, assertion. How, one may legitimately ask, do we venture to make it? The first answer lies in the discovery of a musty notebook of theological musings secreted behind the radiator in Professor Paul Tillich's old office. The notebook has "Theologische Jottings" scrawled on the cover, and it carries the bold if somewhat illegible signature of none other than Franz Bibfeldt! The journal entries begin in January 1917 and are further identified with the line "Die Westliche Front." A closer study of the journal reveals, even more significantly, that marginal glosses throughout the notebook are quite clearly in the hand of Tillich himself. It is apparent from the age of the ink of these glosses, and from their actual content, that this historic document of the early Bibfeldt had been in Tillich's possession since about 1918. Why then, one might ask — as indeed we did — had Tillich not revealed its existence, and why had he hidden it behind the radiator in his office? These were questions that impelled us to embark on a quest both historical and theological.

First of all, we must point out that Bibfeldt's influence on contemporary eco-theology, even given the painstaking and creative work done on his theological influence in these pages and elsewhere, has heretofore gone unacknowledged and unappreciated. Our historical exposition and diachronic elucidation of the roots of Bibfeldt's system — this finely wrought and expertly executed explication of how he, like all seminal thinkers, simultaneously stands firmly within his tradition and yet innovates and changes that tradition — is merely a prolegomenon to any future systematic theology, which will come forth, like a tulip in the spring, as both intellectually rigorous and popularly relevant *Wissenschaft*. In his protoecological theology, as always, Bibfeldt seeks to be — not to put too fine a point on it — trendy. His basic *leitmotif* of "Both/And," best captured in the Bibfeldt family coat of arms ("I dance to the tune that is played"), of course, admits of nothing less.

Thus it remains for us to explore the synchronic side of Bibfeldt's protoecological theology. We must, in short, survey the fundamental elements, the various theological loci, of Bibfeldt's radical and long-hidden yet profoundly influential perspective. In the brief space allotted us, alas, we will, like the farmer on a rainy day, be able to cover precious little ground and thus be able to survey only a few Bibfeldtian *topoi*.

Now, as all Bibfeldt scholars remember, the quest for the historical Bibfeldt has been somewhat derailed ever since the speculative and highly controversial 1976 lecture by David Ousley, "The Quest for the Historical Bibfeldt," relegated it to the realm of myth. Like many other scholars, we have always been uneasy with this mythological turn. The discovery of Bibfeldt's "Westliche Front" journal in the possession of Paul Tillich, therefore, has compelled us to initiate a new quest for the historical Bibfeldt. But more significantly from a theological perspective, the journal makes clear that, beginning with Tillich, the whole course of twentieth-century thought has been seriously and systematically derailed, and that the revolutionary and highly provocative insights of a great thinker have not only been systematically plagiarized but also fundamentally distorted and universally unacknowledged.

What, then, does this remarkable journal contain that emboldens us to hail Franz Bibfeldt as the father of twentieth-century theology, the first to lay the groundwork for what has become an enormously popular eco-theology? Two interlocking and overlapping trajectories need to be pursued: the historical and the theological.

First, the historical. The venue of the "Westliche Front" journal's composition gives us our first substantial historical clue. It shows with certainty that the young Bibfeldt was conscripted into the Kaiser's army at the age of eighteen, and that he found himself far away on the western front during the last two years of the Great War, subject to enemy fire, disease, and innumerable meals of beans. This is significant in itself, but the contents of the journal provide us with even greater insights. In it Bibfeldt reflects at great length on what he calls "my moment of revelation":

> [It was] the moment at which it seemed that the whole cosmos hung together: suspended in time, opened to eternity, punctuated by infinity, traversed by chronology. [It was] the moment when the true nature of the divine became transparent, when the meaning and purpose and goal of existence was stripped of its clothing like a willing prostitute and stood naked before me.

This momentous revelation, Bibfeldt explains, came to him on All Saints' Day, 1917, his twentieth birthday, while he was eating his five-hundredth or so bowl of black beans in the trenches. The mysterious and elusive insight that he had been wrestling with since 1913 suddenly became crystal clear: "God is the ground of all beans."

"Suddenly," he writes, "it all made sense. God is to be found in, with, and under all beans."

This remarkable insight had its origins in 1913, when Franz's father, Friedrich, a semi-distinguished Lutheran pastor, was sent by his bishop to serve the London congregation of the Evangelical Lutheran Church. Before accepting the appointment, the elder Bibfeldt went to London on a three-week trial basis, accompanied by his precocious teenage son Franz. Franz recalls in the journal wandering through the streets of London, absorbed by the sights and sounds of that strange place, feeling, as he put it so poignantly, "like a German in London," and chancing upon an old secondhand bookstore in Charing Cross Lane. As he browsed amongst the shelves, a thin, earth-brown manuscript caught his eye. At that very moment he heard the voice of a child playing outside: "Tolle Lege! Tolle Lege!" (Take it and read!) He writes:

> In that moment the gracious Redeemer planted the seed that was to establish deep roots in the soil so carefully prepared, which in the fullness of time was to break the hard crust of the earth, first as a shoot, then as a stem, then as a leaf, then as stamen, then . . . [he carries on in this vein for some time] until it finally was to bear a rich crop of the ineffable mystery of Bean.

As the testimony of many scholars has made clear, Bibfeldt's methodological acumen and sophistication are legendary, beginning with his doctoral dissertation, "The Problem of the Year Zero." His now famous dictum, "Once method is determined, all else is mere plumbing," has become a cornerstone of the contemporary theological enterprise. Thus it is not surprising that in this most recently discovered installment of his eco-theology, the "Westliche Front" journal, Bibfeldt does not disappoint us: he begins with reflections on method.

Bibfeldt opens his inquiry in the journal with an extended meditation on beans. Beans, he writes, are the ground, the root, the foundation, the linchpin, the acme, the alpha and omega of all method. Taking his cue from an obscure variant reading of Acts 17:28, "In God we live and move and have our beans,"[1] he deduces that there can be no critical

---

1. Bibfeldt explicated this later in his seminal five-volume commentary on the epistle to Philemon, *Der Philemerbrief: Übersetzt und Eklärt: Ein Kritische-Exegetische-Theologische Kommentar.*

correlation of the Christian tradition and common human experience — no correlation of an historical and hermeneutical investigation of classic Christian texts with a transcendental phenomenology of the religious dimension of everyday human existence — without an initial inquiry into the very conditions for the possibility of any method whatsoever. In short, there must be a ground-clearing of sorts, or perhaps "spring cleaning" would be the more apropos metaphor. Bibfeldt later worked out the centrality of beans to methodology in his long-ignored educational manifesto *Long Discourse on the Study of Theology, Philosophy of Religion, Scripture, Church History, Liturgy, Hymnody, Folk Music, Interpretive Dance, Pastoral Care, Parish Administration, Haberdashery, and Etiquette.*[2]

With his methodological moorings securely in place, Bibfeldt, following his Lutheran antecedents, moves on in the journal to theology proper, or the doctrine of God. In Bibfeldt's quadrilateral mind[3] — and in language that Tillich clearly "borrowed" — God is not *a* bean, but Bean-itself. Bibfeldt confidently asserts that God, as the ground of all beans, exists in, with, and under beans of every size, shape, and color.

The loss of Bibfeldt's journal for over seventy years, as well as Tillich's misappropriation of his eco-theology, and the derailment of twentieth-century theology that resulted, can only be a source of *Sehnsucht* for today's theologians, producing only a sense of disappointment and yearning for what might have been. One example with regard to the doctrine of God must suffice: we now have conclusive speculation that Dietrich Bonhoeffer's 1929 *Habilitation* thesis, *Act and Being,* would have been entitled *Acts of Beans* had Bonhoeffer had access to the *ipsissima verba* of Bibfeldt. So great is the loss to modern theology.

With his doctrine of God firmly rooted in fertile soil, Bibfeldt proceeds in the journal to protology, or the doctrine of first things, or, more commonly, the doctrine of creation. His major contribution in this area has been superbly summarized in a little-noticed recent work by Bibfeldt scholar P. T. L. von Keester, *How Many Pinheads Can Dance on*

---

2. Or simply *Long Discourse,* for short.
3. See Robin Lovin's insightful and incisive 1980 essay "Franz Bibfeldt: The Breakdown of Consciousness and the Origins of the Quadrilateral Mind" (originally published in *Jahrbuch für Analyse und Motorcycle Maintenance,* 1979; English trans., *Criterion,* 1980).
4. Disputatio Press, 1990. The *post* in the title, needless to say, does not refer to any recent movement beyond Bibfeldt, since such a move would be logically impossible in the case of so creative and ever-relevant a thinker. The *post,* rather, is a combination of *pro* and *histemi,* and thus means "standing before or preeminent."

An Angel: Scholastic Metaphysics in a Post-Bibfeldtian Theology.[4] We should also mention in this context that Bibfeldt's putative criticism of Karl Barth (that he was a "has been") — which prompted an uncharacteristically miffed Barth to call Bibfeldt "the chameleon of all theologians," akin to Woody Allen's Zelig — must be radically reinterpreted in the light of our new research. Given what we now know, it is much more likely that Bibfeldt actually said, "Barth has beans," a remark showing his utmost approbation of Barth's theological project. In Bibfeldt's considered opinion, we must conclude, Barth's fertile mind contained the seeds of a fully developed eco-theology.

The rudiments of Bibfeldt's anthropology, set forth in the early notebooks, are splendidly outlined in Robin Lovin's aforementioned essay on the breakdown of consciousness and the origins of the quadrilateral mind. And Bibfeldt's hamartiology, or doctrine of sin, is comprehensively summarized in von Keester's recent monograph *Semper-lapsarianismus: Die Sünderlehre in der Theologie Franz Bibfeldts.*[5] Bibfeldt's later reflections on human sin and estrangement are to be found in the renowned volume he co-authored with Robin Leach, *Luther on Vacation: From Worms to Cancun: Travel Motifs in Later Lutheran Theology.*[6] The obvious theme in this work is the human as *viator* — pilgrim and traveler — both finite and fallen, and yet also free and fun-loving. The probable connections between Bibfeldt's research in Cancun and his view of God's "preferential option for the rich," so fetchingly set forth in yet another Lovin contribution,[7] is a theme that cries out for serious exploration in a scholarly monograph — or at least a doctoral dissertation.

Due to limited space, we must omit Bibfeldt's Christology and ecclesiology. But we need to address his eschatology, which is yet another remarkable example of theological creativity, fecundity, and comprehensiveness — and a lasting monument to Bibfeldt's unique ability to embrace all sides of an issue. Consistent with his overarching theme in the "Westliche Front" journal, Bibfeldt authoritatively affirms that conceiving of God as the ground of all beans alleviates virtually every single intractable theological paradox known to humankind. His insights into eschatological problems and their solutions have already borne considerable fruit in his innovative work known as the "pastoral

5. Peccavi Publishing, 1991.
6. Agnes and Gloria Day House, 1975.
7. Robin Lovin, "Franz Bibfeldt and the Future of Political Theology," American Academy of Religion lecture for 1988; see pp. 89-94 of this volume.
8. Cover story of *Newsweek*, 1 May 1978.

theology for the dead,"[8] where his systematic empirical studies show that pastoral care for the dead is significantly enhanced statistically if and only if God is reconceived as *in, with,* and (especially) *under* all beans.

It will not escape the notice of informed and attentive readers that, once again, twentieth-century Western thought suffered a colossal derailment when Bibfeldt's eschatological theology was misused and/or forgotten. To take just one example, Martin Heidegger's magnum opus *Being and Time* should more accurately and eschatologically be rendered — giving credit where it is due, i.e., to Bibfeldt — *Beans on Time,* thereby illustrating the thoroughly ecological motif that in fact runs throughout this esteemed, ponderous, and enigmatic work.[9]

But we must return to the history of Bibfeldt's protoecological theological journal and the Paul Tillich connection. The reader will recall how Bibfeldt's "moment of revelation . . . , when the meaning and purpose and goal of existence was stripped of its clothing like a willing prostitute and stood naked before me," became the verdant ground of his fructive thought. His journal is further laden with delicious and edifying reflections on the structure of beans as explosively revelatory of God. But these leguminous entries end suddenly, two days before the end of the war. At that point in the journal appears a lengthy note written in another hand, that of Paul Tillich:

> This sacramental document was given to me in sacred trust by a young soldier on a night when the foundations of our world were shaken by intensive Allied shelling. He was suffering from severe shell shock, but, recognizing my chaplain's insignia, gave it to me with the almost inaudible words, "Tolle lege! Tolle lege!"
>
> I took it from him just as he was borne away on a stretcher and spent the rest of that night reading its troubling yet ground-breaking revelations, for that is what they truly were. It was as if the wind of the Spirit had broken and flattened me in its draught. "Beans," I gasped, "Ja, beans." I determined to ensure that these insights would

---

9. We would be remiss if we did not take note of a few more subtle indications of Bibfeldt's eco-theological influence on contemporary theologians. In *Blessed Rage for Order* (p. 98), David Tracy refers to the "intelligible ground" and "the final grounding horizon" of all human language and experience; what else can we conclude but that Bibfeldt's eco-theology has, like an overflowing muddy stream, seeped into Tracy's theology? Or when Langdon Gilkey, in his *Maker of Heaven and Earth* (p. 77), with an obvious debt to Tillich/Bibfeldt, refers to God as "underneath everything," what conclusion can we draw but that Gilkey is a crypto-Bibfeldtian?

be preserved and proclaimed, and that the world would hear that God is the ground of all beans.

But the final page of the journal offers an even more telling insight into the mysterious Bibfeldt-Tillich relationship. "Confessions of a bean to Bean-itself" is written in English, and in ink much fresher than that of the rest of the manuscript. It is dated 1965 and signed by Paul Tillich:

> Before my dust returns to dust and my bean is united with all beans, I must confess to a heinous historical injustice. I did try to fulfill my sacred trust to Franz. In the original edition of my first work, *Kairos und Beans*,[10] I remained true to my source and his piercing discernment. I too wrote of "Gott, grund von aller 'beans,'" preserving that wonderful, untranslatable English word. However, my German editor refused to publish a work with so pivotal a concept rendered in English, so he changed it to German and thus mistranslated it into the much weaker *Sein*. I was not able to locate Franz after the war, and presuming he was dead, I decided to leave the matter as it was — a decision I now deeply regret. I hope you will not judge me too harshly.[11]

---

10. A work, unfortunately, never translated and little known outside the inner circle of Tillich devotees.

11. This paragraph concludes Franz Bibfeldt's war journal, "Theologische Jottings: From the Westliche Front," annotated by Paul Tillich (n.d., unpublished).

IV. Culture and Art in Bibfeldt

By the grace of God, the Church moves forward even while constantly side-stepping.

FRANZ BIBFELDT,
Life and Letters

Portrait of Franz Bibfeldt by Siegfried Reinhardt

There's No Business: Franz Bibfeldt and the Place of Religion in Show Business

GLENN HOLLAND

One would hardly expect the run-of-the-mill theologian to have an influence in and on show business, but Bibfeldt is anything but run-of-the-mill. Glenn Holland, who now teaches at Allegheny College, Meadville, Pennsylvania, presented a paper on the subject, which remains as relevant as anything and everything else in the Bibfeldt canon. — ED.

When we seek the place of religion in the wider world beyond the cloisters and candles, the baptisteries and bingo of the Church, to what greater authority can we turn than Franz Bibfeldt? Theologian, scholar, pastor, social critic, biblical exegete, orthopedic shoe salesman — Franz Bibfeldt has been all these and more. If we wish to understand the religious need and the *Angst* of modern women and men in a dreary workaday world, what better helper may we find than the man who hailed the theology of Kierkegaard as "nothing that a month in Acapulco wouldn't cure"?[1] Bibfeldt has long maintained that "the innate spirituality of the human race permeates and illuminates all its activities with a transcendent light that shines from the very center of Being, just as the rising sun shines through my morning Zwieback when I would much rather be having an egg and bacon, but the doctor told

---

1. *Both/And*, trans. H. Mirkin (Chicago: University of Chicago Press, 1951), p. xxi.

me a man my age has to watch his fat intake."[2] Surely then, if anyone can, Franz Bibfeldt can help us find the proper place of religion in show business. As Professor Bibfeldt himself has so often told his students, "All right, all right, come in if you must, but shut the door behind you!"[3]

Franz Bibfeldt has always shown an interest in show business and throughout his career has been keenly aware of the close association between religion and the entertainment industry. As he wrote in "Comforting Thoughts for Those Awaiting Tenure," "Every pastor who preaches has something of the actor in him, every liturgical scholar has something of the stagehand in him, every professor who supervises a Ph.D. dissertation has something of the dog trainer in him."[4]

The sources for Bibfeldt's *dicta* on the study of religion and show business are many. He has written a series of articles on the subject for the *Cambridge Journal of Philosophy in Media*, the *Revue des Maladroites Études Bibliques*, the *Zeitschrift für Verblondjet Theologie*, and *TV Guide*. To those who are concerned about the methodology we shall follow in examining Bibfeldt's work on this subject, they may rest assured that we will steer a middle course. We will neither seek to go "behind the text" nor remain "before the text," but will rather stand "beside the text," treating it as a friend and equal whose opinion we may or may not seek. This is of course Bibfeldt's own approach. One might cite his remark to Jacques Derrida at the Very Important Philosophical Thinkers' Smoker in Paris in 1990: "Text, shmext! Doesn't anyone read books anymore?"[5]

Franz Bibfeldt was drawn early to show business in the form of the theater, when his father took him to a production of Oscar Wilde's *Salome* when he was fourteen. He recorded his youthful enthusiasm in his diary: "The anguish of knowing that the life of John the Baptist hung in the balance was second only to the thrill of seeing Salome's

2. *God: Getting to Know the Creator* (Des Moines: Vanity Press, 1978), p. 17.

3. Author's notes, May 16, 1982.

4. "Comforting Thoughts for Those Awaiting Tenure," in *Publish and Perish: Advice for the College Professor from the Tibetan Book of the Dead*, ed. M. Changara (St. Louis: Religious Academic Press, 1966), p. 165.

5. Bibfeldt quotation taken from Jacques Derrida, "Bibfeldt: Les présuppositions theologiques toutes bouleversées par un critique fou," *Spasmodique* 7, no. 2 (October 1991), copyright 1991 by Jacques Derrida; used by permission. All rights reserved. No part of this quotation may be reprinted or reproduced or utilized in any form or by any electronic, mechanical or other means, now known or hereafter invented, including photocopying and recording or in any information storage or retrieval system, without permission in writing from Traces of Derrida Ltd.

'Dance of the Seven Veils.' Fräulein Schmidt, who played Salome, is a fine big girl and an excellent dancer. You'd never know from listening to Pastor Vogel's sermons that religion could be so exciting."[6] From this experience were born two of young Franz's keenest interests, and religion was soon to become a third.

At university, Franz took an active part in student theatrics, topping his undergraduate career with the lead role in *Charley's Aunt*. This part won him the first of many academic awards: his fellow students elected him Queen of the May. The young Franz first began to see parallels between theater and the realm of religious experience and expression during this same period. An excerpt from a journal recently unearthed from his college sock drawer muses: "Historians of religion tell us that all drama arose from the narration of tribal myths around the communal campfire. The psalms seem to reflect a drama of conflict between the God Jahweh and the chaos monster, resulting in Jahweh's enthronement as King of Creation. European theater began in miracle plays performed on the public green outside the greatest cathedrals in Europe. So why won't Momma let me go to the burlesque in Königfriedrichstrasse?"[7]

Young Franz became interested in the cinema as a graduate student. After seeing D. W. Griffith's great silent masterpiece *Intolerance*, Bibfeldt wrote: "The flickering light playing across the great screen cast moving shadows upon the faces of its enraptured audience, who stared at its larger-than-life images even as the unfortunate Actaeon must have stared at the naked Artemis, with a combination of religious awe and lust. I took the opportunity to eat all the popcorn of the fellow sitting next to me."[8] Bibfeldt had come to understand that mass entertainment is *inherently* religious, both fulfilling the human need for the mythic and satisfying the desire to worship the Transcendent that remains somehow eerily familiar, expressed in the dramatized actions of actor, dancer, or baggy-pants comic.[9]

While on the faculty of Union Theological Seminary, Bibfeldt was inspired by the many overtly religious plays presented on the New York stage, including the original productions of *Green Pastures*, Eliot's *Murder in the Cathedral*, and *Abie's Irish Rose*. It was always Bibfeldt's

6. *Journal*, I:318.
7. *Journal*, VIII (appendix): 417.
8. *Journal*, III:27.
9. See his remarks in "Der Erzbischof und das Fräulein unartig: Die Historien Ungezogen," *Der theologische Witz*, ed. H. A. Schwinesaft (Tübingen: Eine Kleine Nachtpresse, 1963) pp. 27-49.

opinion, however, that all theater would benefit from the inclusion of religious themes and concerns, and that it is the responsibility of the student of religion to assist the playwright when necessary with emendations to the text, whether invited to do so or not. He put his theory into practice while serving as faculty advisor to the two student theatrical groups at Union, the Protestant Players and the Theatre Guild of St. Jude the Obscure. He was always careful, however, to ensure that his "religious" additions were in keeping with the setting and spirit of the original play. Thus, in his production of Shakespeare's *Henry V,* the two soldiers John Bates and Michael Williams spend the night before the Battle of Agincourt comforting themselves with the mystical insights of Meister Eckhart. Bibfeldt even induced Paul Tillich himself to appear as a walk-on character in Bibfeldt's version of *A Streetcar Named Desire* to explain Stanley Kowalski's existential alienation from God to a skeptical Blanche DuBois. Tillich did it as a personal favor to Bibfeldt, whom he always affectionately referred to as "that noodlehead."[10] Tillich later admitted that appearing on stage had not only tested the dynamics of his faith, but had shaken his foundations a bit as well.

Unfortunately, Bibfeldt's flirtation with adding spiritual dimensions to popular drama was curtailed by the short-sightedness of certain playwrights and archaic copyright laws, so he was forced to pursue new interests. He soon investigated the part religion had to play in other sorts of entertainment, but his first love has remained the theater. He recently published an article finding echoes of fertility rites and virgin sacrifice in the Rockettes and other theatrical displays of female pulchritude. His remark that "the world-famous kick-line is just another manifestation of sacred prostitution" earned him the admiration of fellow scholars and a stiff letter from the attorneys of Radio City Music Hall.[11]

Clearly, then, we may see from Franz Bibfeldt's own example that the scholar in religion has much to offer the theater, and indeed all aspects of show business. Bibfeldt's conviction that this is so is a result of the deep influence of Marxism on his thought. Although originally hostile to Marxism in the early thirties, by 1935 Bibfeldt saw this radical philosophy as the only way out of the crisis that was to become the Second World War. Many feel that to associate a scholar of Professor

10. See Paul Tillich, "Der Nudelkopf," *Yale Review of Theology* 9 (June 1960): 3-7, as well as Bibfeldt's reply, *Schlemiel und Schlemazel: K. Barth gegenüber P. Tillich* (Berlin: Gesundheit & Danke, 1961), p. 189.

11. Franz Bibfeldt, "The Rockettes as *Urgeist* and *Urbild,*" *Random Thoughts* 3 (September 1982): 13-29.

Bibfeldt's stature with Marxism is to degrade him, but Bibfeldt defended his views with his typical integrity. He recalled in an interview in 1987, "I was called before the faculty senate and interrogated in detail about my support for Marx. I was frightened, but found the right words coming to me out of the blue. 'My conscience is captive to the Word of God,' I improvised. 'Thus I cannot and will not recant, for going against my conscience is neither safe nor salutary. God help me, I can do no other; here I stand and say: Groucho Marx is the only hope for the future of comedy, although Chico and Harpo are pretty good too. Zeppo? Phooey. Can't even sing.' "[12]

This remark underscores the importance that Bibfeldt attributes to comedy, and anyone who has read much of his work will agree that there is a fine line between the study of religion and comedy. As he said in a career seminar in Berkeley in 1973, "You show me someone who wants to spend a lifetime studying the works of Nikolaus von Amsdorf and I'll show you a clown."[13] All of us who study religion are aware that our field includes elements of the ridiculous as well as the sublime, especially if we have to learn Akkadian or read Schopenhauer.[14] However, Bibfeldt has also pointed out that comedy is a way of "sugar-coating" serious social criticism, as we may see by the examples of Lenny Bruce, Richard Pryor, and Roseanne Arnold, whose comedy has earned more serious social criticism than any other. Comedy may thus provide a vehicle for serious religious discussion as well. Bibfeldt has shown that even the greatest religious teachers used this technique, as we may learn from his articles, including "The Lord of Laughter: Christ as Comedian," "The Power of the Boffo One-Liner in the Thought of Confucius," and "The Buddha: One Wild and Crazy Guy?"[15]

In the same way, Bibfeldt sounds the call for the modern student of religion to use comedy to impart his or her message to the untutored

---

12. "À la recherche du Franz perdu: An Interview with Franz Bibfeldt," *Martimania: Martin Marty's Greatest Hits* (Chicago: Ronco, 1988).

13. Author's notes, apparently September, 1973, but a smudge of what appears to be Yoo-Hoo Chocolate Beverage obscures the date.

14. Cf. Bibfeldt's comments in "Schleiermacher, Schopenhauer, Schelling: Schläferen oder Schlingeln?" *Entlarvung* 32 (July 1947): 456-65.

15. "The Lord of Laughter: Christ as Comedian," *Humorous Theology Quarterly*, 2 (January 1972): 16-31; "The Power of the Boffo One-Liner in the Thought of Confucius," *Theology East and North* 6 (December 1984); "The Buddha: One Wild and Crazy Guy?" *One Hand Clapping* [special humor issue] 3 (November 1969): 3-11; "L'Apôtre Paul: Un Type Fou?" *Revue des Maladroites Études Bibliques* 14 (September 1974): 12-19.

masses. "The simplest religious truths become more easily grasped by the layperson when expressed in humorous terms," Bibfeldt wrote in 1977.[16] "Which remark bears more impact: 'God is ubiquitous' or 'God is so ubiquitous that when He sits around the house, He really sits around the house?' " Elsewhere he summarizes this point: "The student of religion must somehow learn to combine the hair shirt and the Borscht Belt."[17]

Of course, when most people think of show business, they think of television, the Muzak® in the dentist's office of life. There can be no doubt that religion is a mainstay of contemporary television programming,[18] but the mainline denominations (i.e., those that don't practice snake-handling) are not well represented. Franz Bibfeldt has discussed this problem on a number of religious television programs, from "ABC's Wide World of Krishna" to "Monday Morning Kaddish," but since these shows were all aired between one and five in the morning, his views have not received the attention they deserve. As Bibfeldt said on the August 14, 1987 program "Methodists Look at the News," "the capacity of television for disseminating information is enormous, and it is the responsibility of religious professionals — academics, pastors, bartenders — to exploit it to its fullest capacity. The time has come for religious quiz programs."

As usual, Bibfeldt was quick to put his own suggestion into action, before someone else could take the credit or claim the residuals. In association with a Hollywood company, Thumbscrew Productions, Bibfeldt developed a number of specifically religious quiz programs. These included "Leap of Faith," in which contestants climbed up Jacob's Ladder by means of empirical evidence for design in the natural world before making the "Leap of Faith" across the chasm of despair to the postulation of a beneficent divine Creator for major cash prizes. Another popular program was "Zen Master," a quiz in which the winner was the first contestant to stop attempting to answer the questions. Bibfeldt was also responsible for a short-lived quiz show sponsored by the Catholic archdiocese of Chicago, "Let's Make a Novena," in which

---

16. "Pearls before Swine: Great Religious Insights for the Uninitiated," *Pastor's Pasteboard* 37 (June 1977): 34-46.

17. "Liturgy: The Greatest Show on Earth," *Episcopalian Priest,* Special Spring Fashion Preview (spring 1981): 87.

18. Cf. Bibfeldt's articles "Kant and the Viability of Late-Night Religious Television Programming after Johnny Carson," *Cambridge Journal of Philosophy in Media* 12 (June 1992): 30-35; and "Es Geht Mir Gut: Theologie nach Robt. Schuller," *Zeitschrift für Verblondjet Theologie* 31 (May 1981): 65-88.

contestants committed themselves to various devotions in exchange for cash prizes, pilgrimages and plenary indulgences. The members of the audience would dress up as their favorite saints in order to attract the host's attention and get a chance to play the game. Unfortunately, a nasty incident arose in early 1979 when the greyhound of a St. Ferdinand III of Castile attacked the dove of a St. David and ate it in full view of the cameras and a shocked studio audience. The show was quickly replaced by reruns of the animated children's religious program "Jezzy and Ahab," while the erstwhile quiz host, Fr. Monty, was reassigned to a leper colony in Senegal.

Of course, where the scholar of religion can make her greatest contribution is in shaping the minds of the younger generation. An effective medium for this task is children's television. In a speech to the 1983 graduating class of Oecelampadius Institute in Buffalo, Bibfeldt asked, "How many of you are here today because of Captain Kangaroo's daily admonition to say your prayers? How many first gained a sense of the fallenness of man through the brutality of 'Tom and Jerry'? How many first appreciated the 'banality of evil' from watching the futile schemes of Boris and Natasha fail repeatedly to destroy moose and squirrel? Yet today, the moguls of children's television are content to entertain with puppets and cartoons about shapes, colors, and the alphabet. Bert and Ernie are all very well, but they don't bring us any closer to solving the riddle of existence, do they?"[19] This question poses a challenge to all scholars of religion, a challenge to bring to the children of America the benefits to be gained from studying religion: the happy hours spent among the archives of obscure denominations, the sense of accomplishment when a theological point has been carried to its logical conclusion and beyond, the joy of mastering a language no one has spoken for two thousand years, the status of being the world's leading authority on Schwenckfelder hymnody.

In this, as in so many other cases, Professor Bibfeldt has led the way with his own practical example. It was not long ago that he paid a visit to Mister Rogers' "Neighborhood of Make-Believe," where he had a long discussion with the hand-puppet King Friday the Thirteenth about the problem of Job. An unfortunate but not fatal accident involving a high-power cable led to the explosion of the tiny puppet's wooden head and Professor Bibfeldt's hair going Afro from a 20,000-volt electrical charge. As Fred Rogers himself said at the time to his horrified

19. "Everything I Know I Learned from Television," published in the Oecelampadius Institute *Oxyrhynchus*, August 1983, pp. 3-10.

viewers: "Did you like the way Professor Bibfeldt lit up? Can you say 'electro-convulsive shock?' "[20]

There is much more we could say about Franz Bibfeldt's contributions to the world of show business: his analysis of the 1965-66 comedy series "My Mother the Car," based on the theory of reincarnation revealed to Arjuna by Krishna in the Bhagavad Gita; his brilliant analysis of the evolution of Thai Buddhism in the nineteenth century, based entirely on the film version of *The King and I*; his part as spiritual advisor to the cast and crew of *Monty Python's Life of Brian*; and his contributions as the religious affairs columnist for *Daily Variety* in the forties. But enough has already been said to demonstrate Bibfeldt's conviction that every aspect of show business — film, theater, dance, stand-up comedy, television, music, street performance — is necessarily an expression of religious experience and aspirations. If this is so, Bibfeldt argues, then all these fields of endeavor fall within the province of the scholar of religion and may be the proper subject of investigation, analysis, debate, grants, and government-funded projects carried out in plush surroundings at high salaries. In remarks to a group of his colleagues gathered at a cocktail party in Heidelberg on G. W. F. Hegel's one hundred fiftieth birthday to celebrate the fact that the great philosopher had never set foot in that city, Bibfeldt said, "Those of us who study religion must examine the vestiges of religious experience in popular entertainment so as to help average people [*die Dummkopfen*] gain a better insight into their own and humankind's spiritual natures. This is a sacred duty which we must not shirk — unless, of course, we are unable to get someone to pay us for it."[21]

Franz Bibfeldt is thus both patron and example for all those who would not only discover the hidden spirituality in show business, but also aspire to make all forms of popular entertainment overtly and imaginatively religious in character. Bibfeldt encourages us to look forward to a day when no film will be without a clear religious subtext, no dance will be without footnotes to point out its roots in shamanistic rituals, no television situation comedy will be without a puckish priest or a raucous rabbi,[22] no street mime will be without a handout on the Trappist tradition, and best of all, no scholar of religion will be without

20. For Bibfeldt's account of the incident, see "The Liability Policy of Make-Believe: My Lawsuit Against PBS," *TV Guide*, April 19-26, 1989.

21. This remark is quoted by David Tracy, "Franz Bibfeldt: My Most Unforgettable Character," *Reader's Digest*, November 1985, p. 109.

22. For a daring first step in this direction, see Martin Marty, "We Need More Religion In Our Sitcoms," *TV Guide*, December 24-30, 1983, pp. 2-8.

an agent, an expensive sports car, and a bankroll large enough to choke a horse. This vision is the goal of our quest. And if our quest should fail, if we should find ourselves shunned by the very people we hope to enlighten; if the public turns away from our incessant chatter about emcees as Bodhisattvas and car chases as the Eternal Return, about the television set as cultic object and programming the VCR as initiation ritual, and instead decides simply to be entertained — it is then when we must remember that even the greatest scholars have had to face failure. This is true even of Franz Bibfeldt himself. In 1974, after seven years of effort, Bibfeldt finally abandoned his long-cherished dream of bringing a musical based on Richard Hooker's *Laws of Ecclesiastical Polity* (tentatively entitled *Via Media!*) to Broadway.[23] At that moment, when his professional career was at its lowest ebb, Franz Bibfeldt uttered the deathless words that continue to inspire and sustain his disciples: "Well, that's show business!"

---

23. The whole story of Bibfeldt's failed musical was told best by *Variety*, 12 December 1974, under the headline "Sticks Hicks Nix Episc's Kicks."

The Man Who Isn't There:
Some Notes on the Quest for the
Historical Bibfeldt

DENNIS L. LANDON

A further refinement of the Bibfeldt popular culture theme appears
in this essay by Dennis L. Landon, now of Bethany College, West
Virginia. Landon spoke at the time of the nation's bicentennial, so
some of his pop culture references may not be graspable to those
who were not yet conscious in 1976; the editors admit to having
snuck in an updating or two, so the chronology may be a bit jarring
to the sensitive. But then, the sensitive should probably not be
reading this book anyway. — ED.

It is certainly no accident that the topic at hand is the *quest* for the
historical Franz Bibfeldt. Like the quest for the historical Jesus, and
indeed like the great quests of legend — for the Holy Grail, the source
of the Nile, the perfect martini — the closer scholars come to the object
of their pursuit, the further it recedes from them and the more
completely it eludes their grasp. Perhaps the best illustration of our
difficulty, but perhaps also of the promise of our inquiry, comes in this
reflection from Gellett Burgess:

> Yesterday upon the stair,
> I met a man who wasn't there.
> He wasn't there again today,
> I wish, I wish, he'd stay away.

I am hard pressed to think of a better poetic summary of the current state of Bibfeldt scholarship.

The problem is not just that scholars have been unable to locate the essential Bibfeldt; it is even more that they have been looking in all the wrong places — namely, in Europe, where Bibfeldt was born, grew up, and spent his formative years. It should be obvious to anyone sensitive to the thrust of his work that Bibfeldt, the theologian committed to being all things to all men, would not be so narrow as to allow his thought to be formed by his own family, education, and culture. Anyone can do that! To fully understand Bibfeldt we must look first to the *Sitz im Leben* — and then ignore it.

Our thesis is that to bring the real Bibfeldt into focus we must look to this country, and to American popular culture. There we will find the great man not in the desiccated scholarship of the academy, or the effete irrelevance of the church, but in the center of mass society. Only there will we see him in his true role, as theologian of the people.[1]

Theorists of mass culture have long sought the organizing principle of American popular culture. What is it that links Joyce Brothers and David Bowie? Why was Johnny Carson obsessed with the Tidy-Bowl man? How are we to understand Michael Jackson and Joe Pesci as the dialectical twin-*geist* of modernity? I am here to affirm that there is a way, and while I do not intend to develop this theory in all its implications today, I do not shrink from boldly asserting a single, comprehensive, and multivalent principle: Look for the man who isn't there.

Throughout the entire twentieth century in America, Bibfeldt has been the man who wasn't there, and this quality of not-thereness (a quality that theology has yet to adequately explore, let alone notice) is the source of the conceptual power of our theory.

The history of Bibfeldt scholarship has articulated five ways of understanding the relationship of Bibfeldt and his thought to culture. We mean to propose a sixth — after demonstrating the inadequacies of these five.

1. People's theology grows out of people's history, with a single distinction: whereas people's history is an attempt to look beyond what people thought to what they actually did (their behavior), people's theology attempts to capture a thinker's thought in its purity by paying no attention whatever to anything he did. It is an attempt to face human life as it is actually lived (i.e., without thinking about it), and then to look to and isolate the totally irrelevant thought that lies behind behavior. It is a large part of Bibfeldt's genius that his life shows the least connection between thought and action of any contemporary thinker. Those interested in pursuing this further should consult Bibfeldt's recent foray into self-help literature: *Life's Little Deconstruction Book.*

First, those who hold to the concept of "Bibfeldt against culture" have entirely missed the master's flexibility: the theologian who would explicitly take all things into himself could hardly judge the culture that is the exclusive source of his raw materials. The concept "Bibfeldt of culture" is more alluring but no less mistaken: it implies a presence in culture that would never do for our theologian *absconditus*.[2] "Bibfeldt above culture" has its supporters among those who see his thought as neither affirming of nor judgmental of society, which is a good beginning; but they still want to attribute to Bibfeldt an authority that cannot be justified by any close consideration of his work. Bibfeldt himself has rejected even the concept of "Bibfeldt somewhat above culture."[3] "Bibfeldt the transformer of culture" has obvious difficulties, specifically his consistent protestation that his thought is both AC and DC.[4] "Bibfeldt and culture in paradox" comes the closest to our position in its refusal to posit a direct relationship, but its inadequacy is also obvious. Bibfeldt may be many things to many wo/men; he may be enigmatic, abstruse, and contradictory; but he will have no truck with paradox. (A recently discovered letter from Bibfeldt to the late Robert Young affirms this: ". . . when I want paradox, I watch 'Marcus Welby.' "[5])

Our search for an adequate understanding of Bibfeldt and culture led us first to the construct of "Bibfeldt irrelevant to culture," but that fails to allow for his influence. "Bibfeldt oblivious to culture" suggested itself, but there we confront the incredible range of his fan letters and the fact that he clearly believes there is something out there. We needed to find a relationship that takes into account both his love for and his innocence of American culture. Thus we came to a suitable construct, one that incorporates the full compass of Bibfeldt's humble hubris, the total range of his deep shallowness, the construct "Bibfeldt enjoying culture."[6]

2. Obviously, this analysis owes much to the work of Bibfeldt's brother, H. Fritz Bibfeldt.

3. Franz Bibfeldt, "Fear of Flying," *Journal of the Society for Christian Aviation,* March 1968.

4. Franz Bibfeldt, "Out of the Closet and Into the Circuit Diagram," *Publication of the Fellowship of Christian Electricians,* November 1970.

5. The fact that the bulk of Bibfeldt's correspondence is not with other theologians and academics, but with the likes of Young, Lorenzo Lamas, Telly Sevalas, and Monty Hall is indicative of what a Bibfeldt scholar is up against.

6. We do not for a moment admit to a consideration of the suggestion of some of his detractors that the concept should be "Bibfeldt annoying culture." They represent the retained water that swells the ankles of scholarship.

Let us move now to the evidence of Bibfeldt's familiarity and interaction with American culture. We begin with a consideration of the two most successful and paradigmatic studies of the American spirit of the middle 1970s: E. L. Doctorow's novel *Ragtime* and Robert Altman's film *Nashville*. First, it must be understood that the fact that Bibfeldt appears in neither of these works, and that no references are made to him in either, is irrelevant to the question of his significance for them. We must remember here Bibfeldt's oft-enunciated principle of anonymous ubiquity.[7]

Ragtime captured the imagination of the American reading public as well as that of the literary establishment, at least in part through Doctorow's weaving of actual historical characters into a fictional framework that captured the spirit of American life in the 1920s. In the book we meet Emma Goldman, Sanford White, Harry Houdini, and other semi-respectable public figures of that time. It can be shown that Bibfeldt was on intimate terms with all these people. Doctorow obviously left Bibfeldt himself out of the narrative due to (1) Bibfeldt's not being dead, and (2) Bibfeldt's well-known litigiousness. However, the sureness with which Doctorow links characters who never met each other and plays fast and loose with chronology is ample proof of his familiarity not only with Bibfeldt himself but with the master's work on the problem of the year zero. The title of the novel is final evidence of the Bibfeldt influence; had Doctorow not been afraid of acknowledging Franz Bibfeldt as his mentor, the book would certainly have been entitled *Lagtime*.

With *Nashville*, the Bibfeldt influence is more on content than on form, and reveals itself most potently in the song lyrics, which are an essential element of the film. The opening of the movie, in fact, is a direct quote from Bibfeldt's latest article on the American bicentennial:[8]

---

7. Anonymous ubiquity is Bibfeldt's theological corollary to the Heisenberg uncertainty principle: "I can be there and not be recognized, I can be recognized but not be there; I can even be not there and not be recognized." (*Playboy* interview, conducted by Howard Hughes, April 31, 1971.) (This meeting led to a continuing association; Bibfeldt found Hughes an extremely provocative interlocutor. His influence can be seen in several subsequent Bibfeldt publications, most notably in his essay "Notes on Econo-thanatology: Perhaps We *Can* Take It with Us," *Lifeline,* June 1972.)

8. Franz Bibfeldt, "America Would Have Been Here Anyway: Reflections on Continental Stability," *Journal of the Society for Bland and Self-Satisfied History,* October 1975. (Should not be confused with "Reflections on Stable Incontinence," Bibfeldt's theological reflection on chronic bedwetting.)

"We must be doing something right to last two hundred years." Or note the Bibfeldtian lyric that closes the film: "It don't worry me."[9] We need only mention *Nashville*'s 1976 Academy Award-winning song, "I'm Easy," to completely establish our point that Robert Altman is well aware of Bibfeldt's theology of desiring to please and its influence on American culture.[10]

One of the inadequacies of other analyses of Bibfeldt's relation to American culture has been an ignorance of his desperate desire to please, to stand foursquare on both sides of any issue, to try to make everyone happy. It is this very fact — Bibfeldt's concern for the *consumers* of his work and their feelings — that sets him apart from all other theologians, past or present. Giving the public what it wants is both what has attracted Bibfeldt to the American spirit and is the content of his influence on it. We are now ready to explore a few representative details of this lifelong interaction.

You may recall that, during the late 1960s controversy over whether hidden evidence in the Beatles' songs indicated that Paul McCartney was dead, it was Bibfeldt who debunked the theory saying, "Paul McCartney is not dead, he's only sleeping." Sleep has been a continuing preoccupation of this most wide-ranging of intellects. His article "Morpheus and Morphology: Forms of Discourse in Sleep-Talking"[11] led to his acquaintance with Edgar Cayce, whom Bibfeldt once described as "the best listener on earth." It should also be noted that, at the time of Cayce's death, Bibfeldt refused to comment except to say that he had wondered why Cayce had never asked him any questions.

Many have asked for clarification of Bibfeldt's position during the Fundamentalist-Modernist controversy. It appears that his only contribution to the debate was in a letter to P. T. Barnum. In response to Barnum's assertion that "there's a sucker born every minute," Bibfeldt replied, "But they are born again on the half-minute."

It is Bibfeldt's studies of time and its inconsistencies that have intersected most frequently with our popular culture. Bibfeldt was a particularly rabid fan of *Star Trek* (he can be frequently seen at "Trekkie" conventions, dressed as a tribble) and spent a great amount of energy speculating on its implications for his work. He noted, for example,

9. This also indicates the influence on Bibfeldt of the great American semanticist, A. E. Neuman.
10. The fact that Bibfeldt himself is easy, but never its opposite, has been testified to with regret by numerous disappointed theological lecture groupies around the country.
11. In *Kerchief, Cap, and Candle: The Journal of Somno-Psychology*, autumn 1969.

long before other critics had noticed, that the series was a continuing elaboration of the thought of Friedrich Nietzsche (Captain Kirk, the man of emotion and intuition, represents the Dionysian principle, and Mr. Spock the Apollonian), but of greater concern to him was the question of the starship transporter mechanism: Where do the crew of the Enterprise actually go when they "beam down" somewhere? What happens to them between the energization of the machine and their arrival? Is their luggage ever lost? He has come, alas, to no conclusion.

The mystical themes he discovered in *Star Trek* led Bibfeldt into association with various movements for peace of mind, self-actualization, and growth. He experimented with many of the available techniques and movements: he was Rolfed, screamed the primal scream, had transactional analysis (where it was discovered that his parent, adult, and child were indistinguishable from each other and, what is more, formed the three "selves" of a multiple personality calling themselves Moe, Larry, and Curly). Bibfeldt experienced *Gestalt* therapy, having been greatly impressed that Fritz Perls' book was entitled *In and Out of the Garbage Pail*, a metaphor, Bibfeldt said, for both his content and his method. Bibfeldt also spent some time studying with sexologist Alex Comfort, who commended his enthusiasm but suggested remedial work. He was also associated with the self-improvement movement known as est. He found its philosophy (based on the proposition "what is, is; what isn't, isn't") sufficiently sophisticated, but foundered in his attempt to elaborate that neo-Parmenidean insight theologically. The best he could do was, "God either is or is not."

As Bibfeldt first began to experience American television, he became the victim of a circumstantial misunderstanding. Due to his very busy and erratic schedule, he was only able to catch a few shows now available to us only on *Nickelodeon*, including *My Favorite Martian, I Dream of Jeannie, The Flying Nun, Topper, The Girl with Something Extra, My Mother the Car, Mr. Ed,* and *Bewitched*. They all left him with a slightly warped vision of the metaphysical possibilities of American thought; and *Bewitched* also left him with a disconcerting assortment of facial tics. I think it is safe to say that Bibfeldt never recovered from this initial exposure.

This brings us, by extension, to the most unfortunate incident of Bibfeldt's career, an incident that should be instructive to all aspiring scholars. We are all well aware of the master's doctoral thesis, "The Problem of the Year Zero." Obviously, once he had completed it, Bibfeldt went looking for a publisher. After being turned down by the major publishers, he began to circulate the manuscript among the smaller houses, finally attracting some interest at Grove Press. Unfortunately, Bibfeldt knew nothing about the publisher. He took the small check and went on his way. Had he known the ways of publishers and editors, he might have been more wary. The rest we know: Bibfeldt's "The Problem of the Year Zero" was published as *The Story of O*. The error was compounded by the editor's misunderstanding of Bibfeldt's frequent references to the "chains of history," and his insistence that we must "continually submit ourselves to disciplined thought." A passing reference to "the bondage of the will" didn't help matters any. Bibfeldt himself deemed it fortunate that he had used a pseudonym; needless to say, he received no royalties from the movie version of his dissertation.

One realm in which Franz Bibfeldt has not been much in evidence is politics. However, Carl Bernstein's and Bob Woodward's *The Final Days* does contain one Bibfeldtian anecdote: During the last week of the Nixon presidency, as the insomnia-racked commander-in-chief paced the floor of the White House and conversed with the portraits of former presidents, he placed a late-night phone call to Bibfeldt, whose name he found in an NEH listing of theologians. Bibfeldt, ever desiring to please, accepted the collect call and assured the troubled chief executive that yes, what he was feeling probably *was* angst. The magnitude of that contribution to the national nightmare of Watergate may never be fully known.

What, finally, do we know about Bibfeldt the man? The quest ends as it begins. His influence on us is immense, but we seem doomed never to view him whole. Even now, as he begins to receive the scholarly attention he deserves, it is somewhat demoralizing to assess the vast amount of research still to be done. The man who isn't there continues to haunt us and our culture. Our only recourse in the end is to be thankful that he seems to be near us whenever we need him.

Images of Bibfeldt

DAVID MORGAN

Now it is time to turn to the theme of Bibfeldt and art. This we do with a vengeance, since we are in a position to illustrate an essay that addressed the topic head on. David Morgan teaches art history at Valparaiso University in Indiana, and is the artist who, when he failed to make some Bibfeldt sightings, pretended that he had and offers them here as authentic representations. But let him explain. — ED.

"In the postmodern world," Bibfeldt wrote in his now famous *Letters from the Garage*, "originality is a myth best *demythologized*." This oft-quoted passage (which Bibfeldt insists preceded the popularization of the term by another German theologian whose name started with *B*) anticipated the entire discourse on the eclipse of modernism. Bibfeldt's unabashed espousal of imitation is clearly evident in a choice morsel from one of his many collections of aphorisms: "It's better to copy what everyone's doing than look like a moron with no ideas."[1]

Although it will not surprise many to learn that Bibfeldt gleefully trashed originality as a scholarly virtue, the deconstruction of the modern self in postmodern thought poses an intriguing problem when we confront several images of Bibfeldt, or images to which the signifier "Bibfeldt" has been anchored (see figures 1 through 5). In fact, these images exist only as feathery, gray photocopies, their originals having vanished, apparently lost forever, if indeed they ever existed.

---

1. Franz Bibfeldt, *Purity of Mind is to Think Pleasant Thoughts*, trans. Anders Anders (Copenhagen: Hallmark Press, n.d.), p. 1.

Figure 1
Portrait of Franz Bibfeldt by Siegfried Reinhardt

Exhaustive research has failed to produce the original drawings. Only scattered details about the conditions under which the images were originally created have come to light. We are left to improvise, to reconstruct in the most playful and Bibfeldtian mode what these icons of the elusive master might mean.

Bibfeldt himself has remained indifferent toward their origins. This indifference [*in-differ-ence*] derives largely from his unsuccessful attempt to convince the Bundestag to place his face on a German stamp. With the failure of that enterprise, Bibfeldt turned to the idea of illustrating his books with his own countenance. But when he learned that the photocopied drawings would not easily reproduce on the jackets of his projected *Collected Works*, he abandoned all interest in them.

Further research in the extensive archives of the *Riverside Center for Bibfeldt Studies* has produced not a trace of the original drawings. Without exception, Bibfeldt's image occupies the twilight world of cheap reproductions. Take, for instance, an undated cover of the *Center's* mouthpiece, *Bibfeldt Today* (figure 1). Judging from the intricate back-

Figure 2
Portrait of Franz Bibfeldt by David Morgan

ground of his portrait, this well-known image, affectionately dubbed "Atomic Franz," portrayed the master expounding his controversial theory that the universe is best understood as a series of interconnected egg-shaped forms whose integrity is microcosmically expressed in the morphology of Bibfeldt's own head.

A second drawing (figure 2) documents a triumphant moment for Bibfeldt, when he visited the United States to receive an honorary degree in phrenology from Twaddle County Community College. The drawing shows a rather smug Bibfeldt enjoying the recognition of his colleagues for years of work in the phrenological categorization of modern theologians into three types: pinheads, eggheads, and scheisskopfs. His work in this area is literally without peer.

Figure 3

Figure 3 almost certainly dates from Bibfeldt's "pop culture"
phase. Fascinated by the American media and their power to propagate
popular myths such as the sightings of Elvis Presley resurrected, Bibfeldt hit on the idea of a theology of popular culture. He theorized that
popular religious materials appealed to the masses because they were
so cheap — both the materials and the masses. He happened onto a
means of testing his thesis when a distant relative in Nebraska sent
"Onkel Franz" an American biweekly on religion and culture wrapped
around a piece of Confirmation lamb cake. Bibfeldt randomly selected
a woman shopping on market day in Dresden (who, as chance would
have it, happened to be his great Aunt Hilda). He asked her if she would

Figure 4

subscribe to this American newsletter that focused on the interaction of religion and culture, which, though it sounded impressive, he assured her, was by German standards mere intellectual pulp. When his informant pointed out that she did not read English, Bibfeldt replied that neither did the Americans. When she refused to buy the publication, Bibfeldt concluded that American popular culture was markedly inferior to European sensibilities. He tossed the newsletter and treated Aunt Hilda to lunch at McDonalds bei Kreuzkirche.

The fourth image of Bibfeldt which bears at least passing attention stems from an extended romance with the popular culture of Chicago, the "city of pork rinds," as he fondly called it. Cultivating an unrequited love affair with the White Sox, Bibfeldt the adopted South Sider commissioned a local artist to create a baseball card bearing his image (figure 4). The result was so winning that friends in Hyde Park urged him to contact the front office at Comiskey Park. Bibfeldt delivered the image with the offer to address a home game audience on the theology of baseball. The Sox management graciously declined his offer, but noted that the bowtie was a classy addition that elevated the Sox uniform to an unprecedented level of cultural distinction. It was at this time that young divinity professors in Swift Hall adopted the custom of emulating the Bibfeldt trademark.

Bibfeldt's mania for fashion and the proliferation of his visage in mass culture is visualized in no more compelling way than a series of images which plot his physical appearance from 1957 to 1992 (figure 5). The images, lifted from a variety of international tabloids, show the theologian's personal commitment to being *hip*. Proposing a cosmetic variation of McLuhan's thesis, Bibfeldt reasoned that it wasn't what you said, but how you looked when you said it. One of the many unauthorized biographies includes a seemingly endless chapter entitled "Bibfeldt Goes Hollywood," in which our man embarked on a strategy of tailoring his appearance to the whims of fashion in order to bestow on his theologizing what every theologian longs for, that coveted patina of *relevance*. "What's the use of saying anything," Bibfeldt once remarked, "if no one thinks you're important for having said it?" The following captions were taken from the magazines in which the images appeared. The author expresses his thanks to each publisher for permission to reproduce the image and text.

1957   "Skidrow Theologian Frank Bibfault [*sic*] visiting the City of Angels to read a much ballyhooed paper "God is a Howl," at an international conference called 'Theology on the Beat.'"
— *National Enquirer*

1964   "International Theology Guru *Franzi B.* as he appeared recently in a Liverpool club to hear his friends, John, Paul, George, and Ringo. Mr. B. was disappointed to learn that the boys had gone to the U.S. to do the Sullivan show. The groovy man of God was eventually ejected from the club after angering a mob of fans with the rancorous claim that British rock owed its beat to the waltz." — *Sun*

1969   "German churchman Franz Bibfeldt put in a cameo appearance at Woodstock this week. Bibfeldt lost his 'cool' when his rented chopper was stolen and he was forced to hitchhike back to LaGuardia." — *Star*

Figure 5
Portraits of Franz Bibfeldt by David Morgan

1974   "Showing off a luxurious coiffure and a thick mat of chest hair, Saxon Disco King and swinging theologian Franz Bibfeldt danced his way to fame last week at East Germany's annual *Tanz Alle!* competition. Bibfeldt cut a dashing figure in peach and lime-green polyester. Said one observer: 'We knew it was going to be *wunderbar* when he started by throwing his bow tie to the audience . . .'"

— *Die Welt*

1978   "Pop culture icon Franz Bibfeldt appearing as host of *Saturday Night Live*. The German clergyman extraordinaire opened the show by accompanying himself on a xylophone while singing 'Ich bin Conehead, wie heisst Du?' set to the melody of 'Ein feste Berg.' When this received only cool applause from the jaded New York audience, Bibfeldt tried his infamous Philipp Melanchthon impersonation, which fared little better."

— *People*

1985   "Punk theologian Franz Bibfeldt after a recent trip to Berlin. When reprimanded for his appearance by his university's rector, Bibfeldt explained that the whole thing was a terrible mistake. While in Berlin he'd stopped for a haircut. When the friseur said 'Spike'?, Bibfeldt had thought he meant his tea and replied 'Sehr gut!' The epoxied mohawk came off with a large patch of scalp attached and the pink dye took three months to fade away. 'Prussians!' the Saxon churchman exclaimed, 'you just can't trust 'em.'"   — *Scheissblatt*

1992   "Dr. Franz Bibfeldt dressed for male bonding during a recent experience in the manly wilderness of Nebraska's Great Sand Hills. ELCA organizers Butch Linderman and Floyd Goehner welcomed the famous theologian to their weekend retreat where participants were treated to long passages of Bibfeldt's latest book: *Bonding of the Will: Lutheran Thoughts on Men Hugging*."

— *The Lutheran*

An icon of popular fashion, the Andy Warhol of theology, Bibfeldt permeates our visual culture — or at least circles it in an endless holding pattern. Lost in the wispy play of signifiers, our subject who is no longer a subject is approached but never encountered. His presence ever deferred, never more than a trace, the figural construction of "Bibfeldt" is a shadow of one who was, an echo of what could have been but fortunately was not. We find his telltale signs in the wake of every intellectual fad. Failing to anticipate the latest academic fashion, he is nevertheless blessed with an eye for imitating it. Where but in the xerography of mass culture would one expect to find the master of the *postmoderne*?

Yet guessing at yesterday's fads takes its toll, as a sketch of undetermined date suggests (figure 6). This haggard mug reveals the labors of academic ambulance-chasing. But there is something ageless and enduring about the man. As long as the academy stands there will be Bibfeldt, the institution's photocopied *other*, staring at us from the murky world of lectureships and padded footnotes, forever in search of a glitzier resumé.

Figure 6
Portrait of Franz Bibfeldt by Siegfried Reinhardt

V. Landmarks and Landmines in Bibfeldt Scholarship

Whatever is, is right. Whatever is not, is also right.

FRANZ BIBFELDT,
Both/And

Portrait of Franz Bibfeldt by David Morgan

Landmarks and Landmines in Bibfeldt Scholarship

ROBIN W. LOVIN

The American Academy of Religion is the professional organization that annually attracts thousands of scholars in religious studies, most of them teachers at colleges and universities. Like all such professional groups, the AAR generates mores and languages of its own. Robin W. Lovin assumes some of them, penetrates others, and expounds a few in this rather technical piece from the Bibfeldt session at the Academy's meeting in 1988. — ED.

"In the first place, I put for a general inclination of all mankind, a perpetual and restless desire of power after power that ceaseth only in death."

Contrary to what you might suppose, those lines were not written by Franz Bibfeldt. They appear in Thomas Hobbes's *Leviathan,* first published in 1651.

Bibfeldt has on more than one occasion *claimed* that he wrote those lines, but this claim is now regarded, in the most informed scholarly opinion, as extremely dubious. I was once myself inclined toward the theory of Bibfeldtian authorship by a psychological argument, since it seemed to me that what we might call the schizo-schizophrenic characteristics of the text could only have been produced by Bibfeldt's uniquely structured quadrilateral mind, which I have, brilliantly, if I do say so myself, described in one of my early contributions to Bibfeldt scholar-ship.[1]

A conclusive refutation of Bibfeldt's claims to authorship appears, however, in a report of archival research conducted by a team of scholars working in the public library in Oconomowoc, Wisconsin. They point to a copy of *Leviathan* that contains a card recording that the book was charged out to an "F. Bibfeldt" for sixteen days in 1952, and that he paid — under protest — an overdue fine of six cents.

Bibfeldt himself has published a detailed reply to the findings of the Oconomowoc archivists, in which he alleges that the Hobbes text is a forgery and offers an elaborate proof that he is himself the original author. Bibfeldt's case, however, rests on a dubious use of carbon-14 dating techniques according to methods which, were they generally accepted, would date the Shroud of Turin during the reign of the Pharaoh Amenhotep IV.

Despite Bibfeldt's own persistent references to Hobbes as "the pseudo-Bibfeldt," it seems best to conclude that the citation with which I began this lecture is an example of, not to put too fine a point on it, plagiarism. It is, however, nonetheless interesting for all that. For Bibfeldt's claim is that the account of the war of all against all, which Hobbes's *Leviathan* presents as an explanation of human life in the state of nature, is in fact his own participant observer's report on an AAR annual meeting held in New York in the late 1970s.

Just how Bibfeldt would know this remains unclear, since he is not known ever to have actually attended an AAR meeting. Not that he hasn't tried. But Bibfeldt suffers from an inability to master the modern Gregorian calendar system. I don't mean that he can't tell what day it is. I mean that he can't tell what *year* it is. The problem, as many of you know, stems from his dissertation at the University of Worms, "The Problem of the Year Zero." Bibfeldt became the first person in nearly two thousand years to notice that there is nothing between 1 B.C. and 1 A.D. One minute you're a full year before Christ, and then, boom, one minute later, you're into the first year of the Christian era, with nothing in between. Bibfeldt was so distraught by this discovery that his health failed, and he was unable to complete his *Habilitationsschrift*. While in the sanitarium, Bibfeldt did write a series of short essays on wine and cheese that were published as a sort of *Rehabilitationschrift* after his discharge.

---

1. That essay first appeared in the *Jahrbuch für Analyse und Motorcycle Maintenance* in 1979. Some of you may be familiar with the English translation in the University of Chicago's *Criterion* magazine.

The residual problem, however, is that Bibfeldt remains to this day unable to focus on the question of what year it is, and so inevitably arrives either a year early or a year late for events. Just this week, he has been reported wandering aimlessly between the Marriott and Sheraton hotels in Boston, and according to a phone call I received very early this morning, he was ejected late last night from a hospitality suite at a podiatrists' convention in Anaheim, where he had wandered in under the impression that it was the University of Chicago reception. Dennis Landon's depiction of Bibfeldt as the theologian *absconditus* points to the deeper theological meaning of the Bibfeldt's mysterious presence/absence that has marked these gatherings of the AAR, but the management of a string of convention hotels and sixteen angry podiatrists who lost their wallets last night in Anaheim have offered a more concrete, experiential account of the *absconditus* part.

Surely, though, Bibfeldt is at the AAR even as I speak, always present even though perpetually absent. Otherwise, how could we account for the sensitive description of the personal relationships at the heart of academic life which he, not to put too fine a point on it, stole from Hobbes's *Leviathan:* "Grief for the calamity of another is pity, and ariseth from the imagination that the like calamity may befall himself, and is therefore called compassion. . . . Grief for the success of a competitor in wealth, honor, or other good, if it be joined with endeavor to enforce our own abilities to equal or exceed him, is called emulation; but joined with endeavor to supplant or hinder a competitor, is called envy."

Or this observation, drawn from hours of field work in the receptions of learned societies and the cocktail lounges of convention hotels: "Sudden glory is the passion which maketh those grimaces called laughter; and is caused either by some act of their own, that pleaseth them; or by the apprehension of some deformed thing in another, by comparison whereof they suddenly applaud themselves."

Or this, which can only have been arrived at by spending time listening in on interviews at the placement center: "The vainglory which consisteth in the feigning or supposing of abilities in ourselves, which we know are not, is most incident to young men, and nourished by the histories, or fictions, of gallant persons; and is corrected often times by age and employment."

In modern times, as we all know, and as has been so well demonstrated by the high level of argument attained in the recent presidential campaign, the art of politics has achieved a level of refinement that transcends the crude political passions that Hobbes discusses. Bibfeldt's

— how shall I put it — *appropriation* of Hobbes's text cannot be relegated to the tawdry realm of ordinary plagiarism. His is the more subtle purpose of pointing out to us the residual value of Hobbes's now outdated political thought as an introduction to the sociology of knowledge in academic communities. We are all familiar, for example, with Hobbes's characterization of the life of man in a state of nature as "poor, nasty, brutish, and short." Bibfeldt's important contribution has been to develop those terms into a typology for classifying the presentations and responses at the American Academy of Religion.

Most familiar, according to Bibfeldt, is the combination that he refers to as the "Type A Session," characterized by a *poor* paper, followed by a *nasty* response. There is also, however, the "Type B Session," in which a *brutish* paper is followed by a *short* response, and of course, less familiar combinations, such as the short paper with a poor response, the nasty paper with a nasty response, and so on. The four types yield sixteen different possible combinations, and Bibfeldt's writings suggest that steering committees could add zest and variety to the section meetings by assigning a type to each paper proposal, and to the personality of each prospective respondent, and then arranging the sessions so as to maximize the number of different combinations presented. Publishing these ratings in the program book would enable Academy members to plan their attendance at sessions more efficiently, and would also remove much of the air of mystery that now surrounds the question of why some paper proposals are accepted and others are rejected.

Now, I want to pause for just a moment in this exposition of Bibfeldt's — how shall I put it — re-pristinization of Hobbes, to say how much I know the great theologian himself would personally appreciate the warmth of your reception of his ideas this morning. Bibfeldt, as Professor Richard Rosengarten has observed, "seeks agreement with everyone and wants to make everything come out right to ensure that he is always relevant." Bibfeldt, not to put too fine a point on it, likes to be liked.

Those who understand this trait in the great man will appreciate how unpleasant he found the controversy that surrounded his recent attempt to enter the field of Third World theology. Some will have read in *Criterion* of Bibfeldt's "preferential option for the rich." Those who followed the subsequent developments in this line of thinking were, I know, shocked at the Vatican inquiry into Bibfeldt's teaching on these points, and outraged at Cardinal Ratzinger's order silencing him for a period of, as the cardinal put it, "Oh, six or seven years ought to do it."

Bibfeldt, who tries desperately to avoid offending anybody, was deeply distressed by this conclusion to the inquiry. I believe what bothered him most about the silencing order was that he isn't even Catholic. Bibfeldt's own Lutheran bishop attempted to clarify the situation in a conciliatory statement which, while noting that silencing orders are not customary practice in the Lutheran communion, added that we must not be too hasty in judging our brethren, and that this might just prove to be one of those situations in which the Lutherans could learn from the Catholics. The bishop added, and I quote, "I mean, here I stand and all that stuff, but there's gotta be *some* limits, for crying out loud."

Given the deep and painful divisions caused by Bibfeldt's discovery of God's preferential option for the rich, it is important to remember his earlier and more broadly accepted contributions to modern theology. Indeed, given Bibfeldt's penchant for plagiarism, we might also appropriately speak of his contributions to ancient and medieval theology as well. But surely none of these rank quite so high as the war of all against all that Bibfeldt has so vividly described at the heart of our academic enterprise, the perpetual and restless desire of power after power that ceaseth only in death, tenure, or promotion to a named chair; and the penetrating insight of the typology of "poor, nasty, brutish, and short" for describing scholarly contributions.

We must not mistake the magnitude of Bibfeldt's achievement at this point. We are in the presence of a breakthrough comparable to his innovative theory of pastoral care for the dead. At a point in the development of Western scholarship in which the anthropologists have robbed us of Rousseau's noble savage, and the historians have disabused us of the notion that the Germanic tribes ever actually lived in a state that preceded the development of the social contract, Bibfeldt has rediscovered the state of nature, let loose in the halls of the Chicago Hilton and Towers. In the words of the immortal Pogo, "We have met the enemy, and they is us."

Franz Bibfeldt: The Life, and Scholarship on the Life

Summary Abstract

RICHARD ROSENGARTEN

A bibliographical essay is a place for documentation, summing up, and cross-reference. In this bibliographical work of documentation, summing up, and cross-referencing, Richard Rosengarten anticipates the appendix by summarizing much of the literature in this book and making reference to some fugitive pieces no longer in the archive. If the previous essay shows how Bibfeldt belongs to the American Academy of Religion and thus to the whole world, this one brings him close to one site where he has had some influence, the University of Chicago. People more familiar with other Ph.D.-granting schools of religious studies and/or theology can easily translate the temporal tale of woe from Rosengarten's first page to comparable alternative locations and experiences. His startlingly brilliant last paragraph is a most appropriate conclusion to this collection on the theology of Bibfeldt.

Rosengarten is the dean of students of the Divinity School at Chicago. — ED.

Some of us, I know, have rather thin knowledge of Bibfeldt's life and work, excepting, of course, anyone who has taken qualifying examinations, where Bibfeldt is truly and often magnificently omnipresent — and not merely on bibliographies. This lack of awareness is easily accounted for. Contrary to the theory of the faculty that this has to do with the revisions in the master's level curriculum, I submit that simple statistical analysis provides the answer.

In the 1970s, a divinity school student took an average of 12.5 years to complete the doctorate. This translates somewhat roughly into 8.465 years of residence in seminary. Using Bibfeldt's personalized equation for turning years of graduate residence into Bibfeldtian awareness, we arrive at a BF factor — not to be confused with the BS factor, a later Bibfeldt invention — of 3.5.

Now in the '90s, a divinity school student has taken an average of 9.4 years to complete the doctorate. This translates, again somewhat roughly, into 7.982 years of residence, for a BF quotient of 1.6.

My efforts today are directed to raising that quotient through a brief excursus on Bibfeldt's life and the first *Forschungsbericht*, or summary of the scholarship, ever attempted. This material is the result of a thorough investigation of the Bibfeldt files in research libraries and the Foundation offices.

The facts are astonishingly complex. Bibfeldt was born on November 1, 1897, at Sage-Hast bei Groszenkneten, Oldenburg, Niedersachsen, Germany, one day prematurely, having been conceived in the back seat of an 1892 Volkswagen following a Candlemas party. His early education was at Turnverein, where he flunked Indian Clubs and had nothing left to do but go into theology. For example, during a fencing match in *gymnasium*, Bibfeldt jumped during a thrust. Years later he would draw upon this experience in his definitive contribution to Jewish-Christian relations, "Empathy with the Circumcised."

Bibfeldt received his D.D.T. — Doctorate of Digressive Theology — in 1929 from the University of Worms. His doctoral dissertation was on the problem of the year zero, and this existential fact has confused Bibfeldt; thrown off, he arrives one year early or late for events, and has left a trail of nothing but graffiti in seminary and divinity school bathrooms. Throughout the '70s it was generally thought that Bibfeldt worked only in men's rooms, but in 1981 Katie Dvorak demonstrated that Bibfeldt had in fact infiltrated women's rooms as much as five years earlier. Basing her thesis on the assertion that Bibfeldt's linguistic experiments never got past the first four letters of "analysis," and on a close reading of Bibfeldt's definitive contribution to early church history, *Getting to the Bottom of Early Christian Literature*, Dvorak proves that the early fencing incident had more decisive consequences for Bibfeldt than chauvinist interpreters supposed: it was no problem for Bibfeldt to dress in drag and enter the women's rooms. The result was his topology of graffiti, later applied to his *Horsgeschichte* theory of biblical hermeneutics: Profanity, Declaration, Dialogue, Fraudulents, and Accretals.

As you can see from the already digressive direction of this summary, pinning down anything about Bibfeldt is difficult, and so in 1976 an earlier session of this sometimes annual and always unsystematic conference dedicated itself to the quest for the historical Bibfeldt. Joseph Price presented the latest findings on Bibfeldt's massive commentary on the Epistle to Philemon. Published in 1933, *Philemerbrief* devotes one full paragraph to each letter of each word of the epistle, resulting in at least one chapter on each verse. Bibfeldt's most renowned chapter is his 12th, on verse 12, which he interprets as "Onesimus, whom I have sent again: thou therefore receive him, that is, mine own bowels. . . ." Price also discovered a manuscript by Bibfeldt, *A Pragmatist's Paraphrase of the Sayings of Jesus.* Operating on a hermeneutic of reversism, in which "any saying which is too hard to follow is to be understood to mean the opposite of what it literally says," Bibfeldt reinterprets the Sermon on the Mount. Time does not permit a detailed presentation of this work, but selected translations should give you a sense of its general thrust:

Matt. 5:3 "Blessed are the rich in money, for they can build bigger and better churches. Who cares about the Kingdom of God?"

and

Matt. 5:8: "Blessed are those whose external appearance and behavior are impeccable, for they shall look nice when they see God."

Dennis Landon took a more pessimistic view than Price. He argued that the definitive illustration of the quest is found in the poem of Gellett Burgess:

Yesterday upon the stair
I met a man who wasn't there.
He wasn't there again today,
I wish, I wish he'd stay away.

Landon characterizes Bibfeldt as theologian *absconditus*, noting the unpublished but definitive popular biography of Bibfeldt written by Gay Talese, *Blessed Sage for Hire.* It is also Landon who provides us with Bibfeldt's principle of "anonymous ubiquity," his corollary to the

Heisenberg uncertainty principle: "I can be there and not be recognized, I can be recognized but not be there; I can even be not there and not be recognized." Landon also cites Bibfeldt's devotion to the half-asked question and the publication of Bibfeldt's dissertation by a pornographic French press as *The Story of O.*

Nineteen-seventy-nine may prove to be the richest year ever for our understanding of Bibfeldt: no fewer than three significant contributions to scholarship on the great man arrived in this year. Otto Dreydoppel and Janet Summers presented discussions of work on Bibfeldt's theories of pastoral care. Dreydoppel concentrated his attention on Franz's theory of pastoral care of the dead — truly a ground-breaking achievement — which begins with the insight that the dead are the truly silent majority and thus the definitively oppressed group. As the one theologian alive to the dead issue, Bibfeldt, out of gratitude to the dead for their adaptability to his theology, lavished his attention on their needs. He argues that the dead are excellent Rogerian therapists, since their ability to listen patiently is unexceeded; they are also perfect est clients since they can sit still, not just for twelve or sixteen hours, but for really long stretches of time. Bibfeldt also addressed particular pastoral problems of the dead, such as their ennui and their extraordinary tendencies to depression, and extended his sense of pastoral care to social justice: Bibfeldt sponsored several housing discrimination suits on behalf of the dead, noting that they were almost always confined to one-room basement apartments and that previous writings on this matter all had terrible plots. The result was Bibfeldt's definitive work, *The Minister as Mortician.* Finally, Dreydoppel underscores Bibfeldt's particular empathy for the evangelical dead who practice the gift of inert healing and whose slogan is "Died Again."

Janet Summers presented a detailed analysis of Bibfeldt's approach to the living, as summarized in his popular text, *I'm OK; You're a Cretin, or a Slob,* a careful analysis of how Bibfeldt's model of pastoral care is best applied to people who couldn't care less. Summers also noted Bibfeldt's innovative use of a hermeneutic of suspicion, based on his assertion that the baby Jesus sought to fool people, as seen in Luke 2:12: ". . . the baby Jesus was lying in a manger." The scrupulous text critic also notes the hint of conspiracy three verses later: "Mary and Joseph and the baby lying in a manger. . . ."

Nineteen-seventy-nine's third contribution came from Robin Lovin, who presented "Franz Bibfeldt: The Breakdown of Consciousness and the Origins of the Quadrilateral Mind." As Ellen Wondra noted subsequently, the title is a fooler: it refers not to Methodism, but to Bibfeldt's personal cerebral composition, in which the usual two-sided brain is in fact four-sided, combining the usual occupants of poet (right side) and IBM executive (left side) with a composer of television jingles (upper lobe) and a cardsharp (lower lobe).

This, my survey leads me to believe, is one of the major break-throughs in Bibfeldt scholarship. You see, Bibfeldt's is the theology of "Both/And," constructed in response to Kierkegaard's *Either/Or;* when negative reviews of Bibfeldt's *Both/And* appeared, he responded by publishing *Both/And and/or Either/Or* — which received mixed reviews. It was Bibfeldt who answered Barth's thunderous *Nein!* to natural theology with a timorous *Vielleicht?* Bibfeldt seeks agreement with everyone and wants to make everything come out right to ensure that he is always relevant. His coat of arms is Proteus rampant on a weathervane; his motto is "I Dance to the Tune that is Played."

Now it seems to me that Professor Lovin's thesis about Bibfeldt's cerebral composition makes the greatest sense of all this, and I can do no better in this context than to cite his own conclusion: "Unlike the Freudian theories of Erikson or the Piagetian theories used by Fowler and Kohlberg, this [the quadrilateral mind] was a formula that matched the data. Those who know Bibfeldt have often remarked that he seems to be barely conscious. Jaynes's theory leads to the exciting speculation that perhaps he isn't conscious at all."

After keeping a low profile during the years of his tenure review, Professor Lovin returned to the podium for an unprecedented second lecture in the spring of 1987. On this occasion his topic was "Franz Bibfeldt and the Future of Political Theology." This more recent event constitutes the sole part in the 1.6 BF quotient which most of you possess, so I will be brief: suffice it to say that here Lovin traces the emergence of Bibfeldt's empathy for the Third World as arising from a two-week junket to Cancun, which resulted in his new political theology, a preferential option for the rich. Lovin also traces Bibfeldt's clandestine political activity in tantalizingly indirect fashion. Suffice it to say that when Robert MacFarlane makes a clean breast of it about the source of that key-shaped cake and the inscribed Bible that went to Iran, Bibfeldt will be in the news yet again.

In closing, I would like to offer a brief, insincere observation. This review of Bibfeldt has, inappropriately, reminded me of Schweitzer's *The Quest for the Historical Jesus.* As you no doubt recall, it is Schweitzer's thesis that biblical scholars who devoted their efforts to understanding who Jesus was almost always wound up with a Jesus who was precisely what they and their generation fancied themselves to be. May it not be that the same is true with Bibfeldt? Do we not make Bibfeldt in our own image? If so, then what we are given here in Bibfeldt scholarship in fact tells us more about the writer than it does about Franz Bibfeldt himself. This should be the light — or the darkness — in which we consider all Bibfeldt scholarship.

A Partial Franz Bibfeldt Bibliography

Books by Bibfeldt

1927 "The Problem of the Year Zero." Ph.D. dissertation, University of Worms.

1933 *Der Philemerbrief: Ein Exegetisches-Theologisches Kommentar,* 5 vols. Berlin: Loewenbrau Verlag.

1934 *Vielleicht? Antwort an das "Nein" Barths.* Basel: Via Media Verlag.

1936 *The Crooked Way.* London: privately published.

—— *The Variables.* Berlin: privately published.

1937 *Both/And: A Response to Kierkegaard.* Graustark: Dubitare Verlag.

1938 *Either/Or and/or Both/And.* London: Sic et Non Press.

1948 *A Pragmatist's Paraphrase of Selected Sayings of Jesus.* New York: James Publishing Co.

1950 *The Relieved Paradox,* trans. R. H. Clausen. London: Howard Press.

1956 *Purity of Mind is to Think Pleasant Thoughts,* trans. A. Anders. Copenhagen: Hallmark Press.

—— *The Boys of Sumer: Akkadian Origins of the National Pastime,* trans. S. Spencer. Chicago: Addison & Clark.

1957 *Here I Sit: Luther Reconsidered.* St. Louis: privately published.

1958 *Paradoxes Observed.* Chicago: Perspective Press.

1959 *Paradoxes Lost.* Los Angeles: Milton Publishing.

1960 *Paradoxes Regained.* Juneau: Gelidus Publishing.

1961 *Schlemiel und Schlemazel: Barth Gegenüber Tillich.* Berlin: Gesundheit & Danke.

—— *The Relieved Paradox and the State.* Chicago: Sublevatio & Smith.

1962 *The Relieved Paradox and Society.* Atlanta: Mimicus Publishing.

178

1965   *The Fire We Can Light: Religious Reflections on Cremation.* London/Paris: Ardor & Humidus.

1968   *I'm OK, You're DOA.* New York: Mortis Corpus Press.

1969   *I Hear What You're Saying, but I Just Don't Care: Thoughts on Pastoral Counseling.* London/New York: Rogers Press.

1971   *Long Discourse on the Study of Theology, Philosophy of Religion, Scripture, Church History, Liturgy, Hymnody, Folk Music, Interpretive Dance, Pastoral Care, Parish Administration, Haberdashery, and Etiquette.* Chicago: Muy Grande Publishing.

1972   *Crypto-Calvinist Existentialism: Predestined to Eternal Insecurity* (incl. Eng. trans. of Dutch hymn "Who Will Reload the Canons of Dordt?"). Amsterdam: Kok & Beker.

1975   *Howdy, Deutero-Isaiah: Salutation Motifs in Isaiah 40-66.* Tübingen: Specious Press.

1976   *The Food Context of Pastoral Care,* ed. B. Mahan. Bangkok: Panang Press.

——   *Minister as Mortician.* New York: Mortis Corpus.

1978   *Magnum Opus.* London: privately published.

——   *God: Getting to Know the Creator.* Des Moines: Vanity Press.

1981   *Luther on Vacation: From Worms to Cancun,* with preface by Robin Leach. Honolulu: Viator Publishing.

1982   *I Haven't Got a Q: Epistemic Dissonance and the Question of Synoptic Origins.* Oxford/Berlin: privately published.

1984   *Eggnog Hammadi: Newly Discovered Texts Relating to Egyptian Gnostic Season Libations.* Cairo: Pyramid Press.

1986   *Mysticism, Now and Zen.* San Francisco: Galanty Press.

——   *Life's Little Deconstruction Book.* New York/Paris: Dairy Dada Books.

1991   *The Wealth of King Solomon: A Hebrew Scripture Prefiguration of Sports Contracts.* Chicago: Addison & Clark.

1992   *Bonding of the Will: Heterodoxy and Orthodoxy in the Practice of Men Hugging.* Minneapolis: Bly Books.

1993   *Mass-o-Schism: Liturgical Practice in the Anglican and Lefevrite Churches.* Oxford/New York: Genuflection Press.

Books co-authored by Bibfeldt

1959   (with Herman F. Nootiks) *Die Auslegung als eine Glückliche Schatzung.* Sage Hast bei Groszenkneten, Niedersachsen, Oldenburg, Germany: privately published.

1964   (with H. Winfeld Tutte) *Arbeitlose Menschen: Jünger in Theologie und Kirchengeschichte*, preface by M. Daly, introduction by J. Brauer. Berlin: Entmannung Verlag.

1974   (with Hans Küng) *God and the Problem of Freud*. New York: Sic & Non.

1985   (with Donald Trump) *Majoring in the Minor Profits: Fame and Fortune Through Pseudonymous Authorship*. New York: Vanity of Vanities Press.

1990   (with H. Winfield Tutte) *The Execution of Islamic Literary Criticism: The Ayatollah as Man of Letters*. Teheran: Recondite Books.

Unpublished Articles by Bibfeldt

1950   "Empathy with the Circumcised"
1957   "Scatology and Eschatology"
1964   "Theology as the Unsought Answer to the Unasked Question"
1966   "Outline for a Future Examination of New Testament Envoys in the Context of Greco-Roman Diplomatic and Epistolary Conventions: The Example of Timothy, Titus, and Anäis Nin"
1987   "Philanthropic Privilege as the *Imago Dei*"

Books about Bibfeldt

1974   Bibfeldt, V. W. *Theologische Fahrvergnügen: Meine Reise mit Onkel Franz*. Heidelberg: Turnverein Verlag.

1979   Von Keester, P. T. L. *Semperlapsarianismus: Die Sündelehre in der Theologie Bibfeldts*, foreword by J. Swaggart. Baton Rouge: Peccavi Press.

1987   Von Keester, P.T.L. *How Many Pinheads Can Dance on an Angel? Scholastic Metaphysics in a Post-Bibfeldtian World* (humor). Wheaton, IL: Facetious Press.

1988   Whitmore, T. and Bessler, J. *Theologian Absconditus: The Existential Problematics of Franz Bibfeldt*, introduction by R. Rosengarten. Grand Rapids/Chicago: Ex Nihilo Press.

1989   Nootiks, Herman F. *Let the Circle Be Unbroken: The Eisogetical Theology of Franz Bibfeldt*. Berlin: Unsinnig Verlag.

NOTE: All extant essays and lectures on Bibfeldt, heretofore unpublished, are published in this volume.

APPENDICES

Primeval Document

This is the primeval Bibfeldt document. While several of his epigraphs had seen print before December 19, 1951, it was this review, modestly tucked under basketball boxscores, that brought him to the attention of a small but literate (at least athletically literate) audience. We have superimposed the name of the publication and the names on the masthead over the scores, thereby implicating numbers of only apparently innocent people. Here comes Bibfeldt, under "BOOKS."

SEMINARIAN

Concordia Theological Seminary   St. Louis 5, Mo., Dec. 19, 1951   Vol. 43, No. 4

	fg	ft	pf
Zipay	1	0	0
Figuly	1	0	4
	15	17	23

	fg	ft	pf
Otte	8	2	1
Malotky	0	1	0
Kesselmeyer	0	1	2
Siess	1	0	1
	25	17	21

	fg	ft	pf
Berning	1	1	2
Thurston	1	1	3
	14	20	30

	fg	ft	pf
Kaminska	0	1	1
Siess	0	0	0
Ludwig	0	0	0
	21	22	27

Ft. Leonard Wood (53)

	fg	ft	pf
Dempsey	2	1	5
Kluck	1	0	0
Thurby	1	2	0
Klein	5	1	4
Ward	0	2	0
Klærich	5	6	5
Garrett	0	0	2
Anderson	4	2	1
Ehlers	0	3	2
	18	17	19

Concordia (54)

	fg	ft	pf
Schumacher	3	0	4
Haas	2	2	2
Goerss	2	4	5
Wacker	7	1	3
Faszholz	3	4	4
Popp	1	1	4
Otte	2	2	0
	20	14	22

Cape Girardeau State Teachers (52)

	fg	ft	pf
Smith			2
Clippard			1
Engleman			2
Belobraydic			2
Henderson			6
Estes			3
Bradford			2
Wilson			4
Gilbert			1
			21

Concordia (56)

	fg	ft	pf
Schumacher	1	4	2

Central (52)

	fg
Young	6
Burcham	2
Christian	4
Kirby	5
Burgess	0
Saunders	0
Klienert	0
Whited	0
Moffat	0
Dulgeroff	3
Lynch	2
	22

Greenville (61)

	fg	ft	pf
Staff, J.	5	2	5
Mason	3	0	2
Carroll	3	0	3
Kooke	7	1	1
Staff, B.	4	0	2
McCormick	0	5	1
Maroon	3	3	2
	25	11	16

Concordia (69)

	fg	ft	pf
Schumacher	3	1	1
Kaminska	5	2	2
Haas	2	0	3
Wacker	9	3	4
Goerss	3	0	1
Faszholz	3	2	1
Popp	0	2	2
Otte	1	0	0
Malotky	2	1	0
Kesselmeyer	1	0	2
	29	11	16

SEMINARIAN

The Associates

Marty Marty, Editor
Ed Schroeder, Managing Editor
Richard Baepler, Business Manager
Don Meyer
Ken Mahler
Ken Kramer
Dick Koenig
Bob Schultz
Warren Rubel
Siegfried Reinhardt

Staff Writers

Art Simon
Ed Lehman
Paul Heyne
Ralph Skov
Herb Schmidt
Harry Hoeman
Erwin Prange
Roland Miller
Andrew Simcak
Andy Weyermann
Paul J. Schulze
William Friedrich
Norb Hattendorf
D. Wagner Fuelling
Dr. Jaroslav J. Pelikan
Dr. Richard R. Caemmerer

Consultants

Dr. L. J. Sieck
Prof. L. C. Wuerffel

Published monthly, September to June, by the Concordia Students' Association, 801 De Mun, St. Louis 5, Mo. Entered as second class matter, Sept. 30, 1918, at Post Office, St. Louis 3, Mo., under Act of March 3, 1879.

SUBSCRIPTION, $1.50 PER VOLUME

BOOKS

Bibfeldt, Franz. THE RELIEVED PARADOX. *Tr. by R. Cloweson, Howard Press, London, 1950. 144 pp. $2.50.*

NOT SINCE KARL BARTH issued his *Romans* from Safenwil has a continental voice sounded so sudden and surprising a theological note. A *Pfarrherr* like Barth had been, Bibfeldt had been working until quite recently in relative obscurity in little Grossenknetten, Oldenburg. To use Sasse's phrase, Barth was "bone of the liberal theology's bone and flesh of its flesh" when he rose to criticize it. So too the author of *The Relieved Paradox* has come out of the dialectical theology movement to appear as what promises to be its most startling critic. The wide range of his interest and knowledge, which includes music, archaeology, drama, and social interest, enable him to summon a variety of illustration that makes his writing more attractive than the burdened, often oppressive argumentation of the crisis theologians. This color and warmth has assured him an immediate public in the States, and we are given to understand that more of his work in translation will be available here soon.

In this rather slight volume he has outlined the central motif of his attack on the Barthian dialectic. He believes that the emphasis on sharpening tension and paradox has carried all theological expression into an illegitimate and distorted line which does its greatest harm in relation to preaching and through it creates confusion in Christian ethics. He believes that Christian revelation is so clear in its relation to the paradoxes of faith, lending so much weight in each case to one side of the tension, that vigorous homiletical emphasis only "relieves the paradox" and clarifies the confusion.

WHILE CLOSER IN spirit to the Reformed confession and tradition Bibfeldt's viewpoints on inspiration, creation, extra-Christian revelation, and social issues as revealed in this and his German works (where he employs a de-mythologizing in his effort to approximate the *kerygma*) limit his usefulness to all but rather mature theological thinkers. But he indicates a trend to watch, and in that light is called to seminarians' attention at this time. The translation and introduction by Canon Cloweson are dramatic and faithful to the original spirit of the author. —mm

* * *

The idea that the essence of Protestantism is religious individualism is a strange modern misconception. The great Reformers were men under authority. —John C. Bennett.

and his sorrow over the fact that men corrupt it and others reject it because they see only that people use it to escape the law of love, which is the law of life?

You thought we had lost freedom? We have come the round about way which was promised. Not far enough around, but perhaps too far for present purposes. There is no space now to apply what has been said to all the concrete freedoms. However, our doctrine of the calling as indicated above says that we can turn this over to our economists, our political theorists, our philosophers, our people in management and in labor, our husbands and wives, and all the others. Must the church continue to be

The Bibfeldtian Origins of the Pseudo-Thomistic Literature

TODD D. WHITMORE

Readers may have seen that much Bibfeldt scholarship relates the theologian to twentieth-century movements. However, all ages in his sight are equal, and he had an influence on medieval scholastic thought, as it had influence on him. Todd Whitmore, now of the University of Notre Dame, used Bibfeldt Day, 1988, to expound the often deservedly overlooked set of mutual influences, in this case, the *Pseudo-Summa* of Thomas Aquinas. — ED.

Shortly after Vatican II, there were great efforts to retrieve the original texts of Thomas Aquinas in order to challenge the moral rigidity of neo-scholastic casuistry. Finding original texts of the Thomistic corpus that would support such a venture would open up Roman Catholic moral theology to new horizons. The liberal left of the Catholic Church was excited.

On January 4, 1968, sixty-five years after the death of Pope Leo XIII, a heretofore unknown text was found in Leo's crypt in the basement of St. Peter's by a snoopy cleaning lady. The fact that the text was in the crypt of Leo, the pope who made Aquinas the official theologian of the Catholic Church, lent considerable authority to the document.

It was entitled *Summa Contra Lex Mea*, or, loosely translated, *The Summa against Everything Else I Ever Wrote*.

The liberal left of the Church was ecstatic.

The authenticity of the text was later cast into doubt by careful linguistic and historical analysis, because the word "K-Mart" appeared seven times. A quote from renowned medievalist, Professor I. M. Obscure:

> The multiplicitous occurrence of the term "K-Mart" definitely indicated that the text in question is pseudepigraphic. Such numerous references suggest that the concept of discount stores had already shaped the mental outlook of the Middle Ages. This is impossible. Analysis of the finds of archaeological excavations has irrefutably demonstrated that shopping malls only began to appear on the European scene during the fourteenth century, a full one hundred years after Aquinas, being brought in from the East by Muslim bedouins.

The liberal left of the Church was depressed.

Still, it is worth studying these texts. Here, apparently, is an early dissenting voice from within the community of the faithful. The following excerpt, written in the disputational form of Aquinas's *Summa Theologica,* is from the *Pseudo-Summa,* first part of the third part of the ninth part of the sixteenth part, question forty-two, article six, entitled: "Whether Jesus Was a Woman, or Who is the Head of the Family Anyway?"

> Objection 1: The Apostle states that, "The Head of a woman is her husband" (1 Cor. 11:3) and "The husband is the head of the wife as Christ is the head of the Church, his body" (Eph. 5:23). Therefore the husband is the head of the family.
>
> On the contrary, it is stated that a woman without a man is like a fish without a bicycle (traditional source).

> I answer that the procreation of the male offspring requires an x and a y chromosome, while that of the female requires no x.[1] Now chromosomes are made up of both form and matter, with the type being the form, the substance being the matter. As stated elsewhere, God does not consist of a material substance. Therefore, there is no matter through which an x chromosome can be transmitted to Mary. Hence, with no x chromosome, Jesus must necessarily be a woman.

1. EDITOR'S NOTE: Indications of knowledge of modern genetics has also cast doubt on the authenticity of the document.

Furthermore, the Apostle states (1 Cor. 11:3): "The head of every man is Christ." Since Jesus Christ is a woman, then the head of every man is a woman. Moreover, since the meeting of man and woman leads to holy matrimony, the woman is the head of the family.

Reply to Objection 1: The term "man" or "husband" can be understood in two ways, to refer to the chromosomal distribution of x and y, or to whoever wears the pants of the family. The first definition is restricted to material substance, while the second refers to the form. The Apostle here intends the latter meaning. Either male or female material substance — that is, chromosomal distribution — can take the form of wearing the pants of the family. Now it is stated that "the husband is the head of the wife *as Christ is the head of the Church, his body*" (Eph. 5:23). Clearly, then, since Jesus Christ is the head of the Church in *both* form and substance, and she is a woman, the material substance of the woman must be the head of the family in form also, that is, she must wear the pants of the family.

In addition, because the woman is the head "as Christ is the head of the Church," this means that a person bearing the substance of a woman must therefore also take the form of the head of the *Church* (Cf. Col. 1:18 and Eph. 1:22). All passages which refer to the relationship of man and woman, husband and wife, both in scripture and in the Holy Christian Church must be understood in this way.

Finally, this also means that the male material substance must take the form of the woman. That is, for instance, he must do the dishes, and the laundry, and if there be offspring, change the diapers at four in the morning.

This suffices to answer all further objections. [fragment ends]

The early 1980s witnessed a resurgence of the dispute over the authenticity of the document. Certain critics seized on the fact that the text in this last reply refers to diapers and not to pampers, a much later development in the material aspect of child-rearing. This reopened the debate. The liberal left of the Church was hopeful.

The excitement, I am afraid, was a bit premature. Recent evidence — uncovered by a divinity school research assistant — suggests that the true author of the pseudo-Thomistic document is none other than Franz Bibfeldt.

Now, before I go on to detail the evidence, I first need to say that I find it incredible that this man, Bibfeldt, has written hundreds of articles, scores of books, has a full teaching load, trots around the globe giving talks, writes his own weekly column in the widely read journal *The Christian Millennium* under the acronym *B.I.M.B.O.* — Bibfeldt does all of this, and still he has time to create a theologian who does not even exist! But I suppose we should not be surprised by the resourcefulness of academics. Why, just this morning when I was eating breakfast, I flipped on the television set, and there was Big Bird on Sesame Street doing his "same and different" routine. That is where he has a number of objects on a counter and he compares and contrasts them to show how they are "same" and "different," "same" and "different." And it finally dawned on me where David Tracy got the idea for *The Analogical Imagination*.

It shows the resourcefulness of academics, or even the resourcefulness of divinity schools as a whole, as in the attempt to simultaneously increase circulation of the *Religion Journal* and attract more students by devising a Publishers Clearinghouse type of sweepstakes. In a couple of weeks, prospective students will begin receiving oversized envelopes with a caption on the front saying, "You may have already won a university fellowship."

But I digress. On point again, the evidence of Bibfeldt's authorship of the pseudo-Thomistic corpus is hard to refute. First of all, an early draft of the document was found on a floppy disk in his IBM PC. This fact is coupled with the recent disclosure that at the time of the discovery of the document in the crypt of St. Peter's, Bibfeldt, even though Lutheran, was on Fr. Francis Muligan's five-day package pilgrimage trip to Rome. Finally — and this is probably the most conclusive evidence — Bibfeldt is the majority stockholder in the K-Mart company. It appears that the document was intended as a means of subliminal advertising. It is clear that Bibfeldt is here living out his political theology, so well explicated by Robin Lovin, of the "preferential option for the rich."

Incidentally, Bibfeldt is now negotiating with T & T Clark publishers to have K-Mart advertising inserts put into Barth's *Church Dogmatics*. And it is really not a bad marketing strategy. Right after we read about *hearing* the *immediate* and *specific* command of God, we turn the page to *hear* it proclaimed that "jockey shorts are now on sale for only ninety-nine cents a pair."

I close by leaving you with the assurance that, even though the authorship of the pseudo-Thomistic literature is all but certain, the controversy continues. The Vatican has taken it upon itself to try to silence Bibfeldt for a year (despite the fact that he is Lutheran). But Bibfeldt, in his last conversation with the Pope, responded like a good Lutheran, "Here I stand; do you mind moving over a bit?"

Franz Bibfeldt and the Uses
of the Doctoral Exams

ELLEN K. WONDRA

At the American Academy of Religion session in 1988, the pro-
grammers wanted to be sure to relate Bibfeldt to the real world of
the academy. Since Bibfeldt is a "Both/And" thinker, he connects
with both the world of professors and the world of students. Then
doctoral student Ellen Wondra spoke for a generation of newcom-
ers influenced by the German scholar as she showed his relations
to the most traumatic moment students know: the time of doctoral
examinations. — ED.

All of us who spend our lives running around in academic circles are
intimately acquainted — to the point of boredom and nausea — with
the debates about the purpose, content, goals, and philosophy of higher
education in our times. From the "Because we *say* they're great" books
debate and ruminations over whose mind is closed — or is it whose
mind is American? — to dictionaries of cultural literacy, which enable
us all to "pass" without knowing a thing, to our own debates about
whose narratives are pure and impure, to conferences on collections of
papers from symposia responding to reports of studies on the implications and effects of curricula on communities and their many characters:
we are sunk, indeed mired, in weighty and learned considerations of
the social purposes of our work. The culturally literate scholar cannot
help but think of Socrates, the first true academic to drink himself to

death. And the astute theologian cannot help but think of Bibfeldt. For if ever an academic was sunk and mired . . .

Indeed, we turn to Bibfeldt because, as is so often the case, we find that he has rushed in where others fear to tread. For this debate — about the meaning of our work and the rationale for our paychecks — requires all the methodological legerdemain, exhaustive research, incisive analysis, clarity of expression, and originality of insight that students of Bibfeldt have long sought in his work — and so seldom found.

And yet. And yet. Perhaps in this debate our long-expressed confidence in Bibfeldt as a contributing scholar will be vindicated. For only recently a new manuscript has come to light, serendipitously recovered from the botany library of a small community college in northern South Dakota, where Bibfeldt's weighty considerations were being used, apparently, as a leaf press.

But we can be grateful that we have it now: Bibfeldt's own *Long Discourse on the Study of Theology, Philosophy of Religion, Scripture, Church History, Liturgy, Hymnody, Folk Music, Interpretive Dance, Pastoral Care, Parish Administration, Haberdashery, and Etiquette.*[1] Apparently the transcription of a filibuster by Bibfeldt at a faculty retreat high above Cayuga's waters some twenty years ago, the *Long Discourse* gives us a detailed look at Bibfeldt's vision of an educational institution suited to a theory of "Both/And" and a praxis of suffering.

And though it is somewhat daring, nay reckless, for a mere student such as myself to make her AAR debut by presenting material from the illustrious Bibfeldt, surely the advance of knowledge is more important than self-interest, as Bibfeldt has certainly taught us in his own life and practice. I shall confine my reading of the *Long Discourse* to the section that shows surprisingly original thought on Bibfeldt's part. Here, in abbreviated form, then, we have the discussion of "The Five Uses of the Doctoral Exams."

*   *   *

Introduction

We must do everything to establish the doctoral exams, and we must require work. We say that doctoral exams are good and useful, but only in their proper use. The doctoral exams are a light that illumines not

---

1. Hereafter referred to as *Long Discourse*.

the compassionate understanding of the faculty or the knowledge of the students, but the wrath of the faculty, the stupidity of the students and their condemnation in the sight of the faculty, and their possible expulsion. That is as far as the doctoral exams go. After that, the advisor and the job market take over.

1. Restraint of student sin and challenging the faculty

First, the university has ordained doctoral exams, indeed all exams, to restrain sin by preempting all the students' waking time and any of their sleep beyond a mere five hours. When students abstain from sin, they do not do this voluntarily or from the love of virtue but because the length of the bibliographies and their fear of failure leaves them no time to sin. Therefore, restraint from sin is not cleverness but rather an indication of stupidity. The doctoral exams make it abundantly clear that those who desire to take them are not clever but stupid, even insane.

This restraint is necessary and was instituted by the faculty in the interest of faculty time for research but especially to prevent the wisdom of faculty counsel from being hindered by the tumults and seditions of arrogant and ambitious students. This is particularly necessary because, when (through the doctoral exams) the students' stupidity and the wisdom and judgment of the faculty are revealed to them, it is impossible for them not to become impatient, murmur, and express hatred for the faculty and its superior wisdom. Students cannot endure the judgment of the faculty and their own possible failure, and yet they cannot flee, not if they wish to be gainfully employed. So they inevitably fall into blasphemous criticism against the faculty.

So the first function of the doctoral exams is this: at least by fear of punishment to restrain certain students who are untouched by any respect for their betters unless compelled by feeling the dire threat of the doctoral examination reading lists.

2. Destroy false confidence in students' knowledge and ability

What, then, is the second function of the doctoral exams? The destruction of self-confidence — a lovely function indeed! This is the primary purpose of the doctoral exams, that through them students' recognition of their stupidity might grow and become pervasive. Therefore, the chief and proper use of the doctoral exams is to reveal to students their inability, blindness, misery, wickedness, ignorance, arrogance, and contempt of the faculty, the university, and the hiring, tenure and promotion system. . . . Yet this use of the doctoral exams is completely unknown to the master's students, and to all second-year students who go along in the presumption of their own knowledge. But the entire group that has finished course work is crushed with fear. For student rationality becomes haughty with presumption of knowledge, and imagines that on account of this it is pleasing to the faculty; therefore the faculty has to send some Hercules, namely, the doctoral examination reading lists, to attack, subdue, and destroy with full force this monster, which is a rebellious, stubborn, and stiff-necked beast, and must learn that it has been destroyed and damned by its workload. Hence this use of the doctoral exams is extremely beneficial and necessary. For as long as the presumption of knowledge remains in a student, there remains immense pride, self-trust, smugness, hate of the faculty, contempt of faculty teaching schedules, and ignorance of the wisdom of the faculty.

The length of the doctoral examination reading lists takes away all self-esteem from the students. While it shows the faculty's knowledge, that is, the knowledge alone acceptable to the faculty, it warns, informs, convicts, and lastly condemns every student of his own ignorance. For students, blinded and drunk with self-love, not to mention cheap booze, must be compelled to know and confess their own feebleness and impurity. If students are not clearly convinced of their own ignorance, they are puffed up with insane confidence in their own mental powers and can never be induced to recognize their inanity as long as they measure themselves by a reading list of their own choice. But as soon as they begin to compare *their* reading lists with the faculty's lists, they have found something to diminish their bravado. For, however remarkable an opinion of their intelligence they formerly held, they soon know that they are panting under so heavy a weight of books, articles, commentaries, encyclopedias, and notebooks as to stagger and totter, and finally even to fall down and faint away. And they discover that they are a long way from wisdom, and are in fact teeming with a multitude of misconceptions, presuppositions, assumptions and fallacies of which they previously had not even heard. Thus students slough off the arrogance that previously blinded them and encouraged the faculty to admit them in the first place.

3. Drive students into the counsels of the faculty

Therefore, third, the doctoral exams are a preparation for true understanding. For then the faculty can be the guide of the humble, the
miserable, the afflicted, the desperate, and of those who have been
brought down to nothing at all. And it is the desire of the faculty to
exalt the humble, to enlighten the blind, to comfort the miserable and
afflicted, to educate the stupid, to give money to the deserving, and to
send those who are desperate and depressed to some other institution.

For we must say to the students: "After the doctoral exams have
humbled, terrified, and completely crushed you, so that you are on the
brink of despair, then see to it that you know how to use the doctoral
exams correctly; for their function and use is not only to disclose your
stupidity and the justified disgust of the faculty but also to drive you
to the faculty for guidance and a research topic." For the faculty's advice
is a light that illumines minds and makes them productive. It discloses
what the beneficence and the mercy of the faculty are; and what the
benefits of tenure are, and how we are to attain these.

This says that the faculty did not develop doctoral exams to
quench the dimly burning wick but to extend faculty counsel to the
students, to bind up the graduate fellow, and to proclaim a topic to the
ABD. But it takes work and labor for those who have been terrified and
bruised by the doctoral exams to be able to raise themselves up and to
say: "Now I have been crushed and troubled enough. The time of the
doctoral exams has caused me enough misery. Now it is time for listening to the faculty, from whose mouth there come messages of wisdom."
Now they are ready to be teaching assistants.

4. Initiate students into the discipline

While by the deeds of faculty judgment students are restrained at least
from outward rebellion, with minds yet untamed they progress but
slightly while studying for exams, yet become partially broken in by
bearing the burden of all those books. As a consequence, when they are
hired, they are not utterly untutored and uninitiated in academic discipline as if it were something unknown. Though they still have need
of a bridle to restrain them from so slackening the reins on the pursuit
of pleasure and relaxation as to go to the movies more than once a year.
So the doctoral exams are to the pleasure principle like a whip to an
idle and balky ass, to arouse it to work.

5. Lay hold of the promise of the goal

Fifth, the doctoral exams are the best instrument for students to learn more thoroughly each day the nature of the field to which they aspire, and to confirm them in our understanding of it. And not one of our students should escape from this necessity. For no student has heretofore attained to such wisdom as to be unable, from the daily instruction of an advisor, to make fresh progress toward a purer knowledge of the discipline. The teaching assistant will also avail himself of this benefit: by frequent meditation upon the influence of his advisor, to be aroused to obedience, to be strengthened in it, and to be drawn back from the slippery path of self-assertion. In this way the students must press on and lay hold not only of the texts, but the accompanying promise of future success, namely, a tenured full professorship in a university with no intercollegiate athletic program.

*   *   *

Thus the wisdom of Bibfeldt. But we who are veterans of doctoral exams know that Bibfeldt was wrong. Doctoral exams have but one sole and exclusive function: instruction in true knowledge of the good, the true, the beautiful and the holy. And concomitant with this knowledge comes the sure conviction that justification can never be attained by work. Now Bibfeldt's colleagues at the time recognized the severity of his error in greeting his proposals with a resounding "We'll think about it." Subsequently, another faculty member proposed a system quite different from Bibfeldt's, which upheld the one use of the doctoral exams, and it is this system which prevails in all graduate programs in religion even today. As many of us can and do attest from our own experience.

Both This World and the Next: A Sermon

ROBIN D. MATTISON

> Robin Mattison was a pastoral minister for some years before moving to the faculty of Lutheran Theological Seminary in Philadelphia. The Bibfeldt archives turn up this sermon preached July 16, 1978. It ought to dispel any notions held by readers of this book that there are no implications for practical theology or practical living in Bibfeldt's thought, or in what is the opposite of it, as the case may be. — ED.

Madison, WI
July 16, 1978

Dear Friends in Christ,

During this last month I have been vacationing all over the east coast visiting family and friends I have not seen since I moved. One of the persons I met for the first time was a cousin, about thirty-seven years old, who is an economist. I told him I was on my way to Washington, D.C., to participate with the Lutheran Church in America contingent at the rally for the Equal Rights Amendment. We fell into an intense conversation about my planned participation in the march, and his, for he was going too. He saw himself as a kind of lone-ranger ethicist, apart from any church, who mostly unsuccessfully and at best frustratingly was raising social concerns to the people with whom he worked. How — he wanted to know — could I, or he, bear to be involved with social justice issues with the odds, as he put it, so greatly against "Justice's favor"? More specifically, if the ERA failed, how would he ever find the energy to pursue any social justice issue again? And, of course, he wondered as well how I, as a woman, would be able to live with the weight of the nation rejecting equality.

There was an intensity about his questions and a sadness in his self-disclosures which told me that the failure or success of the ERA was precipitating a personal crisis of meaning. He was on the brink of burnout, an imminent casualty of the desire for justice.

The most serious questions he posed to me had to do with why I, who was as concerned about social justice issues as he, was not on the verge of exhaustion, for he saw I had no plans to give up concerns about civil rights even if the ERA *were* defeated. His concerns were clearly appropriate. Since the beginning of my career in ministry ten years ago, I had been raising the same kinds of questions. I felt impelled to push whatever issue was alive for me at the moment, and certain events such as the campus killings at Kent State and Jackson State or the invasion of Cambodia held sway over me and shook my Christian commitment in a major way. But today, I found, this was no longer true. I began to ponder why I wasn't out to singlehandedly save the world anymore. How could I communicate to him what had given me the strength to change? I thought back to all my experiences with Franz Bibfeldt.

Three decades ago and a little more, Dr. Franz Bibfeldt was discovered as the author of a magnum opus known as "The Theology of Both/And," or alternately titled "The Importance of All of the Above," which subsequently appeared in book reviews and library card catalogues. Nothing happened for a long time until the 1970s (these were my student days), but then he was apparently rediscovered. Conferences and parties began to be held in his honor, and his theological slogan of "Both/And" or a rousing "maybe" became known to all. But I, being one of Bibfeldt's loyal followers, prefer to say that he always existed in the hearts of true students of the gospel, if not always in their minds.

Two of Bibfeldt's favorite scriptural passages remain embedded in my mind. In Romans 13:1-10, Paul discusses Christian obligations to the governments that surround us, to the civil authorities that make possible life in community. One is not to deride, says Paul, the structures God offers that bring order and justice to all, Christian and non-Christian alike. In Matthew 22:15, Jesus lets us know that he was concerned that we not set Caesar over against God, either. Jesus uses the denarius handed to him by the Pharisees trying to entrap him as an occasion to expand on man's obligations to civil government and to God. If he says no tribute is owed to Caesar, the Pharisees are ready to catch him for being anti-Roman; if he says the taxes are owed to Caesar, they can catch him for being anti-Jew. But Jesus turned things around by responding in a way that Bibfeldt always loved, "*Give, both* to Caesar what is due Caesar, *and* to God what is due God." Taken completely by surprise, the Pharisees had to back off shamefacedly. Of course, they naturally expected "Either/Or" statements from Jesus. In fact, Judas expected the same: *either* Jesus was to be Messiah-Revolutionary *or* he was in some way against God's people. High priest Caiaphas fell into the same trap of opposite expectations of the faith. *Either* one compromised with the occupying forces of Rome *or* one couldn't save Judaism.

By meditating on these passages, Bibfeldt was inspired to create the theology of "Both/And." Jesus and Paul demonstrated for Bibfeldt three key relationships necessary for the faithful: *both* this world *and* the next; *both* church *and* state; *both* sinfulness *and* righteousness. (A fourth relationship had to do with Scripture itself. Bibfeldt opined that believers were required to read *both* the chapter preceding *and* the chapter following the passage they were actually studying!)

As naturally as was to be expected, reactions to Bibfeldt were *both* strong *and* mixed. While many were relieved to find "Both/And" as part of the theology of the church, others in the believing community were uncomfortable. Theirs was a theology of "Either/Or" as central to the Good News. They stood for *either* law *or* gospel; *either* this world *or* the next; *either* sinful *or* righteous America — *either* love it *or* leave it; *either* convert *or* be damned; *either* set church over state *or* make church separate from state; *either* be a Christian *or* a politician; *either* fight in the war *or* stop calling yourself a Christian! In other words, conflict points were unending.

Meanwhile, Bibfeldt hastened to assure his readers that there were *both* situations where "Either/Or" theology was fitting *and* plenty of situations where "Either/Or" was unfitting for faithfulness. "Either/Or" theology tended to make people unhappy, anxious, defensive and frustrated. Why? Because it posited life as a win/lose situation where one must achieve a certain status, promote a certain lifestyle, etc., before one could truly be loved by God or anyone else. If life was merely a Darwinian struggle of competing forces/forms to be the fittest, then the ability to marshal the most resources, whatever they might be, in order to come out on top was irrefutable proof of righteousness.

As I declared to my cousin when I saw him apparently embroiled in the midst of the "Either/Or" struggle, "What you're really saying when you say '*either* the ERA passes *or* there is no justice' is that the civil loss means a great sense of personal failure for you." If he continued to hold this position, I knew he was on the verge of departing from a life of commitment to one of apathy.

So I decided, right then and there, to share with him how Bibfeldt's theology of "Both/And" had changed my whole conception of the church. Since the church had become for me the community where "Both/And" is the primary realm of discourse, I now saw possibilities opening before me of an ever-widening horizon wherein existed the promise of blending *both* past experience of Israel/God *and* the influx of Christ's kingdom occupying the ever-present moment inundated with hopes of a holy future. This made possible the concept of a community where one entertains *both* glamour *and* terror of tradition, where traditional antagonists of creation — races, sexes, old, young, healthy, ill, educated, illiterate — are summoned by a God found in the symbols of each and all. Intercessory prayer thus is made *both* for the success of social justice causes *and* for the casualties later found on both sides. No doubt new situations may bring new casualties, but I found real freedom in a community committed to support all persons where lone-rangers, such as I had been and as my cousin saw himself, were offered love and support necessary for their compassion to prosper, regardless of their positions or stations.

Thus I began a dialogue with my cousin. Not that he returned to the fold at that moment. I had not asked him that, for that would have violated his integrity as a God-child with the implicit demand, *"either* come back to Jesus *or* else." But seeds were sown on receptive soil; the denarius was seen *both* as Caesar's *and* God's. A way to wholeness was pointed out, and all by virtue of Bibfeldt's "Both/And." I knew he understood much of what Bibfeldt was about. I knew he understood the freedom of "Both/And," the thoughtfully considered "maybe," over against diatribes of *either* right *or* left. All things are possible — for him, for me, for you. Luther knew it, as did Bibfeldt.

This life, therefore, is not righteousness, but growth in righteousness, not health but healing, not being but becoming, not rest but exercise. . . . This is not the end, but it is the road. All does not yet gleam in glory, but all is being purified.

Theologian of the Year, 1994

Each year, *The Door,* a.k.a. *The Wittenburg Door,* an evangelical magazine, gives out its coveted "Theologian of the Year" award. One well-known recipient, for example, was Tammy Faye Bakker of televangelism and mascara fame, who flourished in the 1970s and 1980s and is now forgotten. For its 1994 "Theologian of the Year" award, *The Door* climaxed its sequence by honoring Bibfeldt, many years after he should have received the award. — ED.

He is conservative. He is liberal. He is fundamentalist. He is politically correct. He is patriarchal. He is feminist, hear him roar. When he is in England, he is an evangelical Anglican. When he is in Rome, he is a Catholic. When he is in Switzerland, he is Reformed.

He is Franz Bibfeldt, ecclesiastical chameleon.

He is *The Door*'s 1994 Theologian of the Year.

Bibfeldt is the ideal theologian for the Inoffensive '90s — a truly sensitive decade in which the cardinal sin is offending people. He is the maestro of wishy-washiness — an expert in the fine art of pleasing people, staying relevant, and playing both sides of the fence.

As the esteemed church historian Martin Marty once put it, "Bibfeldt is the complete theologian because he is capable of engaging in complete reversals of positions, depending upon the Zeitgeist."

Bibfeldt is also something of a legend at the University of Chicago, where theological heavyweights gather each year to celebrate Bibfeldt Day with sausage, sauerkraut, and beer. The Donnelley printing family, which has established numerous Chairs for faculty positions, has even made possible a Bibfeldt Stool. The Stool is endowed for $29.95 — a generous fee that

FRANZ BIBFELDT

He came, he saw, he compromised

by Doug Peterson

goes to the person who has the nerve to deliver the annual Bibfeldt lecture.

Bibfeldt's first exposure in the United States was a humble one, coming in 1947 when he was mentioned in the footnote of a student's paper at Concordia Seminary. Not many Americans have had the honor of meeting the great Bibfeldt in person, but he has regularly shown up in bookstore catalogs, Chicago White Sox programs, television credits, and motel marquees. He is also registered with the American Kennel Club as owning an invisible white-haired terrier.

Over the years, Bibfeldt has been showered with accolades, including signed photos from the late Mayor Richard Daley of Chicago, former Vice President Spiro Agnew, and former Senator Charles Percy.

But why all of the attention for this humble theologian, born in 1897 in Sage-Hast bei Groszenkneten, Oldenburg, Niedersachsen, Germany?

Because Bibfeldt is a genius ... or so they say.

Marty once pointed out a truth expressed by F. Scott Fitzgerald: "The test of a first-rate intelligence is the ability to hold two opposed ideas in the mind at the same time

and still retain the ability to function."

"On those terms," Marty said, "Franz Bibfeldt is the proper theologian for tomorrow."

So here is the lowdown on this 20th Century master, drawn from numerous sources — Bibfeldt lectures, press clippings, archival materials, graffiti, etc:

Date Of Baptism: Nov. 1, 1897 — All Saints Day. Bibfeldt's parents chose All Saints Day because they did not want to offend any of the saints.

Boyhood Dream: To be an athlete. Bibfeldt's ability to walk down the middle on all sensitive issues made him a talented gymnast on the balance beam. But when he flunked Indian clubs in disgrace, Bibfeldt gave up sports for theology.

Bibfeldt's Most Regrettable Mistake: Jumping when his opponent

in a dueling match was making a thrust. The resulting scar, which he has never been able to show to anyone but his wife, led to his landmark essay, "Empathy With The Circumcised."

Family Coat of Arms: It features Proteus standing on a weather vane. Proteus, the herdsman of the gods, was terrified of prophesying; and to avoid it, he would keep changing shapes. The Bibfeldt Coat Of Arms also includes the family slogan written in Spanish: "I dance to the tune that is played." Unfortunately, the slogan created a major diplomatic crisis in Japan when it was mistranslated as "Sushi makes me hurl."

Bibfeldt's Most Talked-About Writing: His dissertation, "The Problem With The Year Zero," which noted that no year exists between 1 B.C. and 1 A.D. Disturbed that the cal-

> **H**e is conservative. He is liberal. He is fundamentalist. He is politically correct. He is patriarchal. He is feminist, hear him roar. When he is in England, he is an evangelical Anglican. When he is in Rome, he is a Catholic. When he is in Switzerland, he is Reformed. He is Franz Bibfeldt, ecclesiastical chameleon.

endar had moved two years when only one year had passed, Bibfeldt spent the rest of his life showing up for events either one year early or one year late.

Bibfeldt's Most Significant Contribution To Social Activism: His efforts to help our country's most oppressed group — the truly silent majority — the dead. Bibfeldt fought against housing discrimination for the dead, noting that they invariably end up in low, one-room dark chambers in ghettoized sections of town. He also tackled the potentially divisive issue of ordination of the dead, and he did much to encourage the evangelical dead, who practice inert healing and live by the slogan, "died again."

Most of his thoughts on this issue can be found in the ground-breaking essay, "I'm OK, You're DOA."

Bibfeldt's Most Perceptive Statement About Soren Kierkegaard's Angst-Filled Theology: "It's nothing that a month in Acapulco wouldn't cure."

Bibfeldt's Best Response To Kierkegaard's Book, *Either/Or*: Bibfeldt responded by writing *Both/And*, which argued that contemporary theologians can be "relevant to everything and adapt to anything." When *Both/And* was criticized for not taking a firm stand, Bibfeldt countered with *Both/And And/Or Either/Or*.

Bibfeldt's Favorite Game Shows: "Leap of Faith," in which contestants climb up Jacob's Ladder by means of empirical evidence for design in the natural world before making the "Leap of Faith" across the chasm of despair to the postulation of a beneficent divine Creator for major cash prizes. Also: "Zen Master," a quiz in which the winner is the first contestant to stop attempting to answer the questions.

Favorite Books By Or About Bibfeldt: *Calvinistic Existentialism: Predestined To Eternal Insecurity* (Decree Publishing, 1971); *Staying On Your Toes: Religious Podiatry In The Soul Of John Bunyan* (Cuticle Press, 1988); and *How Many Pinheads Can Dance On An Angel? Scholastic Metaphysics In A Post-Bibfeldtian World* (Reductio Ad Absurdam Press, 1989).

Bibfeldt's Best Attempt At Proving That White European Males Have Been Victimized By Society, Too: He introduced a measure before the German Bundestag titled "A Declaration Of Human Rights For The Ethnically Impaired," a manifesto for the melanin-deprived. Said one observer: "When the mea-

sure failed, although not by much, Bibfeldt was shaken, not stirred."

If this is not enough evidence of the tremendous influence of this singular theologian, then consider Bibfeldt's impact on the field of church history. When a much younger Martin Marty published a review of Bibfeldt's work in a 1951 seminary newspaper, his assignment to London was canceled because of "a lack of maturity." As a result, Marty wound

up in Chicago, where he went on to author close to forty books and thousands of articles, and became a leading authority on the contemporary Church.

Bibfeldt has a way of doing that — changing careers and altering the course of history. But what else do you expect from a theologian of his stature? After all, Bibfeldt is truly a genius. Or, as one Bibfeldt scholar put it, "On the surface he is profound. Deep down he is shallow." ■

The Faces of Bibfeldt

21

A Gallery of Bibfeldt Admirers

Through the years, agents of the Bibfeldt Foundation have acquired celebrity autographs from innocents to Bibfeldt. The Percy and Bernardin autographed publicity photos stand apart because these celebrities seem to be aware that Bibfeldt has a special status on the borderline between fiction and faction. In the argot of the day, they seem to be "in" on the Foundation's lore in a way that the late Mayor Daley and governor Lester Maddox were not. — ED.

To: F.B.
who taught M.M.
everything he knows.
+JLB

To Franz
Bibfeldt—
mentor.] [my Braun and Merton Strietz
a magnificent theologian who stood on
son from April 1 85 Gustav getting
sangh on comman] [from an salen
[   ] Charles Powers

Bibfeldt and the Media

While the Bibfeldt Foundation never seeks publicity, the annual Bibfeldt events have been too visible not to be covered on occasion by Chicago newspaper reporters and sometimes their more remote kin. At times mass communicators in the world of radio and television have also paid attention. From the archives of the Regenstein Library, the University of Chicago, we bring forth several samples. — ED.

CHICAGO DAILY NEWS, Thursday, May 13, 1976

Hail to Franz! UC honors theologian who never was

By James H. Bowman
Daily News Religion Writer

The University of Chicago Divinity School honored one of its best-loved and least-known theologians Wednesday in the annual day of appreciation for Franz Bibfeldt.

Students and faculty, including Dean Joseph Kitigawa and Associate Dean Martin E. Marty, gathered in the dark-paneled Commons Room of Swift Hall to proclaim Bibfeldt's praises.

Instigator of the little-known doctrine of the "was-ness of God" and promoter of the "Both-And" theology, Bibfeldt was hailed by student speakers for his adaptability and relevance.

"His was a theology of 'desiring to please,'" said one of a half a dozen speakers who trooped to the commons podium in the after-

main of a bratwurst-and-sauerkraut and baked potato lunch.

A COPY OF FORMER presidential aide Charles Colson's book "Born Again," which tells Colson's post-Watergate conversion to Christianity, was given to a student in Bibfeldt's honor.

It carried an inscription to the recipient said to be written by Colson himself, complete with reference to Bibfeldt.

Out in the Swift Hall foyer, a display cabinet was filled with Bibfeldt memorabilia, including signed photographs of Mayor Richard J. Daley, former Vice President Spiro Agnew, Sen. Charles Percy and former Georgia Gov. Lester Maddox.

All were "inscribed" to Bibfeldt. So was a picture of the 1971 Playmate of the Year.

There was a letter from a Catholic chancery official dated October, 1971, saying Pope

saying he was interested in a Bibfeldt book—all the way back in 1951.

THERE WAS EVERYTHING to Wednesday's festivities but Franz Bibfeldt, who wasn't there. He wasn't anywhere, in fact, and never was.

Bibfeldt is a creature of a divinity student's imagination, born in 1947. That student was Martin E. Marty—who is a dean and teaches at the University of Chicago Divinity School and has written many books on church history.

The Rev. Dr. Marty created Bibfeldt as a hoax meant to confound the theologians who dared to take himself too seriously.

He was caught up a few times in the trap of his own making Wednesday as students told how Bibfeldt would have praised Dr. Marty's recent book "Pro and Con of Religious America" for its yes-and-no spirit.

Paul VI would be unable to come to that year's Bibfeldt celebration.

There was a wire from a church publisher

Martin E. Marty

BUT MOST OF THE TALK centered on Bibfeldt's contributions to theological lore.

● He adjusted the Sermon on the Mount to fit the American ethos, making it "Blessed are the happy who have everything, because they won't need to be comforted" and "Blessed are the impeccably dressed, because they will look nice when they see God."

● He adapted P. T. Barnum's "A sucker is born every minute," adding, "But one is 'born again' every half-minute."

● He had Jesus saying in the Sermon on the Mount, "I'm Jesus Christ and you're not."

Biographically speaking, Bibfeldt was "born in a Volkswagen trunk of a fundamentalist Protestant bishop-father and a Roman Catholic mother with Pentecostal leanings and in his youth he "sowed wild oats during the week and prayed on Sunday for crop failure," according to speakers.

Spirit of Franz Bibfeldt alive—altho he never was

By James Robison
Religion Editor

MAYOR DALEY, Ed Hanrahan, former Georgia Gov. Lester Maddox, and Playboy's 1971 Playmate of the Year may be surprised to find themselves in the midst of a religious hoax that dates from 1947 and lives today.

But there they all are, their pictures lining the glass case of the entry hall of the University of Chicago Divinity School. Each picture carries an authentic signature and greeting to a theologian who never existed: Franz Bibfeldt.

The signed pictures reportedly had been obtained by a direct request to each personality that he send greetings in honor of the theologian.

"To Franz Bibfeldt—a great and esteemed theologian," wrote Mayor Daley on his autographed picture.

"TO FRANZ Bibfeldt—May we put the universal principles of religion into politics and enjoy true peace among all men" was the greeting from Ed Hanrahan.

Ald. Roman Pucinski beamed forth from a picture autographed by the former congressman: "To Franz Bibfeldt, who is an inspiration to all of us."

The chief architect of the hoax—Dr. Martin E. Marty, associate dean of the divinity school—said he and others have tried to get an autographed photo of the Pope with appropriate greetings to the imaginary theologian Bibfeldt.

BUT A LETTER in the showcase of Bibfeldt memorabilia tells of their failure to bring the pontiff into the hoax.

"I do not feel we could ask the Pope to become involved at this time," read a letter signed by someone [whose name had been blocked out "to protect the innocent"] in the Chicago Archdiocesan Office of the Chancellor.

The hoax began when Dr. Marty was a student at Concordia Seminary in St. Louis in the late 1940s.

TODAY, IT has snowballed into a monumental spoof on theologians worldwide who ofttimes take themselves far too seriously, Dr. Marty said.

This week, the theological takeoff led to the award of an

Robert M. Grant

Martin E. Marty

honorary Franz Bibfeldt degree to Robert M. Grant, New Testament scholar, and a professor at the school, at a Wednesday student-faculty luncheon.

"Bob's whole quest is to say it simply," said Dr. Marty, explaining why Prof. Grant received this year's award. "He's a very erudite man but he gets upset with the jargon, pomposity, and the goobledygook of some theologians."

Dr. Marty said he doesn't like to refer to the Bibfeldt spoof as a hoax because it has never been meant in a "cruel way. We use him very mildly, gently, to satirize the whole

theological system. There's really no malice in it."

It started when a classmate of Dr. Marty's devised a fake footnote citing Franz Bibfeldt in a term paper at Concordia Seminary. The student received an "A" on the paper.

LATER, DR. MARTY, as one of the editors of the seminary magazine, wrote a book review of the imaginary theologian's book, "The Relieved Paradox."

The 1951 review sent several professors scurrying to the library for a copy of the Bibfeldt book and one reportedly even quoted seriously from Bibfeldt in a lecture.

The perpetrators of the Bibfeldt hoax then furthered it by conspiring with the seminary librarian to put catalog cards in the library files; but, of course, the books were always checked out.

When the hoax was discovered, Dr. Marty and friends were called to the seminary president's office for reprimands. Dr. Marty lost his special student assignment to London because he allegedly lacked maturity.

INSTEAD, Dr. Marty was given a church assignment in Chicago where he promptly began graduate theological training leading to his eventual appointment at the University of Chicago.

For that reason, Dr. Marty said, "I say that Bibfeldt had more influence on me than any other theologian."

Referring to the days when the hoax began, Dr. Marty said: "In that decade, our problem was a restrictive, formal theological system. Bibfeldt was intended to take the formality out of the system and soften it."

Today, he said, Bibfeldt serves to attack a more current problem, "theologians who have to be relevant to everybody and everything."

The gospel according to 'Franz Bibfeldt': A divine inspiration

By Clarence Petersen

SHORTLY BEFORE noon, an unusually long line had formed outside the dining room in Swift Hall, the building that houses the University of Chicago Divinity School, and on this day last week held the 1983 Franz Bibfeldt Festival, a satire that has evolved over more than 30 years.

In the adjoining foyer, visitors inspected a glass-topped case containing tributes to Bibfeldt from the late Mayor Richard J. Daley, from Ald. Roman Pucinski and from Playboy's 1971 Playmate of the Year.

There, too, were displayed learned tracts on Bibfeldtian theology and other memorabilia, including what purports to be the May 1, 1978, issue of Newsweek, its cover story headlined "The Pastoral Theology of Franz Bibfeldt."

Few Newsweek subscribers, to say nothing of Newsweek editors, will recall that issue of the magazine, but no recent University of Chicago divinity student is likely to forget it.

NEARLY THE ENTIRE divinity school faculty and student body turned out last week to pay homage to Bibfeldt and hence to the principle that it is one thing to make fun of religion, quite another to make fun of theologians.

An imaginary theologian, Bibfeldt has become a kind of patron ain't of divinity scholars, one of whom, the university's Dr. Martin E. Marty, was present at the creation [the creation of Bibfeldt, that is] and even as an undergraduate at Concordia [Lutheran] Seminary, St. Paul, Minn., became a Bibfeldt apostle.

Though little is known of Bibfeldt outside theological circles, Prof. Jerald Brauer of the divinity school [and chairman of the Bibfeldt Foundation] has introduced Bibfeldtian theology to such internationally known philosophers as Paul Tillich, Joseph Sittler, Karl Barth and Cardinal Leo-Josef Suenens, none of whom is believed to have been unduly impressed.

Theologian Jaroslav Pelikan, the author of "From Luther to Kierkegaard," once announced his intention to write a sequel called "From Kierkegaard to Bibfeldt." Somehow he never got around to it.

BIBFELDT FIRST came to light in the late 1940s

Continued on page 5

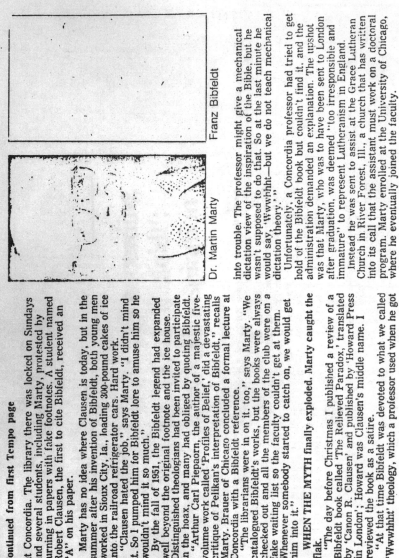

Dr. Martin Marty

Franz Bibfeldt

Continued from first Tempo page

at Concordia. The library there was locked on Sundays and several students, including Marty, protested by turning in papers with fake footnotes. A student named Robert Clausen, the first to cite Bibfeldt, received an "A" on his paper.

Marty has no idea where Clausen is today, but in the summer after his invention of Bibfeldt, both young men worked in Sioux City, Ia., loading 300-pound cakes of ice into the railroad refrigerator cars. Hard work.

"Clausen hated the job," says Marty. "I didn't mind it. So I pumped him for Bibfeldt lore to amuse him so he wouldn't mind it so much."

By the fall of 1951, the Bibfeldt legend had expanded well beyond the original footnote and the ice house. Distinguished theologians had been invited to participate in the hoax, and many had obliged by quoting Bibfeldt.

"Arthur Carl Piepaorn, the author of a majestic five-volume work called 'Profiles of Belief,' did a devastating critique of Pelikan's interpretation of Bibfeldt," recalls Marty. Brauer of Chicago concluded a formal lecture at Concordia with a Bibfeldt reference.

"The librarians were in on it, too," says Marty. "We catalogued Bibfeldt's works, but the books were always checked out and all the members of the club were on a fake waiting list so the faculty couldn't get at them. Whenever somebody started to catch on, we would get him into it."

WHEN THE MYTH finally exploded, Marty caught the flak.

"The day before Christmas I published a review of a Bibfeldt book called 'The Relieved Paradox,' translated by 'Canon R. Clausen' and published by 'Howard Press in London'; Howard was Clausen's middle name. I reviewed the book as a satire.

"At that time Bibfeldt was devoted to what we called 'Wwwhhht' theology, which a professor used when he got

into trouble. The professor might give a mechanical dictation view of the inspiration of the Bible, but he wasn't supposed to do that. So at the last minute he would say, 'Wwwhhht—but we do not teach mechanical dictation theory.' "

Unfortunately, a Concordia professor had tried to get hold of the Bibfeldt book but couldn't find it, and the administration demanded an explanation. The upshot was that Marty, who was to have been sent to London after graduation, was deemed "too irresponsible and immature" to represent Lutheranism in England.

Instead he was sent to assist at the Grace Lutheran Church in River Forest, Ill., a church that has written into its call that the assistant must work on a doctoral program. Marty enrolled at the University of Chicago, where he eventually joined the faculty.

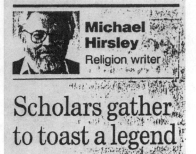

Michael Hirsley
Religion writer

Scholars gather to toast a legend

Once upon a time, there was a newspaper religion writer who was bombarded by letters, notes, calls and other expressions from those who knew the Truth.

Actually, it was just last week. One claimant's inerrant religion was another's cult of falsehood. One's "interesting document" was another's "lost gospel." One prophesied an imminent end of the world, while another insisted the end is nowhere in sight. Everyone cited Scripture.

Comforted by similar selective uses of Scriptures, others offered the Absolute Truth about when life begins, when and what kind of sexual expression is acceptable, and a host of other virtues and sins. A few claimed to speak for, or to actually be, the Messiah.

Discomfitted by all the pious truths, the religion writer muttered to no one in particular, "What part of absolute don't you understand?"

He quickly realized that such an unsympathetic reaction was symptomatic of a larger disease: He had spring fever.

And, as in springtimes past, it was time to visit his favorite theologian.

Franz Bibfeldt has been elusive over the years. But it's a good bet you can catch up with the storied theologian if you just hang around the University of Chicago Divinity School awhile in the first few weeks of spring.

The religion writer parked his car at one of the many "who-knows-if-it's illegal?" curbs on campus, and followed a line of students cutting across a lawn. Near his feet, he noticed a small yellow diamond-shaped sign that read "Holy Martyrs Crossing Only." He gave it due respect as more erudite, but no more effective, than "Keep Off the Grass."

Entering Swift Hall, he checked the religion-related announcements and circulars. There was no immediate sign of Bibfeldt. But clues soon emerged.

A motley line of men and women, young and old, was being hustled into a dining hall, apparently in hopes of not attracting too much attention. But before the door could be shut, out wafted the aroma of sausage and kraut, the unmistakable scent of Sage-Hast bei Groszenknetten, Oldenburg, Niedersachsen, Germany ... the birthplace of Bibfeldt!

The religion writer slipped inside before the assemblage shut itself off from the outside world. And no sooner was he settled at one of the wooden tables decorated with quart bottles of beer than the luncheon speaker's words reassured him that his quest was realized:

Chicago Tribune
16 April 1993

"... Bibfeldt was conceived in the back seat of an old Volkswagen on Feb. 2 after a Candlemas Party in which his father, Friedrich, and his mother, Brunhilda, had apparently thrown all caution, along with their fin-de-siecle prophylactics, to the winds. ..."

As is customary in Bibfeldt lectures, the theologian's early years and initial scholarship were recounted at length while dozens of devotees noshed and imbibed, priming their bodies and minds for this ritual update, known as Bibfeldtian Bullsgeschichte.

Appropriately chosen for this spring's lecture on "The Politically Correct Fundamentalism of Franz Bibfeldt," was R. Scott Appleby, co-director of the Fundamentalism Project at the University of Chicago. Appleby was fresh from making a bunch of TV appearances, including "Nightline," to discuss religious fundamentalism.

He and co-director Martin Marty, professor of modern Christian history at the U. of C., are editing the Project's series of books on religious fundamentalism. Their scholarly subject has become current news, entwined with headlines from Eastern Europe to New York City.

Appleby reminded luncheon guests that timing is everything while fame, particularly media infatuation, is fleeting. What better example, he noted, than Bibfeldt.

Suffering from a rare condition known as calendar-impairment, Bibfeldt habitually wrote about trends, new ideas and other "scholarshtick" observations a year or so after they had been documented elsewhere.

When Bibfeldt chose to slow down more than a decade ago, Appleby said, "references to 'the late Franz Bibfeldt' began to appear in the previously favorable smut press" and his whereabouts became "shrouded less in a veil of secrecy than in a fog of apathy about his comings and goings."

But Appleby and Marty have picked up Bibfeldt's trail and found it remarkably similar, albeit several years behind, their own: Bibfeldt aspires to become an expert on global fundamentalism.

He has been hampered but undaunted in this endeavor, Appleby said, by his lifelong commitment to "a sliding scale of inerrancy" and to "dance to the tune that is played;" and by his admission that "he didn't know a Shiite from a Levite, a Rig-Veda from a Chevy Vega, the Koran from the Koresh. ..."

What sort of man is this revered theologian? Well, put it this way: Reports of Bibfeldt's death are no more exaggerated than those of his existence.

He's a figment of the imaginations of a couple of seminarians who created him 46 years ago as a hoax. One of them was Marty, and he's kept Bibfeldt alive in legend and lectures ever since, to poke fun at both academe and theology. This year, the challenge was accepted by Appleby, perhaps with the knowledge that he's leaving for the University of Notre Dame next year.

Absolute Truth may set you free, but it doesn't always turn you loose.

Dateline America for Sunday, April 13, 1975

Dateline America. I'm Charles Kuralt reporting on the CBS Radio Network. The inspiring story of real estate pioneer Bill Edwards, theologian Franz Bibfeldt, and Professor Josiah Carberry, in a moment.

COMMERCIAL

Dateline, Chicago Illinois. In 1973, Bill Edwards died while investigating a drug ring operating between Hong Kong and Metuchen, New Jersey. At his alma mater, Davidson College, North Carolina, his name and image were enshrined in a memorial. Bill Edwards, real estate pioneer, researcher into zero gravity, millionaire and patriot, was gone. More than that, it was revealed the other day, Bill Edwards never had been. The storied young bachelor was a hoax perpetuated by the jolly class of 1953. At Davidson, they're busy dememorializing old Bill.

They needn't feel bad. Consider the case of Professor Josiah S. Carberry of Brown University. Since 1929, Professor Carberry's penchant for exotic travel has been reported in the Brown Alumni Bulletin, and his treatises have appeared in scholarly journals. Only recently, the aging professor contributed a long thesis on his research into rotatable laboratories for revolutionary experiments. Every time it is reported that Professor Carberry has passed on, he writes an angry letter from Bulgaria or Mozambique denying it.

In the entry hall of the University of Chicago Divinity School, there is a framed picture of Mayor Daley autographed, "To Franz Bibfeldt, a great and esteemed theologian." Alderman Roman Pucinski signed his picture, "To Franz Bibfeldt, who is an inspiration to us all." There are similar greetings from Lester Maddox and from *Playboy's* 1971 Playmate of the Year. Franz Bibfeldt was born as a fake footnote in a term paper in 1940. Reviews of his book, *The Relieved Paradox,* have appeared in print, but those who tried to locate the book at the University of Chicago Library found that it was always checked out. Dr. Bibfeldt's friends at the University say he is used very mildly, gently, to satirize the system. There's no malice in it. Nor, of course, is there malice in the heroic Davidson real estate pioneer, Bill Edwards, nor in the globetrotting Brown University Professor Carberry. They are free spirits in a stuffy world, and in a way, Roman Pucinski was right. They *are* an inspiration to all of us. Now this message.

COMMERCIAL

This has been Dateline America. I'm Charles Kuralt, CBS News.

THE UNIVERSITY OF CHICAGO
CHICAGO · ILLINOIS 60637
THE DIVINITY SCHOOL ASSOCIATION

~~The Divinity School Alumni~~

11 July 1975 ↑

Mr. Charles Collingwood
CBS Radio News
524 W. 57th Street
New York, N.Y. 10019

Dear Mr. Collingwood: *Foundation*

We of the Franz Bibfeldt are always interested and grateful
when our mentor receives publicity, even when placed in
the pejorative category of "hoax." Therefore, we were
very interested to learn from Martin Marty that Professor
Bibfeldt was one of the subjects of a "Dateline America"
report by you on April 14, 1975.

Having endured years of talk about hoax, and much ridicule
from those who abjure his insights, we now follow the
example of Bibfeldt himself (who feels replying to criticism
to be a violation of his hard fought-for ambiguity) and
accept all publicity as worthwhile and gratifying.

Therefore, would it be possible for us to receive a
copy of the script of that April 14 broadcast for our
archives. We would be very grateful.

Sincerely,

Dennis L. Landon, President
The Franz Bibfeldt Society

cc: Martin E. Marty

PS: It is a further disappointment to us that CBS joined
the other networks in their obtuse refusal to cover
Professor Bibfeldt's latest North American visit to
deliver the Crater Lectures at John Jay College.

**CBS
NEWS**

A Division of CBS Inc.
524 West 57 Street
New York, New York 10019
(212) 765-4321

24 July 1975

Dear Mr. Landon:

I am very sorry to say that it was not I who made the broadcast on Dr. Bibfeldt (whom the Lord preserves), but I wish I had. However, because of the reverent tone of your letter and my own theological instincts, I have tracked it down.

The author was Charles Kuralt, a colleague of mine who understands these matters better than I. I enclose the transcript you requested.

Yours sincerely,

Charles Collingwood

Toasts to Bibfeldt

At various Bibfeldt observances over the years, various faculty members (for example, Langdon Gilkey) and various students (for example, Joseph Bessler-Northcutt) have taken their turn at toasting the absent scholar and the gathering. We provide samples.

One such event was a standout. Jerald C. Brauer accepted the Donnelley Stool of Bibfeldt Studies. We reprint the reprintable part of his remarks. — ED.

Toasting the Donnelley Stool

[Jerald Brauer's toast on the Donnelley Stool]

On behalf of the Franz Bibfeldt Foundation, I want to thank Nina Hermann Donnelley, who is present for this presentation, and her husband, James Donnelley, who attends most Bibfeldt gatherings. As is well known, either or both of the Donnelleys will be present in years to come, bringing with them a Christmas stocking that holds the annual yield of the endowment they are offering with this Donnelley Stool in Bibfeldt Studies: $29.95. This is a fixed rate, perhaps the only fixed item in the whole Bibfeldt world. most of all, however, the Foundation appreciates the gift of this fine antique three-legged stool.

Mrs. Donnelley has done Bibfeldt research for some years. In her days as a television reporter, she began to gather memorabilia, including many of the autographs of the eminent admirers of Franz Bibfeldt. Today's endowment and gift of the Donnelley Stool are testimonies to her own admiration for him.

I quote from Bibfeldt's first translated work: "The stool is present from the beginning and will be at the end." A little child sits on a stool. Martin Luther got some of his theological revolutions on a different kind of stool. And when we are old and frail in the legs, as is Franz Bibfeldt, we find that a portable stool comes in handy as we work in the library or attend parades.

In his preface to the cited work, Bibfeldt engaged in his favorite method of comparing and contrasting simple objects from daily life in order to make profound theological observations. In one example, he contrasted chairs — of which the University has two Donnelleys, one of which I occupy — this way: "Chairs are for sitting, stools are for — thinking. Concentration is a problem for the theologian. I sit on my stool and find great thoughts coming my way, as they did to many of my predecessors."

It is fitting that we in the Windy City accept the Donnelley Stool in Bibfeldt Studies. Many know that it is here that Mrs. O'Leary took a stool out into the shed and lit up the whole city. Let us hope that the establishment of the Stool will lead to what Paul Tillich had in mind in a book entitled *The Shaking of the Foundations*, whose tremors will be felt wherever people think.

The Bibfeldt Foundation accepts the Stool in trust, promising to keep it span and spic, ready and polished for use at all times, especially at events such as this one. I propose this as a toast to the Donnelleys and to the absent professor.

A Tribute

Langdon Gilkey

Those of us who have both followed and led the career of Franz Bibfeldt, who have both respected and despised, both read and ignored his work, are both appreciative and saddened by your appearance here today, yesterday, and tomorrow. We both think and feel that both anything and everything (and even nothing) which brings greater fame and infamy to our beloved Bibfeldt is to be both cherished and disregarded. In both the long and the short of it, therefore, we say both thanks and no thanks.

It is the custom that great men of the academy are often honored by the publication of a *Festschrift*; and so it is that those of us who have stood in awe of the achievement of Franz Bibfeldt have a place in this program.

The publication of the *Festschrift* has been an extremely difficult task because the relief paradox requires, of course, that virtually all positions and perspectives be included. Yet, with the current state of the publishing industry, no publisher was willing to take on *that* task. In other words, we were in need of the utilization of the relief paradox itself. We really are quite proud of the results of our efforts. We have contributions from, in the arts: Sir Walter Scott, Alfred Lord Tennyson, William Wordsworth, Robert Browning, Jonathan Swift, Robert Burns, Verdi, Kipling, Byron, and King Lear; from the world of the bench we have contributions from Oliver Wendell Holmes and Louis Brandeis; and from politics we have Prime Minister William Gladstone, President James Buchanan, Aaron Burr, Alexander Hamilton, Benjamin Franklin, Winston Churchill and President Warren Harding. Our only regret was that we could not get a theologian to make a contribution. Yet with all these contributions we have a book of exactly 150 pages.

So at this time it gives me great pleasure to present to you a *Festschrift* in honor of Franz Bibfeldt, requesting that you give it to him whenever you see him next. The title — as I uncover the original copy — is appropriate more to Bibfeldt's character than to the many subjects to which he was drawn. But better that we capture the husk than the essence (to recall Bibfeldt's own response to Harnack), the title is *The Sensuous Dirty Old Man,* which in its own way is not so much a paradox as it is undoubtedly a relief.

LANGDON GILKEY
Nov. 1, 1972

On Reading Bibfeldt: A Toast

Joseph Bessler-Northcutt

Only those who have dealt with China, where dignitaries offer a formal toast per minute, will have any sense of how much is communicated through toasts to Bibfeldt. Sometimes whole hermeneutical discoveries get uncorked with the champagne at Bibfeldt events. In this tribute from one such event, Joseph Bessler-Northcutt offers advice based on theory and discovery. The adjective "Ricoeurian" refers to philosopher Paul Ricoeur's suggestion that scholars should not only study the world "behind" the text, as historians do, or the world "of" the text as literary artists do; they should study the world "in front of" the text. But how, in Bibfeldt's case? — ED.

Rather than fix our attention on any one particular work of Bibfeldt today, I will articulate instead what I consider to be the correct approach to reading the texts of Bibfeldt — a method that addresses quite specifically the unique Bibfeldtian phenomenon of what I will call "the vanishing text."

Now I think it a truism that, as secondary materials proliferate, the primary texts actually tend to recede from view (that is, one reads the commentaries and not the text itself). The case of Bibfeldt, however, offers a profound anomaly. The Bibfeldt texts do not recede; they actually vanish! The world of study they have engendered becomes their only trace. The result of this vanishing phenomenon is that the Ricoeurian "world" in front of the text is empty of content, leaving only the world of *readers,* who must devise a strategy for following the text in its vanishing.

The widening field of Bibfeldt studies is due in part, I believe, to the rapid deployment of literary-critical-philosophical and theological perceptions of writing and reading. In a deconstructive world, these Bibfeldt texts are, I would argue, classic models of *ecriture* sophistication that do not take themselves seriously but model for us an uncanny *ars moriendi* — an art of dying, of passing away — wryly smiling, as it were, at our attempt to separate argument from artifice.

How, then, ought one to read Bibfeldt? I do not wish to default to the time-worn expression "imagination." No doubt a good bit of that helps the Bibfeldt experience. But I believe that one should begin with several shots of Jim Beam, this to provide whatever "proof" one needs to feel grounded in this task. The Beam gives a new twist to the notion of "prooftexting," which is how I refer to my method of reading. Several more shots of the Beam will begin to shift the ground — projected now into the Ricoeurian world in which the self feels *itself* to be an analogous vanishing trace and thus a formal, if artificial repetition of the vanishing text.

Several more shots and one can experience the blurring of boundaries of primordial language receding into itself. This movement toward the Dionysian, of "passing out" beyond the will and the self, will itself leave a certain trace the next morning. This fluid method of reading Bibfeldt, pouring over the text and pursuing the vanishing trace, ultimately reveals the text to be what every student or professor has always known it to be: a headache!

The view of text as headache, as "hangover," of its Dionysian, ecstatic vanishing into nothingness is exemplified *par excellence* in the vanishing texts of Bibfeldt. The reading, mind you, is pure pleasure — the climactic *now* of the text as one reads in excess and enjoys the intoxicating pursuit of Bibfeldt's presence. But the end of our *jouissance* is sobering: Bibfeldt is the paradigm of the text that eludes us, the paradigm of our loss.

But let us gather courage at this our annual celebration, which celebrates itself — the world of Bibfeldt readers, who carry on, who play the game well, who do the best they can to follow the trace. I hope you will now join with me in pursuing the method that leads to the *jouissance* of the Bibfeldtian ideal.

Prost!

Proofs of the Existence of Franz Bibfeldt

Columbus, Ohio, where they don't spell too well. From left to right: Jerald C. Brauer of the Foundation; Leon Lechler, profane Episcopal lawyer; Joseph Fletcher, Bibfeldtian ethicist; and a fourth man, who wisely chose to remain unidentified. (M.E.M. archives)

**Monday
Morning
November 21**

AR

A105 RELIGION IN SOUTH ASIA A105 **SECTION**	**A107 CURRENTS IN A107** **CONTEMPORARY CHRISTOLOGY** **GROUP**

A105   RELIGION IN SOUTH ASIA   A105
SECTION

9:00-11:30   **Lake Ontario**

Theme: *Roles and Images of Hindu Women: A Reappraisal*

Thomas B. Coburn, St. Lawrence University

Frédérique Apffel Marglin, Smith College
Menstruation: "Woman" Deconstructed

Chandra Mudaliar, California State University, Fresno
The Secular State and Women in India

Holly Baker Reynolds, Harvard University
*Community Creators, Community Maintainers: Tamil Women and
    their Ritual Deeds*

Abbie Ziffren, George Washington University
*What is Lost When Feminism is Found: Treatment of Women in Tamil
Fiction*

Respondent: **Harry M. Buck,** Wilson College

A106   THEOLOGY AND RELIGIOUS   A106
REFLECTION SECTION

9:00-11:30   **Boulevard C**

Theme: *The Legacy of Franz Bibfeldt*

Rebecca S. Chopp, Emory University, Candler School of
    Theology, Presiding

Robin W. Lovin, University of Chicago Divinity School
Landmarks and Landmines in Bibfeldt Scholarship

Slide Presentation: *The Life of Franz Bibfeldt*

Respondents:
Franz Bibfeldt, University of Chicago
Hilda Bibfeldt, Chicago, IL

A107   CURRENTS IN   A107
CONTEMPORARY CHRISTOLOGY
GROUP

9:00-11:30   **Continental A**

9:00-10:15
Theme: *Christology and Interreligious Dialogue*

Joseph M. Incandela, St. Mary's College, Presiding

Chester Gillis, Georgetown University
Christology, Soteriology and Ethics in Interreligious Dialogue

Respondent: **Terence J. Martin, Jr.,** St. Mary's College

10:15-11:30
Theme: *Literary Christologies*

Patrick R. Keifert, Luther Northwestern Theological Seminary

H. Frederick Reisz, Jr., Harvard Divinity School
Christ and Cross in Contemporary Poetry: Unconquerable Beseeching

Respondent: **Lynn Poland,** University of Chicago Divinity School

A108   ESOTERICISM AND   A108
PERENNIALISM GROUP

9:00-11:30   **Private Dining Room 4**

Theme: *The Work of Frithjof Schuon*

Joscelyn Godwin, Colgate University, Presiding

James S. Cutsinger, University of South Carolina
*A Knowledge That Wounds Our Nature: The Message of Frithjof
    Schuon*

Respondents:
Charles Courtney, Drew University
Huston Smith, Emeritus, Syracuse University
P. Joseph Cahill, University of Alberta
Seyyed Hossein Nasr, George Washington University

By Way of Response

MARTIN E. MARTY

By this point it may be difficult for the reader to sort out the apocryphal from the pseudoapocryphal in the Bibfeldt legend. One who did attempt this was the co-editor of this book. Some years ago he was asked by Abingdon Press to contribute to a series of spiritual autobiographies, and did it in the form of a book entitled *By Way of Response*. We excerpt here, with the permission of Abingdon, several pages in which he provides what may or may not be a fictional account of the influence Bibfeldt had on him — as one example of Bibfeldt's influence in general. Take it or leave it, dear reader, as an account of reality, or what passes for reality, in the Bibfeldtian world of illusion. — ED.

Then, on the eve of ordination, came a surprising turn and a new influence in life. Yes, surprising but not grim, for the way of response is full of caprice and good nature alongside the violence and discipline. Years later I would see this aspect in a type that Hugo Rahner called God's "grave-merry" person. Such a believer has taken the measure of the cramping boundaries of existence and for that reason, or in spite of it, is a person of tears *and* laughter, a person of invincible security and a kind of spiritual elegance. Perhaps no one can fully embody these extremes, but even an imaginary one can provide excellent company for the journey. I am going to speak about a creature who had more impact on my life than any of the mentors mentioned so far: Rosenstock-Huessy and Buber, Mounier and Marcel, Ortega and Burckhardt, Tillich and Pope John, Paul and ... well, not Paul, then.

One Sunday afternoon, as an act of protest against the closing of the seminary library on weekends before Monday term papers were due, a classmate invented his footnotes for such a paper. The name among them that struck me most was that of "Bibfeldt, Franz." During the next three summers as this inventive friend and I teamed to make a living by icing Burlington railroad cars, I distracted him from the work he found otherwise distasteful by interviewing him about this theologian. Gradually Bibfeldt began to take on consistency and life.

By the final years of seminary we were studding the student magazine with references to our common mentor. His epigraphs appeared as filler, his portrait was scheduled soon to appear. Professor Jaroslav Pelikan, Jr., now of Yale, then of the seminary, solemnly announced that the sequel to his recent book *From Luther to Kierkegaard* was to be *From Kierkegaard to Bibfeldt.* Whereupon Arthur Carl Piepkorn, late author of the mammoth *Profiles in Belief,* with just as solemn a tongue in just as scholarly a cheek, began to take issue with the Pelikan interpretation. The librarian joined the harmless conspiracy by cataloging the corpus of Bibfeldtiana while the bookstore saw to it that Bibfeldt was always "on order" but, as in the library, never available, because of the long waiting lists. As faculty members caught on to the commotion, they added to the lore; so did a couple of publishing houses.

The Bibfeldt invention was never as funny, of course, as we in the thigh-slapping circles that gathered at an adjacent pub liked to think. The history of academic hoaxes is as old and dreary as the academy itself, and the list of invented names in scholarly footnotes threatens to be as long as are authentic ones. But Bibfeldt somehow lived on. He has enjoyed his minutes on the Columbia Broadcasting System, his byline on prime-time television, his name in several lectures or articles and in the donor's list at a Chicago White Sox benefit. Misled notables have autographed their pictures for the Bibfeldt Foundation collection, sometimes acknowledging in their greetings the value of his work for them.

The Bibfeldt ideology has changed after twenty-five years; he embodies the principle of responding-although-he-will-be-changed gone awry. His coat of arms displays the ever-changing god Proteus atop a weathervane, and his motto is the Spanish line, "I dance to the tune that is played." But at mid-century Bibfeldt was most useful for our satirical comment on one aspect of our own system, our own way of reinforcing our House of Muumbi. To cite this here is not to suggest that our own system was uniquely obtuse or perverse —Unitarian and Episcopalian pranksters have discovered targets just as obvious. I have no doubt and some suspicion that latter-day Bibfeldts have even been invented to keep *his* inventors in their place.

It so happened that to reinforce our tribe at the moment when it was emerging in the turbulence of postwar American pluralism, some professors found it more necessary than before to devise props. They then converged on new defenses of the absolute authority of the Bible, literally interpreted on their private premises. The most convenient way to promote full assurance was to minimize the human element in its authorship. God let inspired writers keep their own styles, but they became virtual secretaries to the deity. They were like mechanical subjects of divine dictation, and as such their errant minds were themselves purged from the transmission process. But the mechanical dictation theory was curiously absent from the list of acceptable interpretations, thanks to the survival of older Lutheran, and thus more open, views of biblical authority.

Whenever a professor of the rigid sort would set forth his views on the subject somewhere along "in the seventeenth place," after the preceding sixteen had fit perfectly the template of the mechanical dictation theory, he would assert with sudden and vigorous rhetorical flourishes, "But we do not teach the mechanical dictation theory." That was to take care of that. The colloquialists among the students rudely called Bibfeldtianism a "wwwhhtt" theology because of the suddenness of its address to problems. This way of getting out of a jam was, in more refined language, the relieving of paradox by sanctified rhetorical excess.

Such an idea deserved a home in a book, but since no book existed, at least there must needs be a review. On the day before Christmas break, tucked under the box scores of the seminary basketball teams, was my review of *The Relieved Paradox* by the elusive Professor Bibfeldt. I left school with a heavy vacation agenda. Officials had asked whether my fiancée, my parents, and I would discuss my undertaking an overseas assignment the next year. A small congregation of displaced Baltic people in London awaited a pastor. I already envisioned time at Covent Gardens or the British Museum. A telegram came: would I return to seminary a day early? A couple of professors had grown eager to see the Bibfeldt book, while others were equally suspicious about its existence.

What followed has never been completely revealed. In the world of Bibfeldt, not what happened but what everyone believes happened, matters. It was filtered to us that what we conceived as a satire on a system looked to some like the targeting of a professor or two who were walking parodies of the system. Since we could show that "all of us," not "some of us" were victims, we were simply asked to cease and desist from further propagandizing the Bibfeldt lore. And after we could no longer publicize him, the good-natured victims of the hoax, forgiving all, began to quote him at us. Evidently it was decided, however, that the young candidate for London had proven himself to be too immature and irresponsible to represent the church so far away. He must be seasoned as an apprentice or curate under a salty senior minister.

Coming under that minister's influence was one of the great graces of my life. But one unwelcome hook was attached. The assistants in that parish were expected to continue work for the doctor of philosophy degree. This forced me to the graduate work that helped advance my one-and-the-many project. My story of a journey would sound more portentous were Bibfeldt to remain in the shadows. But he serves numerous functions. If our lives are guided, he helps prove that God works through apparent accidents. Second, he shows that the theologians — like gods — are easier to control if we invent them. . . . Further, Bibfeldt is a reminder that a person need not exist in order to influence lives; had his image not come along, I would be learning Latvian or Lithuanian. And since Bibfeldt was a satiric, not a comic creation, he shows that we believe — as satirists do — that this almost hopeless world is capable of being changed. If W. H. Auden is right, the comic mode, on the other hand, copes with a fated and never so malleable order.

Contributors

R. SCOTT APPLEBY is associate professor of history at the University of Notre Dame. His office is ten yards or so east of Touchdown Jesus' waist, and overlooks the entrance to the football stadium, where much of *Rudy* was filmed. He also directs the university's Cushwa Center, which has just received a grant from a foundation (which would rather remain anonymous) to launch a five-year study of Franz Bibfeldt's recently completed manuscript "How My Mind Has Changed." The study will draw on several disciplines, most notably criminology, sociopathology, and supply-side economics.

JOSEPH BESSLER-NORTHCUTT is the I.B. Rusty Swivel Chair Instructor of Mystical Theology and Spiritual Exercises at Phillips Graduate Seminary on the Tulsa campus (as opposed to the Enid and Honolulu campuses). His dissertation, currently misplaced, "Where in the Hell is Shantung Compound?" is based on Langdon Gilkey's perplexing contribution to Bibfeldt studies. He is also the author of a soon-to-be-unpublished work, *Secret Agents and Sacramental Theology: A Bibfeldtian Approach.*

STEVE BOUMA-PREDIGER, formerly assistant professor of philosophy and Bibfeldt studies at North Park College in Chicago, is currently assistant professor of Bibfeldt studies and religion at Hope College, Holland, Michigan. One of his more popular courses is "Being and Nothingness: The Metaphysics of Sartre and Bibfeldt." His latest book is entitled *Identity Statements and the Self-Reference Problem: The Peculiar Case of Franz Bibfeldt.*

JERALD C. BRAUER has served as chairman of the Franz Bibfeldt

Stiftung since its founding (along with Martin E. Marty as its executive director). Brauer has chaired every Stiftung board meeting that should have been called. He has sat in the Naomi Shenstone Donnelley chair in his Swift Hall office of the Divinity School of the University of Chicago and has always parked his feet on the Franz Bibfeldt Lehrstuhl next to his desk. The Swiss handcarved Lehrstuhl was a gift — handsomely endowed by Nina and Jim Donnelley — and was prominently displayed at the annual Bibfeldt lectures. The income from the Lehrstuhl endowment, $29.95, was presented proudly by one of the Donnelleys to the annual lecturer. In his dual capacity as chairman of the Stiftung and dean of the Divinity School, Brauer sought to persuade Bibfeldt to join the faculty; but each time Bibfeldt forgot to appear for his trial lecture.

OTTO DREYDOPPEL, JR. teaches church history at Moravian Theological Seminary in Bethlehem, Pennsylvania. He is the president — and only member — of the *Unabhängische, Unparteiische, Unwissenschaftliche Gesellschaft für Bibfeldtforschung in der Brudergemeine und Verwandte Glaubensgemeinschaften.*

LANGDON GILKEY is visiting professor at the University of Virginia and emeritus professor of theology at the University of Chicago. He treats both science and religion, ancient and modern theology, Protestant and Catholic thought, God-talk and non-God-talk, and is author of many books, beginning with *Maker of Heaven and Earth* and continuing with works like *Message and Existence, Society and the Sacred,* and *Creationism on Trial: Evolution and God in Little Rock.* He has taught in both North and South, is father of both Amos Welcome and Frouwkje. With so many "both/ands," he is qualified to be a Bibfeldt scholar. He is married only to Ram Rattan Gilkey.

ROBERT M. GRANT has just returned from England, where he found that Bibfeldt is little known nor long remembered. Grant's own situation is retirement, in which he finds Bibfeldt's basic viewpoint of "Neither/Nor" reassuring when "ignorant armies clash by night."

GLENN HOLLAND, after graduating as a drama major from Stanford University in 1974, was for a time gainfully employed as a televison writer in Hollywood. This experience led him naturally to graduate theological study at Oxford University and the Divinity School of the University of Chicago. Currently an associate professor at Allegheney

College, he occupies the Bishop James Mills Thoburn Chair of Religious Studies, which is badly in need of reupholstering.

DENNIS L. LANDON lives in Bethany, West Virginia, where he is executive director of East Central Colleges, an academic consortium which, like Franz Bibfeldt, enhances human life without the inconveniences of actual corporate existence.

ROBIN W. LOVIN, during his years as a member of the faculty at the University of Chicago, came to be known as the most effective lecturer on Bibfeldt, to which the published lectures in this volume attest. His work is so far above that of most other aspirants in the field that one sometimes wonders why he permits it to be associated with the rest. But his generosity works to our benefit. He has, despite that infamous career in Bibfeldt scholarship, managed to secure and hold tenure at several major universities. He is currently lowering the standards of Southern Methodist University, where he is dean of the Perkins School of Theology.

MARTIN E. MARTY is the Fairfax M. Cone Distinguished Service Professor at the University of Chicago. Among his best-known books is *The Pro and Con Book of Religious America*, a work that can be read from either front or (turned upside down) back; this is the most appropriately formatted work in the Corpus Bibfeldtiana. Fate decreed that, with Jerald C. Brauer, he should head the Bibfeldt Foundation, and the Donnelley Stool of Bibfeldt Studies rests in Marty's office, six inches from where he rests, using napping techniques taught by Franz. Marty is also senior editor of *The Christian Century* and the George B. Caldwell Senior Scholar-in-Residence at the Park Ridge Center for the Study of Health, Faith, and Ethics. Marty delivered the *Ur*-Bibfeldt lecture, which is incorporated in this volume.

ROBIN D. MATTISON is presently assistant professor of New Testament at the Lutheran Theological Seminary in Philadelphia. She has engaged in the unrelieved paradox by being a pastor in *both* parish *and* university settings, teaching in *both* Reformed *and* Lutheran seminaries, and consulting with *both* the Lutheran-Reformed dialogue *and* the ELCA's study on human sexuality. At present she is working on the figure of Franz in the Gospel of Matthew, with its strong Greek *Bib*-ginning (Matt. 1:1a).

MARK MILLER-McLEMORE left the Divinity School of the University of Chicago in 1980 and has since been pastor of a small urban parish,

First Christian Church of Chicago Heights, Illinois. This position has given him the opportunity to put some of Bibfeldt's theories of pastoral care into practice with members of the congregation. For a time, for example, the church hosted the only "disco-worship" in the Chicago area. Recently, Miller-McLemore's musical and ministerial interests have shifted. He is currently compiling a comprehensive collection of jokes related to the five-string banjo, a project entering its third volume.

DAVID MORGAN is an art historian at Valparaiso University and currently a member of the Bibfeldt Group, an elite cadre of specialists with nothing better to do than drink Cabernet and pronounce multi-syllabic German words. He has twice visited the residence of Dr. Bibfeldt on research trips to Saxony, only to find the elusive master away from home. Morgan's therapy for a congenital proneness to abstraction is drawing pictures for his friends.

DAVID OUSLEY, unduly influenced by the thought of Franz Bibfeldt, was ordained in that most Bibfeldtian of sects, the Episcopal Church. He presently serves the parish of St. James the Less and is at work on a monograph on the significance of the patron's title: why it should be "the Less" and not "the Short" or "the Unassuming," and whether James the Less ever existed or was merely an invention of St. James the Greater so that he could become "the Greater." Ousley is married with three children: Hilda, Franz, and baby Bibby.

ROBIN PETERSON is a "has-bean" red South African activist, pastor, and theologian. He is currently completing a Ph.D. dissertation at the University of Chicago on "*Kai-roses:* Bibfeldt and the notion of 'right timing' in horticultural liberation theology."

JOSEPH L. PRICE is professor of religious studies at Whittier College and co-editor of *A New Handbook to Christian Theology* (Abingdon, 1992), in whose preface the editors specify the influence of Bibfeldt on their collaboration. Following Bibfeldt's shift from *Heilsgeschichte* to *Bullsgeschichte,* Price has been charged by many with harboring a career goal of becoming chaplain to the Chicago Bulls. Blending interests in *both* religious studies *and* sports, Price's current research focuses, in part, on an analysis of the syntax of "The Last Pennant Before Armageddon," a story published by W. P. Kinsella but thought to be a pseudo-pseudo-Pauline epistle establishing the delay of the *parousia* until the Cubs win the pennant. A forthcoming book he is editing is tentatively entitled *From Season to Season: Sports as Religion in America.*

SAM PORTARO is Episcopal chaplain to the University of Chicago, the ultimate in thankless full-time jobs. He continues to explore new areas of Bibfeldt scholarship, presently conducting a study of the complexities of a little-known problem under the working title "Heterotextual or Homotextual? The Textual Identity of Franz Bibfeldt." Portaro is also composing a new setting for choral evensong based upon the spiritual poems and altar bread recipes of Hilda Braunschweiger-Bibfeldt.

JILL RAITT is the Hilda Braunschweiger-Bibfeldt Professor of Religions, Etc. and Director of the World Center for Missouri Religions, Columbia, Missouri. She is the author of *The Eucharistic Theology of Franz Bibfeldt* (Columbia, MO: WCMR Press, 1972 — all editions lost in the flood of 1971). Professor Raitt has also edited numerous books about etc. and written articles on the same and the related subject, idem. She has published in the most scholarly journals on that subject et al. She is presently working on an edition of the collected letters of Hilda Braunschweiger-Bibfeldt (the source of the letters in this volume) with extended commentary.

L. DALE RICHESIN is an instructor of Old Testament at Chicago Baptist Institute. He is president of the Chicago Anti-Hunger Federation and serves on the board of the Interchurch Refugee and Immigration Ministries. He is co-editor of *The Challenge of Liberation Theology: A First World Response* (Orbis, 1987), co-editor of Interpreting Disciples: Practical Theology and the Disciples of Christ (Texas Christian University Press, 1987), and the author of numerous essays. His forthcoming Bibfeldt writings include *The Confessions of Rev. Smith* (1995/96), *The Pig-Latin Bible* (1996/97), *The Institutes of Jacob, Joseph, and Benjamin* (1997/98), and, with Stephen Hawking, *A Brief History of the History of History* (2000/1).

RICHARD ROSENGARTEN is dean of students at the University of Chicago Divinity School. His current project attempts to establish a bridge between scholarship and administrative work by applying the insights of Bibfeldt's dissertation on the year zero and subsequent dating problems to financial aid commitments for entering students.

MARK G. TOULOUSE and REBEKAH L. MILES, together with their spouses, are co-founders of the Hilda Braunschweiger and Franz Bibfeldt Honky-Tonk Order of Line-Dancing Yuppies, Redeemed Or Lost, Literate/Elliterate, & Ruthlessly Shameless (known by its benefactors and detractors alike as the HOLY ROLLERS), an organization whose 666 members regularly gather on Saturday nights at the world's largest honky-tonk, located in the Fort Worth stockyards. Currently professors at Brite Divinity School, Texas Christian University, both Toulouse and Miles attended the Divinity School of the University of Chicago. Their latest cooperative work, *Metaphysically Challenged: The Bibfeldtian Resolution of the Political Correctness Debate*, inspired by the uncovering of the octagonal mind, appears destined for the nonfiction bestseller list. Their next project will analyze Bibfeldt's recent synthesis of the work of Mary Daly and Tom Oden.

REINDER VAN TIL, Bibfeldt project editor for Wm. B. Eerdmans Publishing Company, has dabbled in *both* theology *and* murder mystery. Along with his collaborator, William Brashler (writing as the pseudonymous Crabbe Evers), he is the inventor of the baseball sleuth/savant Duffy House, who, in a groundbreaking essay on the influence of baseball on contemporary theology, has concluded: "More than any thinker of his generation, the extraordinary Franz Bibfeldt embodies in theological argot the wisdom of Casey Stengel: 'Good pitching will always beat good hitting, and vice versa.'"

TODD D. WHITMORE is a kick return specialist for the University of Notre Dame Fighting Irish. He has not spoken to Franz Bibfeldt, however, since the latter blindsided him in the annual Notre Dame–Tübingen game ("Bibfeldt seemed to come out of nowhere," Whitmore said). Mr. Whitmore is also assistant professor of social ethics in the theology department at Notre Dame.

ELLEN K. WONDRA teaches contemporary unsystematic and impractical theology at Colgate-Rochester Divinity School and/or Bexley Hall and/or Crozier Theological Seminary in Rochester, New York. She is the author of, among other scholarly works, *Encountering the Other: The Theology of Gary Larson* and *Tigers in the Streets of Geneva: Creation and Providence in Calvin and Hobbes*. Professor Wondra was recently appointed to the Anglican–New Age Dialogue, which has yet to crystallize.

NOTE: Royalties earned by this book, if any, will go to the Elsa Marty Memorial Ministry Students' Scholarship at the University of Chicago. Elsa Marty designed and sewed the academic hood that is worn by every Bibfeldt lecturer, but otherwise had the good sense not to be involved with the Foundation. Her regard for students, however, was of long standing and profound, and the Scholarship Fund honors that.